THE PASSION OF
DAVID LYNCH

The
Passion
of
David
Lynch

University of Texas Press   Austin

WILD AT
HEART IN
HOLLYWOOD

Martha P. Nochimson

The publication of this book was
assisted by a grant from the
Andrew W. Mellon Foundation.

Requests for permission to reproduce material from this work
should be sent to Permissions, University of Texas Press,
P.O. Box 7819, Austin, TX 78713-7819.

♾ The paper used in this publication meets the minimum requirements of
American National Standard for Information Sciences—Permanence of
Paper for Printed Library Materials, ANSI Z39.48-1984.

Library of Congress Cataloging-in-Publication Data

Nochimson, Martha.
    The passion of David Lynch : wild at heart in Hollywood / by Martha P.
Nochimson.
        p.   cm.
    Includes bibliographical references and index.
    ISBN 0-292-75566-X (alk. paper). — ISBN 0-292-75565-1 (pbk. : alk.
paper)
    1. Lynch, David, 1946–   — Criticism and interpretation.   I. Title.
PN1998.3.L96N63   1997
791.43′0233′092 — dc21   97-7732

A list of credits for illustrations follows page 271.

To know that balance does not quite rest,
That the mask is strange, however like.

WALLACE STEVENS,
"The Man with the Blue Guitar"

. . . there is a "good ambiguity" in the phenomenon of expression, a spontaneity which accomplishes what appeared to be impossible when we observed only the separate elements, a spontaneity which gathers together the plurality of monads, the past and the present, nature and culture into a single whole. To establish this wonder would be metaphysics itself and would at the same time give us the principle of an ethics.

MAURICE MERLEAU-PONTY,
The Primacy of Perception

Contents

List of Illustrations

Acknowledgments

As Jeffrey Beaumont tells Sandy Williams in *Blue Velvet*, "There are opportunities in life for gaining knowledge and experience. Sometimes you have to take a risk." One opportunity is writing a book, requiring more than one risk but yielding extraordinary gains. Many people helped make the composition of *The Passion of David Lynch: Wild at Heart in Hollywood* a journey to places I had never been before, and I thank them.

First of all, thank you to David Lynch for the telling words, the miraculous silences, for rolling out the Hollywood welcome mat, and most of all for your work.

Thank you to Lynch's associates who spoke with me in a forthcoming and generous manner and often helped in many more ways than they knew: Michael John Anderson, Scott Cameron, John Churchill, Catherine Coulson, Duwayne Dunham, Julie Du-Vic, Frederick Elmes, Robert Engels, Simone Farber, Mark Frost, Ron Garcia, Cori Glazer, Richard Hoover, Toby Keeler, Rodger LaPelle, Dorothy McGinnis, Jack Nance, Deepak Nayar, Tina Rathborne, Peggy Lynch Reavey, Mary Sweeney, and especially to Gay Pope and Debbie Trutnik.

Thank you to the staff at the New York University Innovation Center, particularly Bill Horne, Joseph Hargitai, and Johannes Lang—Photoshops of the World Unite!

Thank you to my students, academic colleagues, and friends who read, reacted, talked, and supported without necessarily agreeing: particularly Lynne and Josh Berrett, Sean Dugan, Sandy

Flitterman-Lewis, Krin Gabbard, Adam Gooder, Bob Guttman, Darren Hopkins, Ann Martin, Anne McMahon, Lynne McVeigh, Carol Moore, Heather O'Leary, Jonathan Rosenbaum, Ann Stetser, Sarah and Irwin Wall, the Mercy College Faculty Development Committee, and the Columbia University Film Seminar.

The author expresses appreciation to the University Seminars at Columbia University for assistance in the preparation of the manuscript for publication. Material drawn from this work was presented to the University Seminar on Cinema and Interdisciplinary Interpretation.

Thank you to Hyperion Books for supplying me with a copy of *Images.* Thank you to Bruce Phillips of Canton, Michigan, and his catalogue, Twin Peaks Collectables, for his stock of Lynchiana that served as such a valuable resource.

Thank you to Ali Hossaini, Jim Burr, and all those at the University of Texas Press who proffered their confidence and counsel.

Finally, mad love and gratitude to my family: my dearest, insightful husband Richard, and my precious children, David and Holly, who must have met the Good Witch; they seem to know what it means to be truly wild at heart.

THE PASSION OF
DAVID LYNCH

David Lynch at a (Feminine) Glance, or Her Eyes Were Moving, but She Didn't Know It

When I began writing this book, I thought I knew my direction, but much changed after a series of encounters with David Lynch. These meetings started with an intense half-hour phone call on January 31, 1992. A year later, March 29–April 1, 1993, I made a series of daily visits to his studio offices in Los Angeles to interview him. In 1996, I observed him directing on the set of *Lost Highway* (January 15–18) and subsequently met him in New York on March 13, and again in Los Angeles on April 12, to hold the conversations for which there had been no time in the hurly-burly of production. Our early meetings confounded many of my expectations, especially of what Lynch would clarify for me about his manner of representing reality in movies. Our later meetings brought both more finely detailed nuances to the revelations of our first encounters and still more revelations.

The comedy of hollow sounds derives From truth and not from satire on our lives.
—WALLACE STEVENS

Before I met Lynch, the prospect of speaking with him filled me with the anticipation of *acquiring* knowledge. I would fill in the gaps of a picture already sketched in my mind. I would *get* an enormously precious something, which I would transmit in my book. As it turned out, much of the value of my time with David Lynch came as a result of *letting go.* The core of my vision as a film critic is a distinctly feminist dissatisfaction with what Hollywood films generally present as reality, particularly regarding the representation of masculinity and femininity. I have in no way surren-

1

dered my dissatisfaction, but I have relinquished some old conceptions about gender issues, Lynch's work, and Hollywood's potential for realism.

First, I had to let go of the customary identification of Lynch's work with that of Joel and Ethan Coen (*Barton Fink,* 1991), Peter Greenaway (*Drowning by Numbers,* 1988), David Mamet (*House of Games,* 1987), Neil Jordan (*Mona Lisa,* 1986), and David Cronenberg (*Naked Lunch,* 1991). All of these filmmakers reveal the labyrinthine self-referentiality of narrative; all despair, in varying ways, of representing any reality beyond that of structure. They may share with Lynch a vibrant distrust of the mimetic illusions of conventional Hollywood realism, but, as my time with Lynch revealed, seminal differences exist that make comparisons relatively trivial.

I also had to let go of some of my presuppositions about realism in Lynch's representation of women. I had thought that, for the most part, Lynch had eliminated realism from his films in a way that deconstructs Hollywood's images of women and men and thus intersects with some feminist attitudes.[1] So I was prepared to talk with Lynch about the deconstruction of sadism and fetishism in *Blue Velvet,* and about the gendered implication of a particular shot-reverse shot in *Wild at Heart* where the camera holds a toilet bowl within the unspecified gaze of perhaps Marietta Fortune, perhaps Sailor Ripley. I had been expecting Lynch to confirm my feeling—in his own terms of course—that his use of this shot pattern subverts Hollywood's use of the shot-reverse shot to establish the controlling male gaze as a biological "reality."[2] But how does one venture this kind of analytic statement with a director who has already declined to pass judgment on whether, in the final cut of his own *Wild at Heart,* Marietta was represented as loving her daughter Lula? "Diane [Ladd, portraying Marietta] thought she did," he said. Don't film directors control these details? I wondered, as my argument about gender representation floated away.

Letting go became the theme of my early visits with Lynch. Much of my preparation turned out to be an obstacle to seeing what was right in front of me. I began to see that what I had come for was to watch (and listen to) Lynch let go. He had no intention of nailing down any truths for me by asserting himself through language. At his most direct, Lynch explained that, when he is

2

directing, ninety percent of the time he doesn't know, intellectu-
ally, what he is doing. However, there is nothing uncertain in him
about the powerful rightness of his artistic choices. His insistence
on letting things happen to him while he works is part of his faith
that film is a place where reality enters when something other than
willfully applied reason does the talking.

I remain astonished both by the seamlessness of his faith and by
its contagiousness. Few of his current and former associates whom
I interviewed have any overall grasp of the films on which they
have worked, and most were baffled by their zest for working on
films about which they were frankly confused. But lack of clarity
hadn't affected the quality of their work. Lynch had made them
feel comfortable about jumping in and moving with the process,
and they had come up with beautiful results. The most theoretical illumination of what Lynch is about came from his first
wife, Peggy Reavey, who told me that he has always been intensely
wary of how we are "dictated to by language and things like language." This sounds like the description of a constructionist/rela-
tivist, who theorizes on the insufficiency of words to connect with
an out-there reality. But the schism that Lynch intuits between the
rational logic of language and existence has led him in quite a different direction.

During my first meetings with Lynch, he created a situation in
which I felt I was bumping up against an invisible force field surrounding meaning. God knows what he felt. I believe I was sometimes cranky with him, and he was sometimes bored with me. But
we came back day after day while the tape rolled in the recorder
that he permitted, indeed encouraged, me to use. After hours of
sending out verbal probes that bounced off an elastic surface instead of engaging him, as I thought they would, *within* a linguistic
grid—self-referential though it might be—I began to feel that he
was talking to me. However, our conversation took an unforeseen
form, generating in me a feeling for which I find a visual analogue
in the delighted surprise of Laura Palmer at her discovery of the
angel in the Red Room at the end of *Twin Peaks: Fire Walk with
Me.* It is this feeling that has led me to follow Lynch into an augmented understanding of reality, meaning, and order in cinema.

In some ways, Lynch is part of a cultural ferment that has been
building since the beginning of the century, when assumptions

about order and meaning began to unravel. His suspicion of language interfaces with the twentieth-century attack on our assumption of a connection between language and an external reality. But if Lynch perceives that language creates its own self-referential reality, he does not imagine that civilization is utterly dependent on it.[3] He does play with the ironic contrasts between the essential insubstantiality of words and the power we grant them. However, unlike most linguistic relativists, Lynch has instinctively shifted to a narrative practice that is essentially optimistic.

Optimism

The development of Lynch's body of work is informed by a realist's optimism that there is an exit from the linguistic labyrinth and that this exit is richly available to us. In our later meetings, Lynch told me this, in so many words, confirming the interpretations of his films that I had evolved in the intervening years. His use of language—and of cinematic vocabulary—suggests that, once we understand that we ourselves have created cultural forms and that they only have the meaning we give them, we are free to understand the forces in the universe that are truly larger than we are and how they connect us to a greater reality.

Lynch intuitively seizes upon logocentrism as the paradigm of cultural imbalances, but he deeply believes that they are not fatal cultural malfunctions. The Lynchian seeker, as either artist or detective—or filmmaker—can always get us out of the labyrinth. We only have to let it happen. Coming in his own way to conclusions that have been formulated by a number of phenomenologists—Maurice Merleau-Ponty and the early Jean-François Lyotard, for example—Lynch acts upon a faith that the illusion of control that language and other cultural structures give us is not as rewarding as losing that illusion and gaining larger, less contingent truths. These truths are always present for us, unless we insist on the fantasy of control and thereby doom ourselves to the sense of disconnectedness we feel if we fool ourselves into believing only in the control that we exert over our own creations.

Lynch's art is the art of removing the blockage to larger truths by deglamorizing and denaturalizing our priorities of remaining in control. Different moments from my interviews with Lynch merge in retrospect as maps routing me past logical impediments to perception. I now see how bound up Lynch's vision of making meaning is with the freedom to respond through the subconscious, by playfully losing control instead of stridently taking charge. One moment of our 1993 conversation made this especially clear, one during which we both looked at the textured surface of *Blue Poles: Number 11, 1952,* a painting by Jackson Pollock full of patches, slashes, lines, drippings, and blobs, with barely a hint of blue (see figure 1). "I don't understand this," I said. "Yes you do," Lynch said. "Your eyes are moving." They must have been, but I had not paid any attention. I had automatically experienced a lack of meaning because I could not stand at the pre-

1. Jackson Pollock, *Blue Poles: Number 11, 1952*—Lynch could see my eyes were moving around this composition.

scribed, controlling viewing distance and read the painting as a rationally controlled system of shapes. Lynch had spontaneously identified the painting as a meaningful representation for me because it had released my moving eye from conventional viewer expectations. *I* saw that I could not contain the painting in some theoretical framework; *he* saw me performing with the painting. He saw as crucial that part of me that my education had taught me is inconsequential to my grasp of meaning.

Looking back on this experience, I have come to the conclusion that Lynch was talking about a *balance* between reason and direct subconscious engagement with the materiality of the paint, not about an *abandonment* of reason. The movement of the eye that Lynch focused on is only possible if it occurs within an intelligence that possesses reason to suspend. The experience is not dependent on a pure form of body or on irrationalism; rather it is dependent on a tension that denotes powerful connectedness. Indeed, for Lynch connectedness is what emerges from the tension between reason and the subconscious.

In encouraging my ability to see with a part of me that precedes my education, Lynch suggested a possible relationship with Jungian thought, and I would say that the label developed by Carl Jung, "the collective unconscious," roughly evokes the kind of connectedness Lynch referred me to as I looked at *Blue Poles*. In fact, on occasion Lynch resorts to this term, as I do in this study, because it is a convenient handle offered by an established cultural vocabulary. However, if I understand him, he would rewrite the term as "collective subconscious." As he says, he is representing a level of nonrational energy on which all kinds of meaningful activity takes place, and for him the word unconscious means "nothing is going on." Furthermore, in referring to this painting, Lynch clearly did not have the universal repertoire of images that Jung catalogued. Thus, I am implying no overall "Jungianism" on Lynch's part when I refer now and then to the collective unconscious. With this exception, I consistently refer to the operation of the nonrational faculties in Lynch's work using his term, the subconscious.

A Lynchian subconscious, but pervasive, connectedness is also suggested by another moment I recall from our conversations. Early in our series of discussions, Lynch emotionally drew back from continuing a point he was making, frustrated by his sense that his words were insufficient because they were ugly; his goal was, he said, to speak to me through the beauty and meaning of the poetic word. Despite his exuberance about the found beauty of the nonverbal, he expressed in this sudden conversational caesura a passionate feeling for verbal form but not for one that stands remote from the materials of verbal sounds and rhythms. Lynch wanted to use language in a way usually associated with plastic artists who discover structure in materiality as they work. In a mere conversation, he keenly felt the impossibility of discovering that form in his words.

I imagine that Lynch might put it this way: there was no time to get out of the way and let that nonrational aspect of words as sensory texture tell him about their poetry. Here is a crucial distinction between his realism and the constructionism of the linguistic relativist. The relativist increases control over language to reveal its tendency toward self-referentiality. Relativist filmmakers like Cronenberg, Greenaway, Mamet, the Coen brothers, Jordan, and Bergman approach their films like watchmakers; they are known for the exquisite micromanagement of each frame. Thus the constructionist seeks to represent at least the reality of his self-referentiality as a thinker even if he cannot force cultural structures to open out onto a reality more enduring. As a matter of course, Cronenberg's films, for example, encourage spectators to go through the usual narrative process as if it were pointing toward some meaning despite the constant presence of dark undertones. They then impress on the audience that this process has been one of disconnection from reality. By contrast, although also exquisite in visual detail, Lynch's films encourage spectators to perceive the hollowness of linguistic structure and then discover a more complex form of connection through the subconscious.

Realism

Lynch's desire to represent meaning by balancing the energy of the subconscious and the logic of the linguistic informs his narratives. His models for this balance were initially the paintings of Francis Bacon, Jackson Pollock, and Edward Hopper, as well as *The Art Spirit,* a theoretical tract by Robert Henri. Of this influence there will be much more in Chapter 1, because to understand Lynch's powerful sense of the benign role of the subconscious in art, we must trace the lessons he learned from the painters he admires for their part in the pleasure he takes in storytelling.

Here, I will lay the foundation for examining the influence of the painters on David Lynch the director by cautioning against the usual comparisons between art and film. Ordinarily, we concentrate on similarities of color, themes, and particular images. However, my conversations with Lynch have led me to believe that such an analysis will mire us in secondary considerations. Lynch has been less affected by the surfaces of his painter ancestors than by the way he understands the role of the subconscious in their work. Indeed, what struck me so forcefully about his response when I appealed to him for help in understanding Pollock was that he said *absolutely nothing* about the painting's surface but directed me toward my subconscious engagement solely *through my eyes.*

However, since artists—particularly Lynch—rarely articulate their underlying definitions, to understand their artistic legacy we will need to determine where Lynch falls within available frameworks of discussing the subconscious.

Understanding Lynch's collaboration with the subconscious hinges on the definition of the subconscious that we adopt, and there are a number in circulation. Although the subconscious is always evoked as distinct from voluntary and rational processes, there is much controversy surrounding this crucial relationship. Lynch's response to the paintings we viewed together, the totality of the time we spent together, his work, and everything he has said publicly all suggest to me that his stance vis à vis the alogical diverges significantly from the dominant understanding of its influence. That is, when he refers to the subconscious, he does not mean what is meant by the logocentric Freudian tradition. The short version of the difference between Lynch's attitude toward the subconscious and the Freudian attitude is that he trusts it and Freudians don't. For those readers versed in psychological theory, a more nuanced discussion follows. (Other readers may not wish to engage in this kind of theoretical discussion and should feel free to skip directly to my application of the lessons from his art education to his films on p. 10).

The Freudian tradition has been utilized by film critics primarily through the lens of Freud's intellectual descendant Jacques Lacan, particularly in reference to Lacan's well-known theory of the mirror stage, which he tells us occurs at the age of roughly eighteen months. Lacan's mirror stage—currently the dominant paradigm of the relations among subconscious, conscious, and image— will not serve us when we talk about David Lynch. In the Lacanian paradigm, the image—our contact with which is initiated by early childhood glimpses of ourselves as a whole shape reflected in the mirror—divorces us from the real. According to Lacan, the seductiveness of the mirror image's alluring wholeness directs our desires toward *an illusion* of totality and away from the erratic surges of energy that are our innate experience of the self. This experience imprints on us our lifelong relationship with the beautiful image and becomes in turn the analogue of our relationship with language and with the primary illusion of inherent meaning. To summarize in a generalization simplified for the purpose of clarity in this discussion, the artist's image, according to the Lacanian view, seduces us, directing our desires toward a consuming passion for our "ego ideal," dooming us to solipsism while we yearn for the illusion of wholeness.

Viewed within this framework, art traps the conscious mind in a net of hopeless desire, and the world of the beautiful object is naught but illusion. As Lacan writes in "The Split between the Eye and the Gaze," "The picture certainly is in my eye, but I am not in the picture" (p. 96). This view of the relationship between the subconscious and narrative suffuses the works of Cronenberg, Greenaway, Jordan, and the Coens, who all keenly feel the enchantment of the illusionist image as well as its despair. They portray in their films the intense pleasures experienced by a spectator in the beauty and coherence of the ideal form that he or she first saw in infancy as Lacan's mirror image. Inevitably, these pleasures lead us to impossible yearnings.

Lynch's responses to Pollock, Bacon, and Hopper tell a different story. Eye and picture *are in each other* as they move together. Lynch has internalized through his experience of their art a sense of narrative image that holds the possibility, not of the doomed quest for an illusory holy grail, but of empathy—among people, and between people and the universe. His belief in the image as a possible bridge to the real does not depend on any abstract framework but rather on a visceral sense of the essential truth of an empathetic—not solipsistic—relationship with art. (In the Lynchian world, solipsism occurs in a relationship with *bad* art.) To clarify this discussion of Lynch, I suggest that the phenomenological model of our conscious and subconscious relationships with the mirror, and the image—as articulated by Maurice Merleau-Ponty—may be quite helpful.

I offer Merleau-Ponty's method, knowing that some readers will find it a credible model but others will not. However, I contend that belief is not the issue. Merleau-Ponty is useful as a clear analogy of how Lynch's imagination seizes on narrative, not as a vain quest for the impossible ideal, but as an empathetic bridge. In "The Child's Relation with Others," Merleau-Ponty theorizes that when children first recognize a mirror reflection they gain the capacity to see a similarity between themselves and others that is less possible before the mirror grants them a sense of wholeness. At that point, an evolved sense of connection—a mature sense of bondedness with the universe—becomes a possibility (pp. 96–155). Here, Merleau-Ponty suggests an alternate, non-Freudian relationship between the beautiful image and the subconscious, one that goes beyond the limitations of language. Lynch has seen this kind of empathy and this kind of hope in the narrative image via his painter influences.

When Lynch told me that my eyes were moving, he was invoking the subconscious as the basis for a sympathetic bond between me and the picture, a bond that would, if I let it, permit the image to become a bridge between me and the world. This is not to say that he sees the subconscious as purely benign. In his work he always seizes upon false dreams and upon the kind of art that divorces the characters from reality and torments them, but he inevitably reveals them to be lesser aspects of the subconscious. During my later meetings with Lynch, he began to talk more directly than he had previously, clearly defining the way these destructive aspects of the subconscious fit into his worldview. There is, he says, a base element in our involuntary energies. It tends to erupt in his work as a danger, but as one that must be encountered before we are released into the productions of the finer levels of the subconscious that are our major connections to the real. By the productions of the finer aspect of subconscious energies Lynch does not mean mimetic surfaces but rather the way such energies in art work to conform us to the life-affirming energies of nature.

The beautiful and true image has the power to join culture and nature. This bond is Lynch's deepest artistic pleasure, found in art that moves him, for example the work of Francis Bacon. Indeed, Lynch's affinity for Bacon offers an opportunity for exploring the former's idea of the beautiful and the image, since Bacon's painting is not beautiful in any ordinary way. It is tempting to look for the connection between Lynch and Bacon in perversity, not loveliness, such as in specific images of open mouths and in the presence of violence in both of their narratives. These resemblances, while present, are almost a homage to the primary influence Lynch has received from Bacon, but they are certainly not the seminal influences. Concentrating on surface resemblances is the trap of illusionist realism which restricts us to its notion of the real in film as solely a matter of surfaces. What is beautiful and true for *Lynch* about Bacon is what was most important to *Bacon* about Bacon— his struggle to engage the viewer in the paint first through the "nerves," in Bacon's words, and only belatedly through thought. Bacon's paintings contain important narrative elements, and Bacon insists on the urgent nature of narrative as a part of his work. But his conscious desire to subordinate the logic of narrative to the subconscious event and to explosive feeling shows how narrative can teach us empathy with the larger forces in the subconscious and the world (see Chapter 1).

In film narrative this has translated for Lynch into a heroic ideal opposed to the prevalent Hollywood understanding of the hero as one who takes control by means of violent domination strategies. For Lynch, a hero tends to be one who can unlearn that absurd cultural lesson, one who can become receptive to life. The Lynchian hero must learn to let go, even though such suspension of the will often leads to the initial terrors of the baser aspects of the involuntary within him or her. We, too, as spectators, must endure the pain, but the faith of the Lynch film is that, inevitably, the hero and the spectator will reach the centering energies of the higher and beautiful element in the human subconscious.

As we shall see in Chapters 2–7, letting go is the form and substance of the Lynch narrative. The spectator is invited to suspend the desire for control by engaging in an empathetic relationship with a protagonist who, as a matter of survival, must learn to permit a channel to the subconscious in order to open the self to the universe. This emphasis obviously challenges numerous cultural priorities. "Take control" is whispered into our cradles by those who wish us well. A problematic aggressiveness is nurtured by this cultural bias; it is also one of the most powerful allies of sexism. The imbalance of value on force to the exclusion of receptivity— often equated with weakness—biases the culture and the movies against much that is associated with women's wisdom. Lynch's belief that the real requires a balance between force and receptivity suspends the usual exclusion of women from the centers of cultural and narrative importance. In his films, the hero must get in touch with—or be—what has been excluded when the conventional Hollywood hero "takes control." Thus Lynch's lessons from his painter influence have led directly to a narrative valuation of femininity and to fresh and encouraging relationships between male and female identity.

In a David Lynch narrative, when the audience feels that it or the protagonists are of "out of control"—a state of being traditionally associated with the perils of femininity and the subconscious—the attitude toward this release bears little resemblance to standard images of losing one's grip. In the Lynchian concept of realism, "being out of control" promotes a connection through the subconscious that leads us beyond the tyranny of the rational illusionism of the real-seeming Lacanian mirror image. The issue of whether one can operate well while "out of control" is central to Lynch's protagonists. For both men and women, this Lynchian practice means a refreshing realism that does away with Hollywood's straightjacketing of gender identity. Lynch denaturalizes and deglamorizes the usual Hollywood definition of control over the individual female and over everything associated with femininity—a definition that presents such control as both a natural good and a healthy masculine prerogative.

In fact, Lynch's vision of the connection between women and the subconscious causes him to portray his female characters as paradigms of connection—generally hard-won—with forces beyond rational control. Frequently, they are models for his male characters to emulate in their need to break their social conditioning. In his films, the character who puts too much faith in will or logic is frequently male and inevitably destructive—the night porter in *The Elephant Man*, the Harkonnen in *Dune*, the police in any Lynch film. (I will suggest in the individual chapters on these films that it is *not* coincidental that all of these cast in a narcissistic/solipsistic light the conventionally validated "masculine" desire to dominate, what I shall call the will-to-control.)

By contrast, in the chapters to follow we shall see that the Lynchian protagonists who engage our affections and move in positive ways also move in abidingly successful ways that are often associated with, affiliated with, or embodied by women. In *The Elephant Man*, Frederick Treves purportedly uses the sanctuary of medical science to save John Merrick, but it is Merrick with his receptive masculine identity, closely associated in the film with women, who has the capacity for moving Treves beyond the constricting logic of his profession. In some ways, Treves's development, leading him past the narrow confines of scientific applications of control, is the real event of the film. Paul Atreides in *Dune* gets his real power from reaching out beyond logic to vision through his subconscious, emulating and connecting with his mother and sister. In *Twin Peaks*, Dale Cooper solves the mystery of Laura Palmer's murder through the modification of his standard FBI procedures by his dreams of Laura and through his crucial affiliation with the Log Lady. Marietta Fortune in *Wild at Heart* is the deviation that proves the rule. Here, it is a woman's catastrophic rejection of her own empathy that threatens the bond with the real. As a result, Lula and Sailor can find release from the downward spiral of the logic of their social entanglements only through their capacity to be receptive to the maternal-like energy of the collective unconscious of society in the form of images from *The Wizard of Oz* and popular music.

The delight in and gratitude to the better energies in popular culture that are expressed in *Wild at Heart* are crucial to Lynch's filmmaking, for, while he runs somewhat against the Hollywood grain, he is at the same time filled with a faith in the extraordinary possibilities within popular culture/Hollywood that he can use for his own vision. Film, for him, contains the potential to truly instill hope in the masses through pleasure, and it is that potential that impels him to be a Hollywood filmmaker. Lynch's works, which consistently recognize clichés for what they are, find the hope for a real offer of something of more permanent value. In a time in which we are bombarded with a sense of meaninglessness and fragmentation, his films are an assertion that this fragmentation is only a surface phenomenon. Lynchian narrative images promoting empathy reveal a fundamental connectedness among people and with the universe. Lynch seeks to avoid the Hollywood trap of creating substitutes for life. Rather, he seeks to use the power of Hollywood to make film narrative a subconscious bridge to real perceptions of life.

Hollywood

The analyses of Lynch's films in the chapters that follow will explore how he uses his aesthetic of the connective image, an image purified of illusions of its own transparency—that is, of the illusion that the image is realistic because it resembles our idea of reality. As we examine his empathetic image, we will find that he uses the images, both visual and aural, of Hollywood culture, with their mass appeal, to bring the greatest consolation to the greatest number of people. Lynch reopens the Hollywood image; he does not merely repeat it. His methods, derived from painters who impressed him as a young student, give him the insight to represent both the mirror-image ideals of the filmic image and the wild energies that disturb it. In this balance, we find that he taps into the vitality of Hollywood *and* is often a corrective to the lies and repressions involved in Hollywood's pretense of a rationalist form of realism.

In his methods, Lynch is foreshadowed and influenced by a significant number of great films made in the heyday of the Hollywood studio system. In these prefigurations, there is an important narrative relationship with both the formulae of Hollywood genres and with the subconscious as an integral part of the film's realism. Such divergence from, but affiliation with, Hollywood film production occurs in the films of Orson Welles and Alfred Hitchcock, two of Lynch's major Hollywood ancestors. Both Welles and Hitchcock were constrained by the studio system. Nevertheless, each altered Hollywood by arriving at a form of realism that, like Lynch's, finds it necessary to incorporate the collision of the subconscious's unmediated energies with Hollywood's. In Chapter 1, I shall explore Welles and Hitchcock as antecedents of the type of Hollywood filmmaking that continues to evolve in Lynch's films. I shall elaborate on Lynch's kinship with his great precursors regarding the role of the subconscious in commercial film and the crafting of the consoling vision demanded by the mass audience so that the vision is real.

By refraining from engaging me within the conventions of the interview, Lynch might have appeared perverse to me if I had not let go of my conventional expectations. This book will suggest the same about the enjoyment of a Lynch film—that the perversity enters when we try to interpret it in the normal manner; simply stated, our eyes are moving, but we don't know it. The general cultural tendency to disregard responses that don't fit the parameters of social control mechanisms—e.g., highly aggressive linguistic structures, logical frameworks, and force—is reflected in the way

repetition of conventional responses blocks perception of Lynch's Intro-
originality.

In the chapters on Lynch's filmworks to
follow, I invite the reader to join me in   **Agenda**
looking closely at the way his narrative appeals to both the authority of cultural clichés and the authority of a reality that is larger
and wilder than society. In this way I hope to rescue Lynch's films
from being overwhelmed, not only by untenable hostile readings
founded on an implacable Lacanian definition of the narrative image, but also by Lynch's "cooler than thou" reputation. Too many
who aspire to "do the Lynch thing" for hip thrills also betray the
empathy his art promotes by turning it into a static (Lacanian)
illusion.

By contrast, Lynch struggles to use the eloquent tools of popular culture to portray unspeakable reality for a mass audience. This
is a struggle from which I have much to gain since so much about
me as a woman has been unspeakable in cultural discourse. However, *all* moviegoers have a stake in Lynch's filmmaking, for nothing is so prevalent—or so I judge from private conversation and
from the media—as the feeling of being invisible in some important respect. Lynch puts us in touch, as a social community, with
many longings that we simultaneously resist and yearn to share
publicly. He has achieved an impressive fluency in moving toward
an inclusive realism that both releases us from being overwhelmed
completely by the seductively estranging ideals of culture and
binds us to an inherent, complex order in the universe.

The comedy of hollow sounds derives
From truth and not from satire on our lives.

Portrait of the Director as a Surfer in the Waves of the Collective Unconscious

When David Lynch tells us, as he does in his every public statement, that he makes films to give his audience a place to dream, he is not waxing metaphorical. Rather, he is referring as directly as he can to a relationship between narrative and image, one that he first saw as a young art student in the work of his early painter ideals—Robert Henri, Francis Bacon, Jackson Pollock, and Edward Hopper—from whom he took much more than inspiration for the still image on canvas.

In the simplest terms, David Lynch the Hollywood film director learned from his fine arts education how to tell stories in the special way that we have come to associate with him. The young David Lynch dreamed of spending his life as a painter. But as he learned to fill a canvas, he was also learning a lesson that propelled him in what some would call a very different direction. From his early influences he took an understanding that narrative can bring us to truth and to each other if it makes us dream. At the same time, and paradoxically, he instinctively gleaned that the logic of narrative can push an artistic expression too close to empty conventions and become a formidable barrier to the dreaming mind. To use narrative as a support for the dream, Lynch takes a page from the painters who inspired him and neutralizes as much as he can of the drive in narrative to take control of a film. In the interviews that Francis Bacon, the most articulate of his early influences, granted to David Sylvester, Bacon sheds much light on Lynch's understanding of narrative when he identifies narrative as an expression of the human will and makes the goal of his art "the will to lose one's will" (p. 13). Bacon's "will to lose one's will" resonates in Lynch's resolute determination "to get out of the way of the paint and let the paint speak," as Lynch phrases it. Lynch approaches directing in a similar manner, working from an instinct similar to the one he saw in Bacon's canvases and bringing to Hollywood the truth of the dream.

All of Lynch's art is characterized by his desire to seek ways of deliberately holding in check the conscious will—a sublime contradiction—in order to diminish the power of the mind to force a deadening influence of clichés into a movie. This ideal accounts for his assertions that ninety percent of the time he doesn't know the reason for his directorial decisions, his way of saying that he frees himself to receive ideas, images, and impulses that his active will *could not* tap into during the directing process. Dreaming, as Lynch means to connect it with his films, requires a conscious "letting go."

In seeking the will to lose his will, Lynch "lets go" of that which most other directors and their audiences commonly identify as the artist's prerogative but which he sees as a certain kind of aggressive control that meets social conventions more than halfway and obviates much of the subconscious's production. We know the power of Lynch's ninety-percent solution from the haunting visual and aural images in his films: curtains and branches rising and falling in the wind, fire, clouds, a hero whose hair literally stands on end, a blue-lipped drowned girl wrapped in plastic, a blonde matron's face smeared with scarlet lipstick, a car wreck lit by headlights on a dark country road. However, none of Lynch's detractors and only a few of his admirers apprehend how significantly Lynch is thereby helping to change the way Hollywood tells stories.

The contempt in which thoughtful people hold Hollywood's stereotypically distorted images of life has much validity, and Lynch understands this aspect of Hollywood very well. However, he also has serious reasons not to turn the critique of Hollywood into a sterile cliché of its own. He apprehends some live coals in mass culture. He is drawn to a Hollywood tradition of touching living places in the collective unconscious in fresh, wholesome, and vital ways. For Lynch, the "letting go" that he brings with him to Hollywood is kindred in spirit to what is already there in the contradictions and intensities that abound in mass entertainment, energy that he perceives as a possible way of opening culture to its truths.

Lynch's insight into the Hollywood movie's capacity for such energy, truth, and beauty is the core of his blazing originality. For he sees in the popular film the potential for the kind of heterogeneous blend of the authority of the rational *and* the authority of the nonrational that Bacon and Pollock created in their painting. Artists like these established a heterogeneous mode of composition as a corrective to the falsifications of traditional aesthetics overly influenced by a logical ideal of harmony. Often accused of being formless, the modern concept of art asserts that in being less rationally ordered it reflects the way we really perceive. Lynch the director has made a similar decision regarding the logic of Hollywood enshrined in decades of formulaic plots and genre conventions. His contribution is that when he directs Hollywood movies, desiring the "will to lose one's will," in the same way that Bacon and Pollock met and transformed the narrative traditions of painting, he meets and transforms all the conventions of Hollywood, discovering new truths within the mass-culture scene where others make false idealizations. Restraining the will, he frees his subconscious and that of the audience, tapping back into the "something else"—as he calls it—very close to the dream that once energized what have now become tired Hollywood clichés. Lynch wants to make movies that will release that original energy to speak to and for us.

Very few artists and critics who identify heterogeneity with artistic health also identify it with Hollywood. Thus, philosophically, Lynch's work is very important because it joins the debate on the side of a small but crucial group of artists and critics who see in the wild drifts of popular culture the capacity for such imaginative forms of meaning. His work is also crucial because it asserts an optimism about cultural narratives that balances the pessimism of two other highly influential twentieth-century modes of thinking that despair of connections between rational/linguistic structure and reality: the Sausurrean linguistic model and the Freudian and Lacanian psychological models. Ferdinand de Saussure proposes that language is an illusion of control to which society desperately clings to avoid perceiving the abyss. The psychological models proposed by Sigmund Freud and Jacques Lacan assert that people invent numerous ways of imagining such control while the inevitable divisions between the human subconscious and its conscious symbolic processes make such mastery a vain, ineradicable longing. Saussure, Freud, and Lacan—and their disciples—designate culture as a kind of solipsism, language as a kind of chimera, and meaning as a phantom. These widely accepted intellectual positions assume a state of affairs in which we are essentially alienated from each other despite a seemingly rich repertoire of linguistic and aesthetic forms of communication. Further, by this light mass culture is deemed by far the worst delusion that something is being said when nothing actually is. By contrast, David Lynch has joined a line of media artists who find in the subconscious the growing tip of a really interesting mass culture. For these artists, emphasizing the subconscious energies mobilized by the conventions of the media is a way of preventing the solipsism that occurs when those conventions are merely mechanically reused and recycled.

These philosophical points are, of course, irrelevant to the pragmatic world of Hollywood, which never questions whether meaning is possible, only whether profits are imminent. But the bottom line is not all that there is to the mass media for David Lynch, and he is in the process of making a reality of his faith. Nor is he an anomaly. David Lynch is not widely perceived as a power and presence in the commercial capital of mass entertainment; most often he is defined as a loose cannon and a marginal aspirant in the California corridors of power. However, nothing could be further from the truth. Lynch is a part of the tradition of a small, significant group of Hollywood directors who have, like Lynch, in their time appeared to the naive eye as merely outrageous, flamboyant, or even decadent while they were in the process of creating new, heterogeneous possibilities for narrative expression. Of his Hollywood precursors, two are particularly relevant to understanding his place in Hollywood. They are Alfred Hitchcock and Orson Welles, who, like Lynch, seemed to stand alone in Hollywood while they changed it forever. (I shall discuss the line of continuity between Lynch and these two Hollywood giants below.) Despite the aggressive role that the will plays in the directorial processes of Hitchcock and Welles, in their films they too experimented with storytelling that de-emphasized the controlling narrative line—that is, the plot—in courting the powers and pleasures of the subconscious in narrative.

Certainly, there are many directors with whom Lynch might be compared. However, comparisons among Hitchcock, Welles, and Lynch are the strongest for heuristic purposes to emphasize the centrality in Hollywood of what Lynch is in the process of accomplishing. These comparisons are not intended to contradict the historical knowledge we have of Hitchcock and Welles as auteurs. Instead, they are meant to emphasize the kinship of these directors with Lynch in the role that the subconscious played in the personal visions with which they shaped their work rather than the control they are known to have imposed on their productions. Given what has been written of Hitchcock and Welles (and by them as well) and what I have experienced firsthand with Lynch, there are significant differences in the behavior on the set of Hitchcock and Welles on the one hand, and of Lynch on the other. However, I contend that the procedural differences concern the differences between the historical epochs in which the earlier directors lived and worked and the new politics of Hollywood that contextualize Lynch. The dark politics of the then-omnipotent studio system and their effect on Welles and Hitchcock have been amply discussed.[1] The films of Welles and Hitchcock are another story. What appeared on the screen built the commercial tradition of struggling with narrative to make it more expansive and more dreamlike in the sense that Lynch employs this term.

Like Hitchcock and Welles before him, Lynch comes to the mass media with hope, as Paul Atreides came to the Water of Life in *Dune*—as to a poison from which many men have died, but which can, if destiny so wills it, be the catalyst for great vision. The individuality of Lynch's path depends on his use of Hollywood materials in a way that will correct what his early influences, and he in his turn, have come to see as an overdependence on a rationalist illusion of control that is ultimately an obstacle to poetic truths. This will become clearer as we explore the theories and practices of Henri, Bacon, Pollock, and Hopper and how Lynch's use of the precedents they set has gained him a place in a history of commercial film alongside Alfred Hitchcock and Orson Welles.[2]

Lynch's gift to Hollywood of more powerful films with more exciting possibilities for mass-culture audiences begins, as

I noted above, with painters who deeply impressed the young
Lynch—Robert Henri, Francis Bacon, Jackson Pollock, and Edward
Hopper. In the following discussion, I will sometimes refer to explicit statements they made about their art, which Lynch may or
may not have read but which he certainly apprehended through
their canvases. At points, I will also discuss how Lynch himself sees
his relationship to them. To eliminate repetitive acknowledgments
of the source of Lynch's self-portrait, in the following pages and
throughout the book it should be understood that when I quote
Lynch, unless otherwise indicated, I am referring to what I my-
self heard when I visited him on the occasions detailed in the
Introduction.

Let us start with the sense of the narrative image that Lynch
took from Robert Henri when, as a student, he read Henri's *The
Art Spirit.* Henri was an American realist painter, whose paintings
document his role in the shift in American art toward the sympathetic representation of ordinary people. However, Henri swayed
several generations of artists not so much with his canvases as with
his book *The Art Spirit,* which speaks of the issue of rational control as a barrier to perception of the real:

> There are moments in a day, when we seem to see beyond the usual
> to become—become clairvoyant. We reach then into reality. Such
> are the greatest moments of our greatest happiness. Such are the
> moments of our greatest wisdom. . . . At such times there is a song
> going on within us, a song to which we listen. It fills us with sur-
> prise. . . . But few are capable of holding themselves in the state of lis-
> tening to their own song. . . . As the song within us is of the utmost
> sensitiveness, it retires in the presence of the cold material intel-
> lect. . . . Yet we live in the memory of these songs which in moments
> of intellectual inadvertence have been possible for us. (p. 45)

Here, in a typical passage, Henri encounters the real only when he
loses control and gets away from what ordinarily passes for language and knowledge.

Happily, Henri's ideas prepared Lynch for greater "intellectual
inadvertence" in the canvases of Francis Bacon. As an art student,

21

as Lynch tells it, he encountered in Bacon's work a new world of possibilities. When Bacon listened to the interior song, it suggested that realism was only possible if the representation was not restricted by the *domination* of any form of narrative over the image. For Bacon, reality lay in the connection between the artist's nervous system and the language of the world, as uninsulated by the brain and the will as possible. To represent a narrative reality that implicates the forms of reason but is not first processed rationally, Bacon selected images from such diverse sources as classical narrative motifs (e.g., Oedipus), a poem by T. S. Eliot, dental photographs, Muybridge's anatomical studies of the human body, and the genre of portrait painting. Beginning with powerful narrative in his paintings, he courted that in himself that would engage the hard-edged rationality of the forms with something beyond his will. Some call the resulting images distortion; Lynch calls them beautiful and especially values the movement on the Bacon canvas.

A more precise grasp of Lynch's enigmatic attribution of velocity to unmoving canvas is possible if we consult the extensive interviews of Francis Bacon by David Sylvester and combine them with what Lynch said to me about Bacon's *Triptych Inspired by T. S. Eliot's Poem "Sweeney Agonistes."* From the Sylvester transcripts, we can see that the motion Lynch perceives in Bacon's canvases is intimately connected to the "will to lose one's will." In these interviews, Bacon reveals that the artist gains vitality from the willed escape from self-control and that this escape generates the motion in the narrative image in his paintings:

> . . . suddenly this thing clicked, and became exactly like this image I was trying to record. But not out of any conscious will, nor was it anything to do with illustrational painting. What has never yet been analyzed is why this particular way of painting is more poignant than illustration. I suppose because it has a life completely of its own. It lives on its own, like the image one's trying to trap; it lives on its own, and therefore transfers the essence of the image more poignantly. So that the artist may be able to open up or rather, should I say, unlock the valves of feeling and therefore return the onlooker to life more violently. (Sylvester p. 17)

For Bacon, narrative reality is inherent in the way that the image can cut through the static of its own conventions and those of the coherent self to reach the movement of feelings, the energies of the subconscious, and the nerves. That is only possible if the artist permits such fissures to occur in the composing process. If the illustrative nature of the image takes charge through the domination of the painting by the artist's will, nothing can come of the artist's work but a boring reflection of his own intellectual limits: "some paint comes across directly onto the nervous system and other paint tells you the story in a long diatribe through the brain. . . . The moment the story is elaborated, the boredom sets in; the story talks louder than the paint" (Sylvester pp. 18–22).

In talking to me about *Triptych,* Lynch, unaware of these

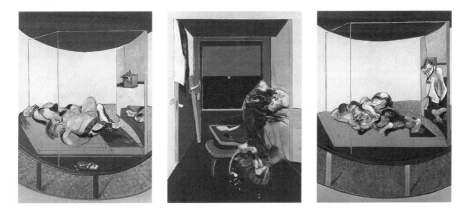

2–4. Francis Bacon, *Triptych Inspired by T. S. Eliot's Poem "Sweeney Agonistes,"* 1967. Lynch focuses on the "fast" and "slow" areas of the center panel.

Sylvester interviews, reveals how close *in process* his art is to Bacon's. First, foremost, and always, Lynch relates all of his impressions of Bacon's canvases to motion (see figures 2–4). He turns his attention first to the center of the three panels. In it, we see a chair draped with meat and a brown coat. On the seat of the chair sits a squarish object, and at the foot of the chair is another object much like a carryall, opened with objects protruding from within and scattered around it. This grouping sits in front of an opening that is both a door and a window. Lynch is captivated by the beauty of the textures in the triptych's center image and the way the "meat hooks onto this brown shape which hooks onto this thing and the way the eye just kind of flies around; it's unbelievable." He speaks of how this center image works with the right and left panels, concentrating on the way

23

the eye moves around the "fast" and "slow" areas of the pictorial fields. The figure of the chair, Lynch identifies as fast, the floor area as slow. One must not, he says, have too much fast area; that would not work, and, he says, Bacon never does that. Lynch focuses on the movement of the eye among the three panels of the triptych. What draws him in is the movement, an engagement of the eye with a beauty that is not in geometrical stasis but in the flow created by these unmoving images. This has been true since Lynch began to paint, according to Peggy Reavey.

One of the pertinent aspects of Lynch's commentary on Bacon is how little he concerns himself with the surfaces of Bacon's canvases—that is, Bacon's use of Eliot's poetry in the images, or Eliot's use of the images of Agamemnon and Clytemnestra. The center of Lynch's interest is process, what he perceives as Bacon's riveting relationship to "the paint," which he iterates and reiterates is "doing its thing," a process that produces a work of art that is exactly right, that seems not to have been painted by a human being but to have found its perfect configuration. Lynch's inheritance from Bacon is not his subject matter or color palette or specific images, but the tension created by the collision between the narrative and the non-narrative elements of painting.

Lynch speaks passionately about this tension when he discusses his own art, through which he yearns to move beyond familiar boundaries to a place where he can escape cultural overdependence on reason and its stale clichés. He speaks of the necessity for figures in the painting that are "painted in such a way that you know that they're figures but they're completely new, and so you really see them. It's much more than a figure; there's way more room for interpretation and there's a huge, big world that's opened up, and you add in so much on your own, and that's why they're frightening, because there's no other reason for them to be frightening; they're only paint."

The opening of a "huge, big world," as representational form that bends and breaks under pressure from the subconscious—*but never disappears*—is the essence of Lynch's narrative, as is well expressed in his favorite image of a duck's body as a circuit of narrative energy. The body of a duck makes the viewer's eye travel around it in a perfect flow, in the same way that Bacon creates his art. According to Lynch:

When you picture a duck you picture a bill, and a head, and a neck and a body and legs. . . . The bill is a certain color and a certain length and a certain texture. And it is completely different [from anything else on the duck], although there is something in the color and the texture that is a little similar to the legs of the duck and it is very important that that is the way that is. Then the head comes up out of that. . . . And the head comes up and comes down into this fantastic S curve. And the feathers on the head are kind of short and swift because it's faster, the bill and the head have to be a faster area. It can't be very big. The head is slower, and the neck has that S curve that lets you come down to the body. The body is kind of uneventful in a way. It can't have too much fast area. It's a big kind of fluffy kind of smooth area. And then it has these more complicated textures in the feet. And the texture is reminiscent of the bill and it returns back to the bill and makes this trip. The eye wants to go down the S curve and it gets to the feet and it makes the whole trip.

Lynch's prose poem about the duck concerns the empathy between eye and form, the shape that art achieves when the cultural inheritance of the artist and nature are in dialogue with each other. Lynch's sense of beauty and movement heterogeneously contains within it an allusion to the logical, geometrical perfection of the circle, but, here, it is not dominated by the limits of symmetry. Lynch's duck is a circuit of beauty, moved by the asymmetry of the parts. It is important that the bill is not like the legs but yet reminiscent of them, so that the return of the eye from the legs to the bill, the making of "the whole trip," is motivated by a spontaneous mystery of resemblance and difference, not by the mechanically reproducible repetition of symmetry.

But flow is not the whole story. Indeed there is no story without the element that challenges our understanding of how the pieces relate to each other—the greatest link between the spectator and reality is the mystery of how the eye of the duck fits into the balance of the duck's body. In moving from the bill to the head, down the S curve, around the body to the legs and feet, and back to the bill, we would seem to have the organic form of the duck. And yet Lynch asserts that the secret of the ocular rapture is the eye of the duck, disconnected from the connected lines of the duck's body but the glowing impetus for all the movement that radiates mysteriously around it.

The eye's desire to move around the "fantastic" S curve is the contact with reality, both a function of the recognizable shape and something that cannot be read through a cultural coding dealing with the invisible relationship between the sparkling eye and the form of the outline. Lynch explicitly connects this movement with what moves in film narrative. He has made this connection in numerous interviews in which he speaks, as he spoke to me, of the "eye-of-the-duck" scene.

The desire to make his paintings move, in the context of a Baconian understanding of movement and narrative, generated not only his career change but his painterlike definition of the crucial moment of his films as an "eye-of-the-duck" scene, while more conventional directors focus on a narrative moment, the climax. In his films, his "eye-of-the-duck" scene is the necessary prelude to closure but not in the way that the climax is. The three scenes he identifies as this narrative necessity in his work will illustrate for the reader the necessity of thinking differently about narrative structure in Lynch's films: in *Blue Velvet,* the scene at Ben's place; in *The Elephant Man,* the scene in which the title character attends a musical fantasy pantomime in one of London's West End theaters; and in *Wild at Heart,* Sailor and Lula's discovery of a dying girl in the middle of an automobile wreck. While the dramatic climax is clearly related to the plot, all of these scenes appear to be gratuitous. But they are so only if one considers narrative as a conflict to be resolved by the will of the protagonist. In fact, these scenes make narrative a function of both will and the nonrational sensibilities beyond volition. As the eye-of-the-duck scenes are discussed below, we will see that they are precisely the scenes in which the protagonists lose their will in the flow of narrative events. If we can break through the cultural fear of such a moment, we can see how felicitous this moment can be. For it is in this moment that the protagonists either accept losing control and head toward a positive outcome, or reject losing control and begin a slide down the slippery slope of despair.

The fear that there is chaos beyond the culturally imposed will is groundless in the works of both Bacon and Lynch. For Lynch, as for Bacon, cultural forms become real once they are infused with the energy of the artist's subconscious. Of some interest is Lynch's aesthetic inspiration by an artist who himself had impulses associated with filmmaking. Bacon was fascinated with photography, particularly with that of Eadweard Muybridge, whose photographic studies contain the essential concept of cinematic movement, and he greatly desired to paint in frame series: "I see images in series, and I suppose I could go on long beyond the triptych and do five or six together, but I find the triptych is a more balanced unit" (Sylvester p. 84). But here it is appropriate to note that what Lynch did not take from the older painter is also of interest. While Lynch's heterogeneity appears to have roots in Bacon's struggle with narrative and visual forms, he did not take on the substance of his inspiration's vision. Bacon's vision is suffused with homoerotic emotion and an excruciating sense of deterioration. By contrast, Lynch's vision is heterosexual and ultimately joyful.

The spirit of play and joy in Lynch's heterogeneous sense of reality is closer to the ebullient canvases of another of his painter inspirations, Jackson Pollock. Pollock's statement about his art also illuminates Lynch's feelings about his own painting as well as about his films:

> When I am *in* my painting, I'm not aware of what I'm doing. It is only after a sort of 'get acquainted' period that I see what I have been about. I have no fears about making changes, *destroying the image* [emphasis added], etc., because the painting has a life of its own. I try to let it come through. It is only when I lose contact with the painting that the result is a mess. Otherwise there is pure harmony, an easy give and take, and the painting comes out well. (Frank p. 68)

Lynch resembles Pollock in their mutual joyful submission to the life of the work. Lynch's reluctance to talk about art "because there is always so much more" is part of his sense that the unrelieved rationality of language forges a distortion of reality that might make him lose contact with the work and concoct a mess. His description of Pollock's *Blue Poles: Number 11, 1952* suggests how deeply he feels that authenticity is the confluence of nature and culture when the artist's will-to-control is humbled by a respect for an external reality: "It's like nature. . . . He's painting but he's not getting in the way of the paint. He's not making it be just like him. It's bigger than him. It's like nature's working on it; he's working with nature and with paint. And so the whole thing has a wild dance that's so organic, and yet he's putting enough control

in it so that he's acting and reacting and nature's acting and reacting, and it's like a heavy symphony where the whole is more than
the sum of the parts."

Pollock's influence on Lynch is less visible than Bacon's. We
can find the surfaces of Baconian images by the score in Lynch's
work—particularly Lynch's emphasis on the mouth, the lips, the
cry, and what this does to our perception of the facial form, as in
the soft-focus, flowing image of Frank Booth roaring in *Blue
Velvet*. Pollock's significant contribution is more the sense that the
crux of narrative is the surrender of the protagonist's will that we
see especially in the eye-of-the-duck scenes, as when Jeffrey learns
what he needs to know as Frank Booth's utter captive at Ben's place
(*Blue Velvet*), or when Lula is completely overcome by witnessing
the death of a victim of an automobile crash (*Wild at Heart*), or
when John Merrick is held captive by a fanciful musical pantomime (*The Elephant Man*).

By contrast, the influence of Edward Hopper on Lynch seems so
obvious that it is easy to miss its complexity. Many of Lynch's
frames actually resemble the small-town scenes of Hopper's canvases: *Sunday Morning, Four Lane Road, Western Motel,* and *House
by the Railroad,* to name but four images recognizable in Lynch's
films. However, this surface interface is secondary in importance
to Hopper's experimentation with the collision between the cultural and the subconscious by means of the carnivalization of
familiar appearances. Hopper's images of railroad tracks, small-
town facades, offices, apartment bedrooms, cafes, and people situated in anonymous public spaces tantalize us because they look so
mimetic and yet at the same time suggest a way in which cultural
spaces like houses, cafes, and even the surrounding cultivated land
are like theater sets. For Hopper, the ordinary image of reality is
vivified by his ability to remind us of what is not seen. This is
sometimes available as a shadow, or as a suffusion of light, or in
the evocation of carnivalesque performance in what passes for the
representation of reality in society. The performance-like pose of
the ordinary woman sitting on her balcony in *Second Story Light*
conveys a sense of watching an actress in the spotlight, similar to
what we get from other paintings of women alone in minimally
furnished, isolated rooms—e.g., *Morning Sun*. These paintings

are primarily addressed to a perspective that does not accept mimetic realism but yet acknowledges its power in culture.

For the theory that expresses the relationship between the carnivalesque and the representation of the real, we will have to turn to Mikhail Bakhtin:

> Carnival is the place for working out, in a concretely sensuous, half-real and half-way-acted form, a *new mode of interrelationship between individuals,* counterposed to the all-powerful socio-hierarchical relationships of noncarnival life. [In carnivalized representation] The behavior, gesture, and discourse of a person . . . defining them totally in noncarnival life . . . become eccentric and inappropriate. *Eccentricity* is a special category of the carnival sense of the world, organically connected with the category of familiar contact; it permits—in concretely sensuous form—the latent sides of human nature to reveal and express themselves. (Bakhtin p. 123)

Here, Bakhtin captures concisely what Lynch learned from Hopper—to view the heterogeneous clash between culture and the subconscious from the perspective of the subconscious, a perspective from which ordinary pragmatic rituals of bureaucratic and mercantile processes are flattened and defamiliarized. Such is the Hopperlike carnivalesque in the behavior of Detective Williams in *Blue Velvet:* "Yes, Jeffrey, that's an ear." Such is the feeling we get about the ordinary, yet suddenly comic, apparition of flatbed trucks carrying logs in *Twin Peaks,* and about the unspeakable strangeness of a man buying an axe in the Beaumont's hardware store in *Blue Velvet.*

Lynch's inheritance from Bacon, Pollock, and Hopper is reflected in its purest form in his own paintings. On his canvases, narrative aspects of the image are rendered as if we were already freed from stock responses, leaving us with innocent eyes that comprehend culture as the tracings of bounded form miraculously quite stable in a sea of perpetual motion. A 1992 painting called *So This Is Love* is typical of Lynch's depiction of reality through heterogeneous use of paint materials. *So This Is Love* literally bears a title that conjures up sentimental, glossy-magazine illustrations in the letters that are pasted across the image in little squares such that the words take on the texture of visual mosaic. The image itself—a network of stick figures against a ground of grey, streaked non-geometrically with white and black brushstrokes—strains against the sentimental resonances of the title. The figures evoke a landscape in which a child is standing in his yard over which an airplane flies with a white-grey jet trail "moving" into the top center of the composition. The stick-figure child is evoked in grey-white brushstroke legs beginning below the position of the house and rising above the airplane, torsoless and topped by a white circle of a head and two small stick arms. The cut-out title letters are pasted along a line parallel to that of one of the character's legs, but at a distance (see figure 5). The network of shapes represents the image of a child whose elon-

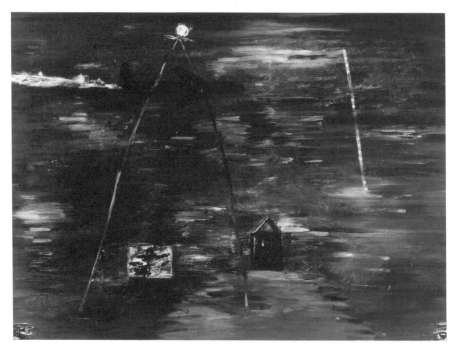

5. David Lynch, *So This Is Love*, 1992.
A larger order holds in place many equivocal, human-made structures.

gated legs permit his head to rise into the sky even higher than a passing airplane.

The minimalist stick renderings of a human figure, house, and airplane, as well as the culturally resonant title of the picture pasted onto a field of greys, blacks, and whites, have mistakenly been read by critics as the statement of a pessimist. Comments on Lynch's painting in the catalogue of the exhibition of his paintings and photographs at the Sala Parapallo in Spain, reflect the moralizing of darkness as evil when they refer to the works as images of "the abyss . . . within ourselves" (Lynch p. 14) and of the landscape of a "terror-stricken" child (p. 22).

However, an alternate reading, one that credits the influence of Lynch's painter influences, particularly of Bacon and Pollock, suggests that the canvas invokes the child's eye in us that dances around the surface of the canvas unimpeded by any demands for mimetic, Rockwellian realism. In this sort of reading, one might discern a kind of imitation of the duck's S curve. Perhaps the trajectory of the plane quickly brings the eye into the canvas to the point at which the elongated leg of the child leads the moving eye down a slide to the slow area of the house and the rectangle and then back up the other leg, which is whiter and faster, to the elation of the almost floating circle of the head from which the eye shoots to the descending trail of letters. This reading privileges the desire of the eye to flow around a system of shapes. It also privileges the spirit of the eye's flow, which evokes the endurance of drastic ups and downs, as well as a spatial and temporal relationship that exists in pulsating energies; this is a context without compass points, without even the indication of firm ground. To our amazement, the configuration of shapes is centripetal; nothing, not even the letters, which are so distant from the shapes, threatens to float away, although there exists no visible force that keeps all of this together.

The miracle of the image is the possibility of narrative coherence. With no possible grounding in any solidity, how does the configuration of shapes stay together? How is wholeness inherent in a configuration so heterogeneous in nature? The painting is the testimony to the miracle of wholeness in dissonance. Of Lynch's many paintings of stick figures in a shimmery grey darkness, some are exuberant like this one. Others, like *Shadow of a Twisted Hand across My House* (1988), connote the conductivity of pain and violence through these unfathomably coherent systems of heterogeneous relationships. However, it is not the rational interpretation of greyness as fearful and suffering that represents the pain or violence, but rather the manner in which the painful constriction of energy in the interrelationships of forms creates pathways for the eye.

In representing the real through the interplay of unbound energies and bound cultural forms, Lynch alludes to the twentieth-century fear that the culture we have built is not grounded on rock. In representing the mysteries of coherence despite the reality of cultural inability to control wild forces, he comforts us with the revelation that stabilizing forces far beyond the kinds of controls that human beings can willfully assert are in play and guarantee a viable place for human culture in the universe.

Losing It/Finding It on Screen

Reassurances also live at the heart of the storytelling in Lynch's movies.[3] In directing, Lynch has developed from his painting legacy in a way that resembles Hitchcock and Welles, who also use the realm of mass culture to reveal the limits of social structures only to reassure us about how much more is "out there" and to let us know that what is beyond our control is often a palliative to the suffering that human beings endure from limits they impose. It is no accident that the three of them are most attracted to bringing changes to the genres that are most closely connected with the subconscious and therefore offer the most opportunities for heterogeneity: the horror film, the melodrama, the psychological thriller, film noir, and the suspense film, genres that are permeated with the sense of "something out there"—actually *in* there, that is, the subconscious.

Hitchcock, Welles, and Lynch are monumentally important to these genres in particular because conventional Hollywood has mined them in ways that exploit and manipulate the audience to draw from them thrills and chills of fear, an amusement-park attitude toward entertainment that depends on the logic that what lies beyond reason is a threat. Hollywood has typically depicted the larger energies of the subconscious in these kinds of films through a conventional, moralizing plot that effects control over the *nonrational* by coding it as the *irrational,* that is, something defined as lacking because it is not rational and so must be controlled or even erased at the climactic moment. The sensory experiences of darkness and lack of visibility as well as of light and open space that are so important and beautifully used in Welles, Hitchcock, and Lynch are, in conventional films, diminished by being coded as bad (darkness) and good (light). Because Hollywood has thus trained us to feel intense anxiety about darkness until it is dissipated by light, many habitually assume that such is also the case with Lynch's films, an assumption commonly made relative to the works of Welles and Hitchcock as well. However, the work of these three in these genres is so outstanding because it forms a Hollywood lineage that challenges our mass conditioning to simplistic, reductive, logical labeling of energies, a conditioning that impedes the free flow of the subconscious in facilitating our perceptions of our world and of our emotional situations within it.

Lynch's Hollywood forebears took the labels off darkness and light by losing rather than incorporating the influence of painting. Initially, both Welles and Hitchcock were attracted to the uneasy shadows and odd perspectives of the German expressionist canvas. However, if expressionism originally included a hopeful approach to the subconscious, Hollywood has used its shadows and veils to represent the subconscious as a dangerous internal force that must be checked. Only in their earlier work did Welles and Hitchcock use expressionism to evoke enclosed spaces of shadows and distortions that primarily serve to titillate a rational dependence on light and total visibility as a sign of security in the manner that a carnival spookhouse does—the audience thrills to a "safe" sensation of danger, knowing that social controls are actually in place. As they evolved, Welles and Hitchcock abandoned learned correspondences between light and safety and between darkness and danger, gaining the kind of authentic intensity that occurs when cultural controls are actually removed in a way that prefigures Lynch (discussed further below). Thus, both Welles and Hitchcock eventually embraced the heterogeneous tensions between culture and the subconscious by *rejecting* their painter influences, or at least rejecting the way expressionism had been used in mass culture to evoke fear of what the mind cannot control or label.

The three all arrived at some important similarities in losing, or at least complicating, reductionist labeling. They most obviously resemble each other in the unusual intensity of audience response to their alteration of bad/good-dark/light narrative polarities. Lynch's filming of many of his most threatening scenes in full light intensifies the shock to the audience's nervous system, as in *Blue Velvet* where, although Lynch uses virtual three-point lighting, violence lurks just beneath the surface of every word and gesture at Ben's place. BOB materializes in the sun-drenched living room of the Hayward home in *Twin Peaks,* and when he appears in darkness he is suffused with a light within which there are no shadows (see figure 6). Here is where the power of Lynch meets the intensity of the Welles who, in *Touch of Evil,* depicts the shining of light into darkness as a sinister attack when the heroine is fixed in the beam of a flashlight in the darkness of her room. Here is where Lynch meets the later, virtually shadowless, non-claustrophobic Hitchcock whose depiction of the brutal murderer in *Psycho* is powerful because it is set in the value-free light of a bathroom. We can also see the connection between Lynch's directorial instincts and the vicious wife-killing in *Rear Window* that takes

6. BOB materializes out of the sun-drenched Hayward living room.

place in the blind space of a completely exposed courtyard, as well as the crop duster that comes at the hero of *North by Northwest* out of the cloudless sky over a wide, empty plain. Similarly, the swarms of flying creatures in *The Birds* appear in a vast expanse of perfectly blue daylight sky, not from out of some dark, gloomy night. Hitchcock's use of light here does not imply a reversal of the old categories—i.e., light is evil—but that morality is irrelevant to the experience of dark and light.

Unmoralized, unlabeled space that impacts directly on the nerves, avoiding the learned associations between dark and evil, brings with it a liberating, sometimes euphoric, feeling but also an uncanny sensation of disorientation. This is an important part of the shock of Lynch's first film, *Eraserhead,* which is still puzzling to filmgoers who try to "read" its darknesses, in which protagonist Henry Spencer ambulates and cogitates, within the usual definition of darkness as evil or fearful. In *Eraserhead,* Lynch's film frame opens for the spectator the physiological depth of darkness (see figures 7 and 8). Its visceral quality is the focus as we look at how dark darkness is (see Chapter 6). Concurrently, we also see light and hear sound in this unlabeled way, as part of the narrative experience.

But this disorientation is not merely a part of an aesthetic of shock. It also offers a refreshed mode of perception that expresses

34

to us a vision that our comfort does not lie exclusively in social forms, for beyond them is not a void—compare Columbus insisting that he would not sail off the edge of the earth—but abundant larger realities. Indeed, Lynch suggests that our fear comes from our unreal dependence on the boundaries we have created for ourselves. If we return to *So This Is Love,* we can see the roots of the challenge to this dependence in the pervasive Lynchian image of air in his painting.

In *So This Is Love,* Lynch's use of the stick shapes reduces the importance of the ordinarily foregrounded cultural forms—the minimalist narrative of the house, the human figure, and the plane—and augments the presence of the background, here a streaked greyness that fills the canvas. Our education has taught us to make a logical association between grey and depression, perhaps fear, or some other negative emotional state. However, if we let go of whatever rational associations culture urges us to tack onto this pervasive streaking of the canvas—to whatever extent we can—and we dream, in the Lynchian sense, then we are free. We are free to note that the absolute saturation of the canvas around, behind, and in the recognizable forms is a representation of the air as if air were suddenly visible as the materiality that it is, imperceptible to the rational eye though it may be.

7–8. Dark and light in *Eraserhead* are tonal prompts to the subconscious, not moral cues.

Hereby, Lynch grants us a meditation on the mystery of structure in space. The painting fills us with wonder at how a space so completely full of air can still contain structures. And we can take this a step further so that this painting is a way of representing another presence that we cannot rationally see when we are seeing—the subconscious. The reading of this canvas in terms of the depression associated with grey maintains the spirit of illusionism which codes grey as fear. We limit our sense of wonder about the universe if we cling to illusionist realism in this painting. The same can be said about literalism in our interpretations of Lynch's films. In the films and in the paintings, miraculously, air and solid form can occupy the same space; miraculously, reason and the subconscious are simultaneously operative.

Lynch's films are full of overt references to what I shall call the "language of the wind," a visual evocation of free energy, ordinarily invisible, in tension with the narrow confines of cultural form, ordinarily all that *is* visible. For example, his influence on *Twin Peaks* fills the screen with the pleasure of air in the recurring sensory images of the rising and falling of the Douglas fir boughs in the wind, and of the traffic light swinging on a wire. The pleasurable presence of what is "out there" is part of all of his films— think of the clouds in *The Elephant Man,* the floating figures of hope in *Wild at Heart* and *Fire Walk with Me,* and space in *Dune.*

Lynch's use of sound, another function of air, also fills his cinema with the pleasure of what exists beyond ordinary mimetic images of the real. He is not interested in what the illusionist understands as realistic sound. For him, film sound is not the illusion of a perfect mimesis of sound effects; it is another reflection of the multiple dimensionality of the film frame. Thus the mixed sound track of a Lynch film is full of hums, rumbles, throbs, pulsations, and the sound of wind in addition to typical sound effects, such as doors opening and footsteps, and a musical score that make the track sound as fully occupied as the film frame looks. In this way, sound deepens the visual depiction of the miracle that narrative representation can contain so much outside of bounded image and narrative.

Lynch's de-emphasis of foreground objects to make way for perception of the air creates a hole in the film frame into which the subconscious may enter, finding its own reflection as a similar unremarked omnipresence. When air is no longer an irrelevant backdrop for cultural clichés which ordinarily pass in Hollywood film for the whole of reality, those clichés are relativized. This is Lynch's way of freeing film narrative to play with the social labels on which conventional illusionist narrative and characterization depend, without losing that element of storytelling altogether.

What is conventionally designated as "character" exists in the films of Welles, Hitchcock, and Lynch, but it is expanded to reveal how so much of what is traditionally accepted as character in movies is actually ritualized behavior—compulsion that take its force from some illusion of coherence, not from a direct foundation in a larger reality. The existence of a character on the border between logic and the subconscious is responsible for the unusual texture of the Lynchian scene, and, as we shall soon see, is a development of what Welles and Hitchcock achieved in their films. An example is the interchange between hero Jeffrey Beaumont and heroine Sandy Williams in a car outside a church in *Blue Velvet*. This scene walks a puzzling fine line between its stereotypical appeal to stock melodramatic response and an aura of artifice that appears to threaten its own conventionality.

At this point in *Blue Velvet*, Jeffrey, with Sandy's help, has broken into the home of Dorothy Vallens, a woman connected with a strange crime, in order to investigate the case, and now he is reporting back to Sandy. Two young adults, Jeffrey and Sandy are assuming roles in what started out as a kind of game of playing detective. Thus, this scene is played out against a rich Hollywood context of detective movies and coming-of-age adventure movies in which the adversary is external and all of the hero's will is necessary to find the adversary and put the pieces of the puzzle together. But, atypically, well before the film reaches its climactic moment, Jeffrey has found the villain, Frank Booth, and knows the whole story. The problem is that he is still reeling from involuntary emotions that have been unleashed in him by a sexual attraction to Dorothy that renders him more like Frank than the ideal detective who will bring Frank to justice.

The tension between Jeffrey's uncontrolled impulses and the stereotypical masculine role of detective comes out in a most undetective-like, plaintive line that inevitably provokes audience laughter: "Why are there people like Frank? Why is there so much trouble in this world?" The cry situates him right on the boundary line between his feelings and his pose. The questions, absurd for a detective, are disguised but unwilled cries of self-doubt. When Sandy responds by telling him of a good omen in her dream about robins who bring light and love to a dark world, she plays an ordinary, stereotypical feminine role of maternal comforter. However, she too is both absurd and endearing.

Lynch is neither making fun of this scene nor simply tweaking the youthful earnestness of his protagonists. He is instead representing the characters' (and audience's) authentic difficulty with the male and female roles that mediate their existence both as representations of the real and as narrative mechanisms. This difficulty comes out explicitly when, with pure gratitude for Sandy's solicitous attitude even if it doesn't bear on his problem, Jeffrey tells her she's a "neat girl," and Sandy replies, "You are too." Both are aware of the gender confusion, which Sandy quickly corrects, but they are also so filled with emotions toward each other that their feelings are grounded even if confused for different reasons about how they fit into the plot action. The narrative pleasures here are potentially very great, for these scenes portray the discomfort we all feel with our social roles as well as with the dichotomy of our reaction to popular culture as both emotionally gratifying and a little less real than an amusement park.

Lynch is not representing the bizarre but rather the reality we actually know. It is the reductive illusionist image to which we have become acculturated that is bizarre in its exclusions. Perhaps we are experiencing the shock of recognition of our own learned habits of perception when we think that Lynch films are strange. His exposure of the mapping in a narrative film changes the way we identify with narrative film much to our benefit. In a Lynch film, we identify less with the plot and more with the characters' uncanny experiences of the roles they are driven by the plot to play; the narrative is no longer the invisible norm of the movie experience. Indeed, the structure of narrative becomes visible as a series of tensions between invisible urges and visible, rigidly set cultural identities and parameters.

Through its powerful presence in the Lynch film, heterogeneous clashes between cliché and subconscious energy open up the usual categories of characters. The familiar strong, silent hero; the femme fatale; the ingenue (male and female); the hard-boiled detective; and the remaining stock figures are in the film, but newly visible as poses with which the characters struggle. Thus, as spectators, we simultaneously have the illusory reality of Hollywood's heroes and heroines and a validation of our subconscious sense that they are created forms.

Adding to the heterogeneous tensions in the viewer's relationship to the characters, Lynch frequently addresses involuntary bodily actions that shift the spectator's belief not only in the characters but also in common gender constructs. Jeffrey's incorporation of the conventions of the detective film in his plan to investigate the ear is juxtaposed with the involuntary urge to urinate. This act creates a recognizable tension between the role of the masculine heroic stereotype and the masculine body. Jeffrey has taken on the glamorous detective role in a calculated way, and his involuntary need to relieve himself keeps him from hearing a warning signal at a crucial time. In *Wild at Heart,* the involuntary process of vomiting creates a tension between the direct sensory presence of the bodies of Lula and Marietta and their contrived styles of glamor and also brings their bodies into the action of the film quite apart from the calculations of their appearances. In *Twin Peaks,* there is a similar tension between Dale Cooper's involuntary physiological reactions to odors, tastes, and gunshot wounds and his conventional heroic role. Of course, the contradictions of uncontrollable physiology and the determined shape of the narrative role are at the heart of *The Elephant Man,* not only in John Merrick's ordeal of survival, but also in the pointed ambivalence of his role-playing of Romeo with the glamorous actress Mrs. Kendal.

Remarkably, these strains in character representation do not diminish our pleasure in narrative but rather heighten it in a dynamic way. In *Blue Velvet,* our pleasure in Jeffrey Beaumont is augmented when he takes time out from being a conventional young hero in order to urinate, and there is more gratification because more than scatological humor exists here. Much of what we learn about heroism in this film evolves when Jeffrey's penis takes on a life of its own. This involuntary energy collides with his more conscious dramatic and conventionally heroic purposes.

This pleasure that heterogeneity brings to familiar conventions of heroism finds a correlative pleasure in Lynch's depiction of the femme fatale. Illusionist films project all of their fear of losing control onto her. By contrast, in *Blue Velvet* we are just as aware of Jeffrey's body as an equally unsettling locus of disturbance. At the same time, the mystery of Dorothy's consciousness of her role, a consciousness which she cannot act on but which is strongly present in the film, changes the nature of the conventional object-role of the desirable woman. While we, the audience, preserve our stereotypical identification with the narrative desire of the hero, that identification becomes intensely problematic when the film creates a resemblance between the desires of the hero and those of the villain. When the hero and the villain both desire to abuse Dorothy, and Dorothy welcomes it, old gender roles are present, but new discomforts with those roles are also in place.

Lynch's disquieting representation of gender stereotypes within the plot has caused critics like Danny Peary and Roger Ebert to feel discomfort or even disgust with *Blue Velvet.* Lynch appears to them to be fostering misogyny or glorifying sexual violence. But in fact, the film is provoking an intense separation between the enjoyment of the film and enjoyment of abusing women, gratifications that are often conflated in conventional realist film. Furthermore, *Blue Velvet* also offers an alternative to women in the audience, who are most often limited to the two possibilities that Hollywood usually gives its female spectator: identification either with the gender-appropriate passive object (victim) of sexual force, or with the gender-contradictory agent, that is, the man exerting the force. In *Blue Velvet,* the female spectator can identify with the problematic relationship of the hero with the desirable beauty and with the beauty's problematic relationship with herself. Later, in *Wild at Heart* and *Fire Walk with Me,* Lynch goes further, creating audience identifications that are fully alienated from the abusive realities behind conventional gratifications created by a heroine who is an object of desire. Instead, we identify with all that is unclassifiable by those poses—the seeker in the detective who crosses the detective's ordinary rational limits, and the secret within character structure, a secret that radiates something mysterious beyond the stereotypical icons of love and beauty.

With the conventional "role" no longer a unifying, stabilizing element in the Lynch film, new character realities emerge that link character to the flow of subconscious energies as well as to the rigid structure of stock narrative types. In the continuity of his films, there emerge two possible relationships to the subconscious positions that exist in tension with conventional character and plot: the seeker and the secret. The seeker and the secret offer a place for a collective unconscious connectedness that partakes of a reality that both includes the familiar history of narrative clichés and transcends their mechanistic limits. Lynch's seeker-protagonists resemble the conventional hero in a variety of ways, but their reality in the film is not founded exclusively on a resemblance to cultural definitions of heroism but also on the character's active difficulty with that position. These seeker-protagonists drive a plot that calls for action that they cannot perform without crossing limits that have been culturally preset for them. Jeffrey Beaumont in *Blue Velvet* is one of Lynch's seeker-protagonists. Others in his work are the little boy in *The Grandmother,* Dr. Frederick Treves in *The Elephant Man,* Paul Atreides in *Dune,* Dale Cooper in *Twin Peaks,* and Sailor Ripley in *Wild at Heart.* To some extent, Henry Spencer in *Eraserhead* is also a member of this classification, but he is also a member of Lynch's other category of mass-media protagonist.

This other Lynchian category of protagonist is the bearer of the secret. The secret-as-protagonist enters into the Lynchian canon partially through Henry Spencer but also previously as the girl dreaming in Lynch's student film, *The Alphabet.* Subsequent bearers of the secret are John Merrick in *The Elephant Man,* Lula Fortune in *Wild at Heart,* the broken-hearted woman in *Industrial Symphony No. 1,* and Laura Palmer in *Fire Walk with Me.* This difficult and challenging Lynchian protagonist is usually passive in the illusionist film, the object of both some sort of attack and some sort of heroic protection. In the Lynch film, this position becomes highly active as a voyage of discovery. The Lynchian story of the secret protagonist permits this character to make the painful and difficult discovery of the connection between his or her suffering and malign elements in purportedly benign social institutions. The ultimate challenge this character must meet is to reconcile his or her radical, but mysteriously covert, exclusion from social systems with survival.

However, as alien to Hollywood as all this may seem, Lynch's forthrightness is the strangest aspect of it. Covertly, precedent for his complication of the conventional hero, heroine, and femme fatale already exists abundantly in the most evolved films of Hitchcock and Welles. Although the studio system precluded overt shaking of our confidence in labels as an obvious narrative strategy, such practices and the resulting tensions in stereotypical representation are very much a part of the hidden life of the works of Lynch's Hollywood predecessors. To make manifest these resemblances, I have selected, for heuristic purposes, one film by Welles and one by Hitchcock, each an especially clear example of the family relationship among these three filmmakers in regard to the subconscious, defamiliarization, and narrative pleasure.

The Lady from Shanghai (1948) is one of Welles's most obvious precursors to Lynch's entry into Hollywood, introducing the audience as the film begins to an early "seeker" protagonist, Mike O'Hara (Orson Welles), who acts very much like an ancestor of the Lynchian seeker-protagonist when he walks into what is clearly the contrivance of narrative. This contrivance exists in tension with hero Mike O'Hara as an authentic consciousness aware that he is being reduced to a scripted network of relationships. The separation of his larger consciousness from the script he feels forced to play is represented by a disembodied voice-over. Initially, O'Hara's voice-over narration, speaking retrospectively, dwindles into Hollywood playacting as it imitates sound-synchronized dialogue when O'Hara is shown meeting the irresistible Elsa Bannister (Rita Hayworth) as he walks near her horse-drawn carriage in Central Park. When synchronized dialogue takes over, the carnivalesque relationship continues; for example, after Elsa's carriage is waylaid by a gang of young toughs, she and Mike consciously act out the clichés of romantic encounters between heroic knights and fair ladies in distress. The film calls attention to how Mike's yearning for love and meaningful action is falsified by cultural clichés—a situation revealed as near-fatal by the end of the story.

The somewhat bizarre carnivalesque performances at the beginning of *The Birds* (1963) are similar. The meeting between heroine Melanie Daniels (Tippi Hedren) and hero Mitch Brenner (Rod Taylor) in a San Francisco bird shop is a series of gestures and poses, as each thinks he or she is fooling the other. Briefly, Mitch thinks she is a salesperson, and Melanie then pretends to be exactly that, not knowing that Mitch has already realized his mistake. The charade intensifies later when Melanie tries to take the initiative in role-playing as she visits the Brenner home in the small town of Bodega Bay, where her performance will play itself out. Here, however, the carnivalized social interchange will ultimately reveal not a seeker in the maze, but the secret of Melanie's simultaneous emotional marginality and appearance as the hallmark of glamor. Both of these films foreshadow Lynch as they gratify the spectator with a greater understanding of the "roles" people play in their lives, as with Melanie's role as the "secret" of female mystery.

In his depiction of Melanie, Hitchcock comes even closer than Welles does to prefiguring Lynch. *The Birds* presents an attack that has its mysteriously wholesome side. The birds destroy the magazine-glossy town of Bodega Bay, which has already been represented to us as an illusion of social order, full of posing, inexpressible longings, and long silences. Most impressively—if also most mysteriously—the birds liberate Melanie, the most tormented of the characters whose secret is the most submerged. While other characters can say what is wrong, Melanie's suffering is communicated most powerfully without language—by a back view as she hides the expression of her profound grief at her abandonment by her mother.

Through Melanie, a Hitchcockian forebear of the Lynchian secret character, we get our sharpest experience of a profitable, painful empathy with the loss of control, particularly in the scene in the Brenner attic in which the birds attack her. In the attic, "something else" about Melanie emerges from behind the gestures and mechanisms of her mannered role as the glamor queen. This scene gives the spectator the experience of a nerve center under the social veneer—here, an identification with the feminine, which is rare in media culture—so visceral an experience for the audience that it is difficult for a first-time viewer to refrain from the impulse to repel the birds from the face as Melanie must. Patently, she, not the force that attacks her, is the point of audience identification. The carnivalization of her glamor—her illusion of control—is analogous to the carnivalization of the pretty town. As the characters' narrative roles peel away to abject terror before the birds, we are left with Melanie as the precursor of the Lynchian secret bearer and with many questions about glamor and about its narrative role.

Like Welles and Hitchcock, Lynch takes a positive attitude toward what is "out there/in there" and probes our possibilities by penetrating the barriers that are supposed to protect us from the unknown. As we examine *The Grandmother, Eraserhead, The Elephant Man, Dune, Blue Velvet, Twin Peaks,* and *Wild at Heart,* we will see that through his seekers Lynch's films embolden us about facing the daunting prospect of crossing cultural parameters. As we examine *The Alphabet, Eraserhead, The Elephant Man, Wild at Heart,* and *Fire Walk with Me,* we will see through his secret-bearing characters into what is *excluded within* the parameters of culture in a way that reveals the invisibility of marginality as only an illusion of logic.

For Lynch, inclusiveness is also the basis of hope. *The Alphabet,* his first student film, is a short work that enigmatically evokes the suffering caused by a narrowly construed rationalist culture and concludes on an indeterminate, but pessimistic, note (see Chapter 6). However, in his succeeding works, while he is increasingly graphic about the magnitude of the problems of the human condition, he is also increasingly hopeful about the human capacity for endurance and survival. Significantly, it is this optimism that accounts for the complexity of his narrative structures.

As a result of this complexity, one of the parameters I have found a need to question as a given in my analyses of Lynch's work is the standard of economy to which criticism is generally held, a standard with which I generally concur. Reason tells us that in discussing each film we ought to dispense with as many of the details of the film as possible, opting for those few well-chosen references to the film that will make the point. In this light, the best interpretation is always one that is as tightly logical as possible. From the perspective of logic, the proliferation of detail in an analysis always smacks of inefficiency and redundancy. However, Lynch's ninety-percent solution threatens to make logical elegance a parody of itself when it seeks to illuminate films like his, the entire purpose of which is to resist the control of expression by the logic of language. Criticism, as we understand it conventionally, is not suited to the heterogeneous work of art. To understand the progress of the Lynchian seeker and/or secret, we must slow down the flight of the crow of logic and break its straight line or else we will fly right over Lynch's narrative process instead of engaging it.

This is by way of a prologue to the following chapters of analysis, which defer more than is usual to the structure of the elements in each film. I have tried to tell a coherent critical "story" about the individual works. However, I have also struggled with the tendency of the critic's logical narrative to obscure the open places and flow of Lynch's structures. In other words, I am playing with the possibilities of critical heterogeneity. I am aware that it may look to some extent like a lack of economy or a critique "out of control" in the light of conventional expectations. However, I am convinced that to compress the analysis in a conventional way would be to give more weight than we dare to the reductionist tendencies in reason and logic if we wish to appreciate the Lynchian fiction.

Further, in discussing Lynch's individual works, although I will use a chronological plan, it will not be a traditional one. That is, I will reverse chronology and proceed backward. I have selected a reverse chronological plan because it strikes me that Lynch's boldness in his early films and his struggle with his first Hollywood assignments will be more interesting to discuss once we have firmly established the achievement of the later films. However, it also seems to me that it would be unwise to begin with Lynch's last released film at this writing, *Fire Walk with Me*. *Fire Walk with Me*, although it does mark a high point of his mapping of narrative reality, is bedeviled by many current misunderstandings. A clearer perception of that film will also benefit from some preliminary exposure to Lynch's more accessible work. I have therefore decided to adopt a modified reverse chronology by beginning with *Wild at Heart* (1990), to anchor our explorations in his less controversial mature work, and to push backward in reverse chronological sequence to *The Alphabet* (1966). When we have established this inclusive spectrum of Lynch's work, we will be in a position to appreciate *Fire Walk with Me* in terms of Lynch's development as a filmmaker.

We now have a substantial body of work by Lynch which takes seriously the place of the collective unconscious in the narrative experience of popular culture. It encourages us to engage in a collective cultural life in which we use, but are not completely contained by, the labeling and categories developed by rational systems. In so doing, Lynch continues the work of Welles and Hitchcock to end the impasse between the humanizing potential of popular culture and the tendency of the mass-media industry to clog that space with stultifyingly repetitive, stereotypical texts. The urgent nature of this hope spices Lynch's pleasure in Hollywood filmmaking and the pleasure in the critical task of exploring the fresh realities of his films.

2

"I Just Met the Good
Witch"

WILD AT HEART

Wild at Heart (1990) is an accomplished Lynchian romance in which the hero transcends his limitations and becomes a seeker, and the heroine, moving beyond the traditional controls on her, attains the power of a secret-bearer of major importance. A portentous expansion of the possibilities of Hollywood film, *Wild at Heart* grows out of David Lynch's mature narrative sense of the hardships and rewards of letting "something else" speak to us. This original Hollywood movie, which reflects on both the power and the mystery of its traditions, invites us to a richly articulated, darkly comic festival of "the will to lose one's will."

Wild at Heart concerns a young couple, Lula Pace Fortune (Laura Dern) and Sailor Ripley (Nicolas Cage), who are in what seems to be an impossible situation. They live in extreme danger because Lula's insanely controlling, homicidal mother, Marietta Pace Fortune (Diane Ladd), wants to separate them permanently.[1] Having gained her own freedom by arranging Lula's father's murder, Marietta is in the process of putting out a contract on Sailor. Compounding the couple's woes, Sailor, as willful as Marietta, continually endangers Lula and himself by bolting wildly into one catastrophic danger after another. Lula's alternatives—a mother's love stained by father's blood, and blissful sexual love in a mine field—are not very promising. Sailor's alternatives—self-detonation or hostile takeover—are equally grim. Moreover, the film darkly reflects the world around Lula, Sailor, and Marietta as a world in which human will is governed by either uncontrollable violence or unyielding depravity.

This larger picture of the culture is of great importance in this film. The plot may be driven by Marietta's various attempts to part Lula from Sailor, but what is on the line for the spectator is the human capacity for positive action. Lynch takes the spectator to the edge and beyond with Lula, Sailor, and Marietta, but ultimately gives people and culture a thumb's up. The how and the why of Lula and Sailor's happy destiny despite the many perils they face create a chronicle in which the language of popular culture brings a curative subconscious into play in a world savaged by the twin Lynchian demons of control and will.

In order to give us a perspective on the ultimate union of the lovers, *Wild at Heart* turns familiar Hollywood options upside down. The seemingly insuperable obstacles to Sailor and Lula's happiness would be surmounted in a standard Hollywood film only if the hero *takes control*. However, in Lynch's film, on the road to love Sailor must learn to *lose control* or face the consequences of forever abandoning the delicate connection with Lula that has been given to the two of them through no design or effort of their own. *Wild at Heart* focuses on the necessary experience of being *overcome*—by love, by our original bond with our mothers, and by the elements of the collective unconscious that bind rather than separate us. This perspective diverges dramatically from the typical Hollywood warning about the incompatibility between nonrational energy (frequently associated with the maternal) and orderly, "normal" life. The logic of the illusionist film, asserted as reality, mandates that the protagonist forcefully guard the "normal" parameters established by reason. Conversely, in *Wild at Heart,* although Lynch exuberantly and quite pointedly represents his narrative within the context of the Hollywood film, he uses that tradition to invert itself.

Heroism as an act of will, control, and force is seriously questioned, perhaps abolished, in the first scene of the movie, when Sailor protects himself and Lula in the time-honored Hollywood way, by "beating the hell" out of his opponent. Even though his antagonist is trying to kill him, Sailor's behavior is visible here as an ugly display of force that makes the audience very uneasy since he greatly exceeds the requirements of self-defense. The film takes Sailor beyond the stereotypical role of the hero and dangerously close to that of the criminal as his actions become increasingly fraught with the counter-productive deficits of violence.

Sailor's difficulties with the conventional heroic role transform him into a Lynchian seeker. As such, he becomes a figure who survives the absurdity of the standard pose through the compelling nature of his emotional and subconscious receptivity to the larger forces of love and connection. Simultaneously, Lula transcends the stock role of the heroine who is conventionally the desired object of control. The clichéd heroine's role is deromanticized in the film as we see her suffer terribly from those, including Sailor, who try to control her. Lula emerges as a Lynchian bearer of the secret, more compelling to us because of her participation in the covert energies of the subconscious that exist within social structures rather than because of the usual charms of the heroine, that is, surface glamor. Lula's glamor, like Sailor's heroic pose, establishes false parameters, as we will see below. The greater reality of the Lynchian heroine is the energy that is simultaneously present with the glamor. In Lula's case, it is a secret force both sexual and spiritual that bonds her and Sailor to a maternal, subconscious energy that will save both of them.

Critical blindness to Lynch's carnivalization of Rambo-like heroism and his priority on the maternal in this film is the glaring flaw in the classification many critics have made of *Wild at Heart* as a "road picture."[2] True, Sailor and Lula take to the road to escape Marietta, but the "road film" is dedicated to the reality of the damn-the-torpedoes heroic assertion that requires no connectedness to location and time. Sailor and Lula on the road permit us to see the futility of such disconnected derring-do. *Wild at Heart* is actually closer to the genre of the maternal melodrama, though much transformed by Lynch. However, the melodrama's fascination with maternal energy is usually comparable to the curiosity generated by a circus animal act in which the energy of a wild beast exists to be tamed.[3]

This is not true in Lynch's film, though it might seem to be at first. Certainly, Sailor and Lula spend the film combating Marietta's feral interference in their lives. However, *Wild at Heart* divides the maternal force. Their futures and the narrative can fully create themselves only if the two can free themselves of Marietta without disconnecting themselves from the anchoring *subconscious* reality of maternity. Marietta's maternity is a dangerous rage-to-control directed at Lula. But there is another maternal energy in the film, an embracing force that is the less obvious secret of this same violent social order. This second source of maternal energy is available in nature, one of the conventional analogies for the mother. Less conventionally, Lynch also represents this energy in the secret reserves of culture—in popular music and in the sustaining images from remembered Hollywood movies. Specifically, it exists in the funny, hopeful visitation of Glinda (Sheryl Lee), the Good Witch from *The Wizard of Oz,* who comes to Sailor as a vision and thus inspires the film's happy ending.

When Sailor and Lula are finally free to be together toward the end of the film, their union is, strangely, as dubious as ever. The child that they share should be a conclusive bond, but willful logic, in the form of Sailor's absurd misreading of Lula's emotionality, continues to threaten their tender alliance. What makes cohesion possible comes out of the air and the collective unconscious of popular culture. It is also represented as another resonance of maternal energy that Lula has opened for Sailor throughout the film with her visions of *The Wizard of Oz.*

Sailor patronizes Lula's visions as a foolish, illogical part of her charm. But finally, her seeming eccentricity is her gift to him of well-being, a gift, however, that he cannot accept until he has relaxed his willfulness. In a humorous inversion of the standard slap at the hysterical heroine that brings her "back to normal rationality," Sailor needs to be on the receiving end of a punch in order to enter into the blessings of the subconscious. When Sailor leaves Lula for what appears to be the last time, he encounters a street gang, provokes them unnecessarily, and is knocked out. Here, Glinda abruptly appears to Sailor and turns the story around. "But I'm wild at heart," he moans to the Good Witch, meaning that he is deficient in "parental guidance" and thus a destined wanderer. The Good Witch reframes his self-characterization: "If you're truly wild at heart, you'll fight for your dreams. Don't turn away from love, Sailor." Sailor finds his happy ending as he heeds the Good Witch and returns to Lula.

The determining appearance of Glinda has seemed to some

spectators and critics to be a sophomoric use of *The Wizard of Oz*. However, in this closure, so full of genuine Lynchian energy, Lynch celebrates the collective unconscious that selects its own icons on its own terms from what the power structure of Hollywood proposes. Lula and Sailor have fastened onto images from this part of the popular-culture reserves as their vehicle to their subconscious forces. This event represents Lynch's vision of popular culture as the place where "something else" speaks to us and balances the controlling obsessions of our society. He believes that certain mass-media representations, although created by technology and human volition, eventually become forces independent of social control and intrinsic to the lives of ordinary people in spectacularly unforeseen ways.

When Glinda crosses the line between metaphoric image and plot by intervening in the course of story events and reinterpreting his life for the commitment-shy Sailor, her reinterpretation is by no means a narrative transgression in the world of Lynch's film; rather, it has been fully prepared for, and it creates the *meaning* of the film. Indeed, through Lula's visions it has been a continuing, peripheral presence. With Glinda's reinterpretation of the film's narrative destiny, what previously existed only in Lula's dream life now crosses into the plane of action. When Glinda appears to Sailor, she is the last and only hope for him to save himself from the vestiges of conventional heroism that cling to him even after all that has transpired in the story. Ordinary logic keeps him a prisoner of old, "normal," alienating patterns. Thus, an image from society's subconscious brings about the happy ending, superseding the literal deficits of both the culturally defined mother and the conscious cultural order. This, not the particular image, is the point of Glinda's scene.

Glinda is a comic vision, carnivalized through a goofy distortion, reflecting how old images from the mass media populate our dreams. (The crucially comic aspects deriving from Glinda's obviously artificial appearance will be further discussed below.) Nevertheless, she represents the reality that the willful characters have previously blocked. Her appearance is actually Lynch's way of experimenting with lessons he took from Bacon, Pollock, and Hopper about the subconscious and narrative form. Glinda is the long-awaited entry into events—too burdened by the corrupting, raging will—of the fruitful maternal subconscious. She is even more than Sailor's access to his nonrational wellsprings; she is also the film's access to the reality of a meeting of social mediation and the subconscious in that twilight zone in which the human future is created. *Wild at Heart* is Lynch's return via the language of popular culture to the near perfection of his first feature-length film, *Eraserhead*. This first film built the inevitability of its narrative structure on his subconscious connection with the materials of his own mythology; *Wild at Heart*, on the other hand, is built on the inevitability of his subconscious connection—and the spectator's—with the materials of the mass media.

Thus, narrative destiny in this film is not represented by Lula's will or Sailor's, both of which are pervasively flawed. Nor is it founded on Marietta's corrupt will. Rather, the narrative path honors the claims of both intentionality and the energies and intelligences that are provided to us. All of the film's elements support this core heterogeneity. The images that rivet our imagination tend to complicate rather than further the plot: immensely magnified, close-up images of cigarette ash, shoes, light bulbs, and the visceral tones of Marietta's body smeared with lipstick and gleaming red. Even the villains exist in the plot as distracting, physiological presences. The aural and visual tonalities of these villains—rapist/seducer Bobby Peru (Willem Dafoe); Marcello Santos (J. E. Freeman), an operatic homicidal maniac; and the highly stylized sadistic voyeur, Mr. Reindeer (W. Morgan Sheppard)—are as important as their conventional narrative functions. Similarly, we are inundated with the tactile aspects of the allusions to *The Wizard of Oz*, as well as with the correlations between the two narratives—the tonalities of the music associated with the iconic images and the tactile elements of the film frame. That is, Lynch prevents the narrative aspect of, for example, the image of the Wicked Witch's crystal ball from suppressing its sensory aspect, as is standard practice in Hollywood. Instead, the impact of the refraction of light through the crystal is at least as engaging as the significance the image may have to the story. In proliferating this kind of complex representation of images, Lynch prohibits the customary dominance of narrative and encourages a richer, more heterogeneous movie experience.

In tracing the operations of control and the subconscious in

Wild at Heart, we see Lynch characteristically seeding the nucleus of the Hollywood film with the lessons of his early influences about the gain in reality when representation realizes itself by the will to lose its will. Because of the cultural importance of subduing the subconscious, the body, and anything else that moves of its own accord, loss of will is usually presented in the stories we tell ourselves as a form of defeat or transgression. In *Wild at Heart,* Lynch exuberantly redefines this seeming loss as the potential abundance at the core of our humanity. As the narrative works its way through the involuntary processes of the characters, the collective unconscious of mass-media conventions, and the preconscious of the spectator, the redemption of the corrupt will's old crimes becomes possible. This possibility is inherent in the maternal connection that creates our capacity to cross the line between the rational and the preconscious—a border crossing that is our irrevocable truth.

Cape Fear: Somewhere near the Border

The optimism of the story of Sailor and Lula in *Wild at Heart* emerges where all Lynchian life arises, on the border between rational surfaces and subconscious depths, where convergence of the two makes everyone "wild at heart and weird on top." On the border, old patterns are subject to the pressures of the new through the competing force of deeper energies. If narrative conventions are the paternal forces of cultural continuity, the border is where they meet the maternal matrix of narrative and cultural renewal.

Renewal at the border is neither a safe nor a reassuring operation. The potentially disconcerting aspect of renewal is its challenge to habitual appearances of normality. The vitality of the interface between the images and energies of the subconscious and the conventions and mechanisms of the will shows itself in carnivalized form, that is, in eccentricity. This is certainly true of the story of Sailor and Lula from the moment it begins, as screen titles tell us, at Cape Fear, somewhere near the border between two states. More specifically, the film opens in a place that marks a threshold—the vestibule of a large dance hall and its staircase. This place of exchange and movement between locations is a fluid location in which no one has a "rightful" place. Here, there exists only a reflection of the social definitions that we believe hold us in place in the perhaps apocryphal location that is not on the border. The border, to borrow from Mikhail Bakhtin, is the place of the carnivalesque, which permits "in concretely sensuous form—the latent sides of human nature to reveal and express themselves" (Bakhtin p. 123).

The action on the stairs at the beginning of *Wild at Heart* immediately defines the film's action and tone by this borderline site of carnivalesque eccentricity. Bob Ray Lemon (Gregg Dandridge), a hit man paid by Marietta, assaults Sailor midway on the flight of stairs, while Lula is caught between the bloody fight and Marietta, who is peering anxiously through a door-way at the top of the stairs. The scene abounds in the latent sensual forces of the characters that create another carniva-lesque border between the energy of the flesh and the externals of appearance. The deep texture of Marietta's obsessive inter-est in the fight crosses the line between internal and external in her carnivalesque look: a thick coat of makeup; her long, clawlike, painted nails; her unnaturally smooth wig of pale blonde hair; and her costumelike cocktail dress and rhinestone necklace (see figure 9).

9. Marietta carnivalized, playing a role in her own life.

10. Sailor pointing, life as spectacle.

The heterogeneous collision of per-formance and gut emotion molds Sail-or's gestures and facial expressions. When Sailor has defended himself against Bob Ray Lemon by killing him, he turns to-ward Marietta, knowing her role in what has just happened, and points toward her (see figure 10). His entire body is speak-ing in this performance-like gesture that identifies Marietta as the instigator of the action. The excesses of Lula's physical gestures of fear and horror also display the same performance-like body position. As a result of this overtly dra-matic behavior of the characters, the film begins by focusing us on surfaces and depths even more than on forward action, resulting in the experience of a narrative that drives as much toward revelation of what is beneath appearances as it does toward the conclusion.

Wild at Heart keeps us at the borders between the visceral energies of Lula, Sailor, and Marietta and their narrative roles, thus providing us with profound narrative inversions. As Marietta chases Lula and Sailor, she appears to be the winner in the game of pursuit she has constructed. But even as she approaches triumph, the disarray of her subconscious energies predicts the sudden reversal of her fortunes that she finally suffers. The opposite is true of Sailor and Lula as they run from Marietta. They seem to be losing the game, but in the final reversals they alone achieve satisfaction.

Marietta's ultimate disintegration is predicted by her disastrous relationship to the involuntary aspects of her being. On the other hand, Sailor and Lula's relationship to their subconscious energies foreshadows sweet resurgence. Their happy ending is predominantly represented by their sexuality, which defines one rare area of pure harmony between the will and the subconscious in this film. The sex scenes between Sailor and Lula represent their physical passion as a privileged, virtually seamless act. Their sexuality defines a place in the heart of the border where we come as close to the unity of involuntary and voluntary in the connection between mother and child as is possible in the adult world. There are no carnival disguises of constructed romance, no artifacts of conventional sexual representation and language naturalized by Hollywood as "real" images of romance. When Sailor and Lula are involved in lovemaking, all that is in the film frame besides their flesh is color unconstrained by narrative shape—a warm golden radiance. The visceral palpability of the air, usually the element that reveals the strain between energy and form, is barely in tension with character action. The tension between the masculine and feminine roles in sex is represented by the collision of their bodies and by a pizzicato guitar at the very lowest end of the octaves. This produces a thumping sound, a minimum edge of dissonance consistent with a narrative that suggests a world totally alive with heterogeneous complexity.[4] This sexual authenticity is nearly seamless, conforming to the pleasures of narrative and distinguishing Sailor and Lula as the focus of audience sympathy, thus validating their position as protagonists in this film.

Extraordinary balance predicting their final happiness is already present in their sexuality. Through the events of the plot they rediscover this balance in their external lives by dealing not only with the violence that Marietta's willful strategies create but also with the clash between purposeful action and the uncontrollable forces in themselves. Not just through Marietta but also through Sailor and Lula, we see how they must cope with their own acculturation to a world of absurd logic. Sometimes debilitating social logic is directly related to less wholesome aspects of mass-cultural intervention, such as advertising. Puffing away, Sailor tells Lula that his mother died of cancer from smoking when he was very young. In response, Lula takes a sympathetic drag on *her* cancer stick and then asks, "What brand she smoke?" Sometimes that logic shows itself as a perversity of the individual will. In the afterglow of intimacy, Lula lies to Sailor for no discernable reason about an incident in her past—being raped while very young, a rape that she claims her mother never knew about. However, a flashback reveals Marietta's murderous rage on discovering this very rape. Sailor also withholds truths from Lula despite the near completeness of their sexual commitment. He refrains from telling her about an incident just prior to Bob Ray Lemon's attack on him in the dance hall, when Marietta threatened to kill him for witnessing the fire that she had set in order to kill Lula's father. Even the purity of the sex between Lula and Sailor is partially mapped by the deviant will when later in the film Lula gets "hotter than Georgia asphalt," excited by a story Sailor tells about "bad boy" sex with a prostitute who stimulates her customers with a room full of "assault weapons and spankhouse [*sic*] magazines"— icons of mastery.

These tensions in Sailor and Lula's relationship are never resolved because, despite their moments of sexual grace, they too are part of the dissonant world as it actually exists. The willful way of the world produces aberrations at which Sailor and Lula can sometimes laugh, but when they are on the spot, they too—to their detriment—put their trust in the strength of their will in a world that seems to be out of control. Their problem is that, as the evidence increases that the will is a very untrustworthy ally, they do not question the desire to take control. They chuckle over Lula's story about her cousin Dell (Crispin Glover), who wants every day of the year to be Christmas and is so seized by this desire that he spends his life conflating this wish with reality. Dell is so obsessed with what he wants that the refusal of the larger reality to conform itself to his demands prompts him to imagine aliens— men in black rubber gloves—who are continually thwarting him. His fights with these "aliens" are really just battles with an empty pair of rubber gloves that he himself has placed in his own way. No one ever sees the result of Dell's fixations because he just disappears. But laughing at Dell as "one of the lessons on life" is one thing for Sailor and Lula; confronting the alienating will in themselves is another.

When the lessons of life come closer to home, the problem of the human will magnifies. Sailor and Lula misunderstand the will as the ultimate reality, while they find themselves stymied by its paradoxes at every turn. Until the end of the film, when the hopeful truths emerge, Lula and Sailor feel more and more hopeless and defeated by the "realities" of power. This is the significance of the downward turn in their lives that follows their presence at the last moments of the life of a girl they encounter by chance on the road to Big Tuna, Texas, as she dies in the wreckage of a car accident. When Lula and Sailor come upon the overturned car, lit by the still-functioning headlights, they find corpses draped in and over the wreckage and Julie Day (Sherilyn Fenn), a girl of about Lula's age, wandering through this disaster. Julie, bleeding profusely from the head, alternately screams for Robert, her lover, and worries that her mother will "kill" her for losing her purse. Completely oblivious to her dying body, Julie continues until she dies to operate within a defined context in which she is under her mother's orders to consign objects to their proper places. Her attempt to make order while she exists in some twilight zone on the border between life and death renders the human will a self-parody. To the horror of Sailor and Lula, the life drains out of the girl while she is still trying to return her possessions to their normal locations.

This scene has only the slimmest relationship to the plot, but it is, paradoxically, crucial—Lynch's definition of the major turning

point of his films, the "eye-of-the-duck" scene (see Chapter 1). In
Wild at Heart, the eye-of-the-duck scene sends Sailor and Lula's
lives into a descending spiral, which they must experience before
they can achieve a happy ending. This "eye of the duck" is the release of the baser elements of the subconscious into Sailor and
Lula's life, seemingly a catastrophe for them but actually a necessary encounter for the seekers and secrets preceding the encounter
of the higher and finer elements of our imagination.[5]

It is no coincidence that the car crash exposes Lula to the failure
of the will of a girl, the pattern of whose situation replicates her
own—that of being caught between the authority of the mother
and the accident-prone boyfriend. As she dies, the girl alternates
between yelling, "ROBERT!" and worrying about what her mother
will say when she learns that her daughter has lost her purse and
has "sticky stuff"—i.e., blood—in her hair. Lula takes the seemingly fortuitous car wreck as a global pronouncement of destiny
on her own helplessness.

By interpreting the car wreck as a jinx, Lula demonstrates what
sustaining stories mean to us. Alone and unaided, our subconscious resources are inordinately constrained by circumstances.
Within those confines, the logic of culture, with its technology and
its politics of power, tyrannizes our consciousness through a sense
that the whole world is about will. In this eye-of-the-duck scene,
the limited consciousness fosters in Lula, who ordinarily has access to subconscious energies, a panic that her will is not sufficient.
And she continues her misinterpretations under the pressure of
ensuing events after she and Sailor arrive at their next stopping
place, a motel in Big Tuna, Texas. First, Lula discovers that she is
pregnant. At this point in the story, she considers this a depressing
invasion of her body beyond her control, suggested when she
writes a note to Sailor about her condition, unable to speak the
words. Her association of pregnancy with a transgression of her
control of her body is also evident in her memory during this
scene of a forced abortion after she was raped by "Uncle Pooch."[6]
In addition to this, in the next scene, Lula is horribly violated by
Bobby Peru, the "black angel" as she calls him, who, appearing at
the motel in the guise of a new buddy for Sailor, is actually the hit
man there on Marietta's behalf to kill him.

Angels are conventionally beyond human control but still protective. Dark angel Peru, willfully inflicted on Lula and Sailor by Marietta, has a threatening message for Lula. Peru invades Sailor and Lula's room while Lula is alone, asking to "take a piss in her 'head.'" His immediate qualification that he is referring to the toilet in her room and not to "her head, her hair, and all," is more than slightly threatening. The threat is realized when he loiters in her room after relieving himself. After guessing correctly that she is pregnant, he seizes her in an iron grip, demanding that she repeat the words, "Fuck me," to him. Lula resists, but using calculated manipulation of her breast and genitalia, Peru produces a mechanical sexual response, wringing the words from her (see

11. Bobby (like the country) Peru strips Lula of her will.

figure 11). Peru immediately releases her, expressing bashful glee as if he had just told her a wonderful joke, and promising to "fuck her" when he has more time. Lula is so defeated by being victimized this way that, when she realizes that Sailor is also in danger of becoming Peru's victim, she cannot summon the energy to aid him.

At the same time, Sailor's "heroic" will is seduced into an illusion of asserting itself by the same Bobby Peru. Sailor succumbs to Peru's plan to get easy money—a nest egg for the coming baby—by armed robbery. Sailor is not killed by Peru during the heist as Peru had planned, but he is sent to prison again. Once Peru has brought him down on behalf of Marietta, we can see that history repeats itself and things only get worse. This separation from Lula lasts three times as long as his first jail sentence (after he killed Bob Ray Lemon) and comes at a time when she needs him most. Her worst fears about her helplessness appear to be all too true when she is recovered by Marietta and embraced by Santos, the pair she now knows killed her father.

During the eye-of-the-duck scene, Lula misinterprets her lack of control as a sign that immediately debilitates her. But later, losing control works quite differently for her and for Sailor. Indeed, for the spectator, the dying girl's futility shows how deeply we are marked by cultural illusions about order. Even as death comes to Julie Day, she can only act on the basis of a social conditioning

unbalanced by a priority on volition. As her life is leaving her, she
absurdly wants to put things back in their "rightful" places. The
interpretation that our conditioning leads us to absurdities is supported by the context of the film, as we, the spectators, see the insubstantiality of what passes for success by means of the logic that
demoralized Lula. Marietta's exertions seem to culminate in victory at the train station when she and Santos take Lula as their
prize. However, she ultimately demonstrates that the seeming triumphs of the will, and the machines and order created by will, are
pyrrhic victories. Marietta's volition traces a very shaky line of
conquest along her subconscious inner forces by which it is finally
absorbed as Lula is ultimately lost to her.

Lula misunderstands her situation as she appears to fail; Marietta also misunderstands her own success. As Marietta acts out her
determination, she pays a terrible price, but, failing to attend to
the value of anything but the logic of success, she never questions
the pain and suffering caused by her plans. Her debasement of
what is generative in her is reflected throughout the film in what
is inflicted on her and on the world by the ugly acts of carnage
perpetrated supposedly on her behalf by Mr. Reindeer, Marcello
Santos, and Santos's agents Juana and Reggie.

In *Wild at Heart,* the tyranny of volitional control is drawn
in pointedly gender-specific terms as it begets a clear perversion
of both masculine and feminine roles. The masculine power of
Mr. Reindeer and Santos is represented in the rich baritone of
their voices, while their pleasures in power and assertion of control have a vicious depthlessness to them. Reindeer is the head of
a harem, a patriarch who reduces the mother's role to that of a
housekeeper managing his women and the daughter's role to that
of an object of the purely voyeuristic gaze. His scene of pleasure is
depicted as he sits on the toilet with his pants down, drinking a
cup of tea and looking at a girl dancing for him with her breasts
exposed to his view. Santos, as the man of action and Marietta's
would-be protector, can take pleasure only in what he destroys or
reviles, chortling with professional satisfaction over the best way to
inflict "lots of irreparable brain damage" and enjoying active disregard for Marietta's feelings, whom he thinks of as both *his girl*
and a "crazy fuckin' bitch." He takes her contract on Sailor for
pleasure, the pleasure of exerting power as he orders the killing of

Sailor and of Johnnie Farragut (Harry Dean Stanton), Marietta's boyfriend. This is part of a perverse romantic pleasure of serving Marietta and of possessing her at the same time. But the true horror of the overvalued will is represented in the atrocities of Marietta's success. The more she asserts herself, the greater and more irreversible is her distance from the gratification of desire. This apocalyptic swerve is clear in the way her doubling of her efforts results in the unplanned, unwanted murder of Johnnie Farragut. His murder is unusually peripheral to the plot for a scene that is given such play. It is, rather, a counter-narrative event, for it empties the value of the plot energies that Marietta sets in motion. The result of an overzealous narrative thrust, it would not have taken place at all if Marietta had been satisfied with merely interfering in her daughter's life, for which purpose she had already dispatched Johnnie. However, knowing that Johnnie will only bring Lula back and not murder Sailor, she then sends Santos out on the same assignment, even as unknowing Johnnie is on the trail of the couple in New Orleans.

Santos is only too willing to kill, and he resolves not only to kill Sailor but also to throw in Johnnie's murder for good measure. There are weak plot reasons, and other very powerful reasons, for this initiative. Santos says that Johnnie's intimacy with Marietta is a threat because, if Johnnie learns about her many criminal connections with Santos, he will surely turn the two of them over to the law. (Santos and Marietta deal drugs and colluded to kill her husband.) But this is a peripheral consideration, almost a distraction from the spectacle of perverse, solipsistic energies set off by Marietta's carnival of the will that we see in the scene when Johnnie is killed by Juana and Reggie at Santos's behest.

As Johnnie sits bound in a chair in a dark room somewhere in New Orleans, Juana (Grace Zabriskie) and Reggie (Calvin Lockhart) use him as part of their foreplay for sex, and they show him Santos's ring for Santos's gratification. The scene is a shocking one, perhaps one of the most assaultive scenes in all of Lynch's films, and most likely construed as pornographic by those members of the preview audiences who walked out on the film at this point. This negative reaction caused Lynch to delete several frames, making a rare concession to a form of censorship.[7] But, significantly, the effect of the scene defines it as distinctly unpornographic since it collapses the spectator's distance from the screen rather than giving the controlling voyeuristic distance that is the norm for pornography. Moreover, very much as in the climactic scene when Melanie is attacked in the attic in Hitchcock's *The Birds*, the spectator does not occupy the position of the controlling force in this scene (see Chapter 1). Here, the object of control is not doubly controlled by simultaneously being the spectator's object of control. The spectacle is the couple inflicting the violence and supposedly asserting the control.

Johnnie's death scene is shot and edited such that the spectator is in Johnnie's position and everything that attacks him also attacks the spectator. As Juana torments him, her face, distorted by gut-level screaming and a tongue flicking obscenely, is inches from the camera of which Johnnie is the invisible point of origin and a surrogate for the spectator (see figure 12). As Juana moves toward Johnnie with a grotesquely obscene stroking of his cheek, as she and Reggie pant lasciviously and uncontrollably, as they clutch and kiss each other, and as the gun points at Johnnie's head, the spectator empathizes with Johnnie, occupying his point of view. Together with Farragut, we are the target when Reggie says apologetically, "I can't stop her, Johnnie," as Juana commands Reggie to "fuck me now; I can't wait no longer." The assaultive spectacle is amplified by the sound, an intricately mixed track of distorted twanging, crashing, growling, and whispering, as well as the signature Lynch sound—the wind. Within the sound mélange is the articulation of the name Santos, creating his presence in the scene.[8]

12. The spectator occupies the place of Juana's victim, along with Johnnie Farragut.

Here, the spectator is given a sensory experience of sexuality perverted by will from which there is no escape through the normative controlling distance of watching movies. The portrayal of Johnnie's murder is not pornographic because it positions us as the victim of, and thus painfully aware of, the abuses of pornography. The spectator cannot enjoy this scene as a scandalous, secret transgression. Juana's masturbatory sexual gratification as Reggie

pulls the trigger of the gun pointing at Johnnie—and the spectator—is the film's palpably sickening rejection of the uselessness
and depravity of the coercive pseudoerotics of the will-to-control.[9]
Narratively, the spectacle of Johnnie's murder functions most
pertinently as a representation of the larger context of Marietta's
will which informs the linear plot. Johnnie dies as a consequence
of his involvement with her, but it is continuous with, not diver-
gent from, the bondage scenario that represents his attraction to
her. The sexuality between Marietta and Johnnie is exactly the opposite of that between Sailor and Lula. Although Johnnie, a mature
man of at least Marietta's age, is richly evoked in most ways as a
man and not a boy, in his relationship with Marietta he is infan-
tilized. Marietta is for him a mommy-seductress, playing peek-a-
boo with a Johnnie who is suddenly childlike when she pseudo-
erotically manipulates him to her will. She is not unlike Bobby
Peru in the "fuck me" scene when she negotiates with the unwill-
ing Farragut to send him after Sailor and Lula. She mechanically
stimulates him to a manufactured sexual excitement that is not
fulfilled—emerging from behind a coffee table as a growling animal dressed like a starlet, slipping into his embrace but withholding any real sensual contact. Johnnie's death virtually parodies his
life with Marietta. Bound helplessly in a chair, he is toyed with by
Juana as she alternately strokes and threatens him, suggesting in
the context of the film's themes about maternity another parody
of the mother and the child in the high chair. Moreover, as with
Reggie and Juana's simultaneous victimization by sexual compulsion and willful exercise of control over Johnnie's life, Marietta's
characterization as a homicidally domineering mother also reflects
the paradoxical tyranny of the will over the willful.

Just as Marietta's iron grip ironically closes around Johnnie in
an unwanted fashion, it also turns against her, internally cutting
her into pieces with each of her external attacks on Lula and Sailor.
To express this, Diane Ladd's body speaks a completely different
language than her lines. For example, Marietta cringes inside of
the seductive appearance she has put on as part of her negotiations
with Santos which later drive her to try unsuccessfully to default
on the contract. As she outwardly encourages him to go on the
murderous rampage he enjoys, she is inwardly in turmoil.

Marietta's fragmentation is especially evident when Santos proposes killing Johnnie in addition to Sailor. It is impossible to know whether her increasing agitation about whether Santos will kill Johnnie against her wishes comes from a real feeling for Johnnie or from her willfulness. Does she love Johnnie or is she rejecting a development that did not originate with her and is therefore out of her control? Clearly though, as she strives to regain control from Santos, separate energies are moving faster within her and rising to the surface. Crossing the border between will and the subconscious, these energies drive her to paint her upper body with dark red lipstick. She smears her skin a lurid blood color, framing her white satin, 1950s starlet nightgown, and covers her face framed by her "glamorous" platinum hair, starting first at the wrist pulsepoints where the heartbeat resonates.

Marietta's rage-to-control has put her on top of the narrative, but as she wins plot points she grows more and more radically confused and increasingly alienated from significant parts of herself. In the aftermath of her "victory," as Sailor is about to be released from prison, Marietta's energies have degenerated to a point of no return. Her Barbie-doll hair has lost its shape and is now a fright wig. No longer made-up, she looks as confused on the surface as she always has been internally. Her characteristic reliance on alcohol has deteriorated her speech and coordination, and she lurches about, holding her drink precariously and speaking with difficulty. Still screaming for Lula to stay away from Sailor, she must now face the truth that there is something bigger and more pervasive in this world than determination no matter how much violence it packs. There is a better place than the microcosm within which Marietta attempts to incarcerate Lula; astonishingly, it is the same place.

A Better Place: The Power of E. and Oz

The popular press associates Lynch with the dark side of the soul; however, in his films the nadir of existence is always coexistent with the most intense hopes and possibilities. In his work, the latter is typically a mystery of the air, an omnipresent reminder that any bounded location is always also unbounded by virtue of the air that flows in it. In *Wild at Heart*, we see a rich Lynchian representation of air as the ground of the essential subconscious space in which we move past the will-to-control. Marietta burns that space with her controlling will, while Sailor and Lula receive from it the blessings of our unbounded energies—here, the "power of E." (as Sailor refers to Elvis Presley) and of Oz. Characteristically, Lynch in this film asks us to stop blocking our sensibilities by allowing reductive familiarity with the sight of ordinary appearances of the air to deny us the truth of astonishment.

As we see air in his paintings, we also see it in his films. It becomes manifest in flames under the pressure of will, and in music, color, and Glinda in the flow of the subconscious. The fire in the film is, of course, a relatively banal narrative element through which Marietta rids herself of her husband Clyde when Santos sets him aflame and burns down their home. Images of this fire that haunt Lula's memory are also flatly narrative as the vehicle for her understanding of her mother's crime. But when we see greatly magnified close-up shots of matches being struck, we are shown that fire is also a visceral image of consuming, willfully imposed acceleration of the air to intense movement and color that occupies a part of the border where will compresses space and time into holocaust. Later, with Glinda and the song that Sailor sings to Lula, the same air is the site in which the forms of the subconscious emerge, bringing meaning to the characters, stabilizing and informing instead of annihilating.

Annihilation and creativity are always and everywhere synchronous in the air. The same air that Marietta and Santos can force to ignite can operate beyond the limits of will to bring with it a (fragile) form of utopian bliss as a temporary alternative to the violence of the daily wars of existence. The utopian possibilities are part of Sailor and Lula's story. They inhabit the gentle carnivalesque comedy of the scene at the Hurricane, a club to which Sailor and Lula go to dance before they hit the road. These possibilities also inform the darker scene in which Lula and Sailor park at the side of the road and dance away their frustrations with the harrowing events described on every station on the car radio except the music station.

At the Hurricane, as Sailor and Lula gyrate wildly to the music, the punk who drifts between them threatens to bring into a blissful, almost sexual moment the aggressions that shadow their lives. However, unlike in the opening scene, Sailor does not pull out all the stops as he did with Bob Ray Lemon, whom he continued to beat to a bloody pulp even after he had effectively disarmed and defused the threat. In this scene, Sailor economically defeats the punk with the minimum effort required and then celebrates his victory with a song. Taking the microphone, Sailor sings one of Elvis Presley's signature songs, "Love Me," while bathed in a golden spotlight with Lula, reminiscent of their lovemaking, as the other girls present undulate and shriek.

The difference is what is in the air in these two scenes. In the opening scene, it is Marietta's incendiary will, boiling out of her electric blue satin glamor gown. At the Hurricane, it is the bliss of music. The distinction is made even more literally at the roadside later in the film. By changing the station, Sailor fills the air with music instead of what Lula was subjected to on every other station—news narratives that speak of a hopeless world. One turn of the dial makes her privy to a story about a murderer having sex with the corpse of his victim; another turn informs her about crocodiles being sent into the Ganges to eat the turtles who were originally released into the river to devour corpses. The music moves from the harsh rock chords on the radio to the soaring main-title theme, as the camera pulls back to survey a panoramic integration of earth and sky, of which Sailor and Lula are but a small, organic harmony. In music, Lula and Sailor find a fleeting cultural bridge to a better place that alters the condition of where they are, just as the Hurricane does, even if it does not provide permanent shelter.[10]

In the light of this privileged place of music, we can begin to understand the puzzling happy ending of the film which seems to parody itself and thereby the viewer's feelings for Sailor and Lula that have been established during the film. In the final frames, Sailor sings "Love Me Tender," the song he has told Lula he will sing only to his wife, thus signifying his commitment to her while they absurdly stand on the hood of her car in the middle of a traffic jam. The ridiculous location of this romantic denouement is rendered even more incongruous by Sailor's swollen, probably broken, nose which juts out grotesquely—a nose clearly enlarged by putty and clearly created by a makeup artist. This final scene may take the Hollywood film a little faster and a little further toward an evolved form than many critics and fans are ready for. However, the heterogeneous mapping of the denouement is a validation of a hopeful connection to the maternal subconscious that is not possible within the "normal" Hollywood illusions of narrative.

Sailor's nose creates a new understanding of realism in closure. Here, closure becomes a comic, privileged moment when the problematic fit between the warfare of culture and the subconscious energies of nature is at its most sublime and its most ridiculous. Sailor and Lula can only find each other in such a moment of hiatus, when nature and culture are completely balanced. So too can the audience find a kind of freedom and structure together in the simultaneous mapping of the illusionist gratifications of a happy ending and a contrasting reminder that we are looking at the devices created by cultural control.

At the end of *Wild at Heart,* instead of a character willfully bringing the film to a close, all the aggressively willful characters are erased from the film, leaving only the internal debilitating tendency toward will that we have seen in Lula and Sailor. First, Sailor and Lula are freed from Marietta's will by its own self-consumption. Next, they are also freed of their internal resemblance to her by a narrative that ultimately gives up its own will-to-control by acknowledging itself as only a representation of what is in the air.

We can see this dynamic if we carefully address the end of *Wild at Heart* within the context that it has established of representing all action on the border between acts of will that are made to happen and events that evolve from involuntary wellsprings. Lula and Sailor find their way back to each other because Lula's motherhood gives them and the narrative another chance to establish a new, uncorrupted foundation in the origins of human strength and vitality, that is, the maternal subconscious. Lula takes the first steps when her pregnancy revives her strength and provides her energy beyond volition. First, she insists on having the baby against her mother's initial objections. Next, she insists on his name, Pace. Significantly, Pace is her mother's maiden name, and the naming of her child links Lula with her mother's potential strength, not with the perverse engine of destruction Marietta made of herself. Then, when Sailor is released from prison, Lula refuses to obey her mother's repeated order that she not reunite with him.

66

But as in the eye-of-the-duck scene, Lula unaided by something larger than herself is not enough. Initially, the reunion between Sailor and Lula does not bode well. As she drives Pace (Glenn Walker Harris, Jr.) to meet Sailor at the train station, the bad omen of the auto wreck and Julie Day's death resonates when Lula has a near miss with another car. Immediately afterward, she drives by a car that has crashed, leaving the occupant bleeding and mangled while a man hopelessly maimed by a former traffic accident commiserates with what may be a corpse. Once Lula finds Sailor at the train station, things still seem perilously out of control. Sailor interprets her churning emotions as a sign that they have no future together, which only makes Lula more overwrought.

Thus, Lula and Sailor begin to act out a stereotypical scenario that blocks what is real in their relationship. In the face of her "feminine vacillation," he takes control of the situation in a "manly" way and gives his son the first and last lesson he expects to give him—how to be a man: "If ever something don't feel right to you, remember what Pancho said to the Cisco Kid, 'Let's went [*sic*] before we're dancing at the end of a rope without music.'" Sailor leaves Lula calling "hysterically" and ineffectually after him as he returns stoically to the station. The mapping of what "don't feel right" in this scene leaves narrative on the border between control and the involuntary. The experience of the involuntary as not "feeling right" brings Sailor to the brink of disaster, that is, he is actually refusing to feel in order to impose control. For the spectator, it is the robotlike calm of his words and the automaton-like motion of his body as he walks toward the station that do not *feel* right.

Catastrophe is averted when Sailor becomes liberated from conventional heroic posturing and matures as a Lynchian seeker. Everything he needs to free himself from imposing a detrimental control comes to him without his willing it in the empty street over which he moves. A gang appears out of nowhere, and, feeling intimidated, Sailor plays the macho role, demanding of the kids, "What do you faggots want?" The street kids do not take well to his abusive gambit and beat him to unconsciousness. In Lynchian fashion, this loss of control literally brings Sailor back to Lula.

Throughout the film, Lula has carried the secret of what is happening to her by means of images from *The Wizard of Oz*. These cultural gifts help her to know and to express her reality before she has language and thought to do so. Wordlessly, the images of Oz create truth for her out of a power that is rooted in the subconscious. Thus, even before she is clear on all the particulars of her mother's crime, she is intuitively clear about Marietta when the air brings to her on a rush of wind an image of her mother as the Wicked Witch. Similarly, Lula's red shoes click together as Dorothy's did when she found the power to go home, a clear articulation of Lula's wish for a better place after the humiliation she has experienced at the hands of Bobby Peru. In a literal sense, Lula has no home to which to return, but beyond logic there is the home of the imagination.

13. Lula's eyes send Sailor a nonverbal message.

14. Sailor's false nose: we know it's a movie, but all the same. . . .

Lula takes recourse to this better home when she erases her mother's image from *Wild at Heart* by throwing a drink at Marietta's picture. Her mapping of herself with Dorothy, the heroine of popular culture, suggests that her bid for freedom, in part, originates beyond her own ego. She takes her strength from *The Wizard of Oz*, a common reservoir that allows her to move beyond the confines of her experience. The possibility to do so is what she must communicate to Sailor, which she again does wordlessly, as Lynch tells us through extreme close-ups of her eyes just before Sailor rejects her and then as he reverses himself (see figure 13). As Lula's eyes contain the possibility of moving past linguistic impediments toward connection, the message is thus sent. It is received later when it is processed by Sailor's subconscious into the image of Glinda.

Sailor's progress toward real "wildness"—that is, freedom from the oppressive aspects of culture—is measured through a number of encounters that point toward the one with the gang. This is the fourth in a series of battles that brings Sailor ever closer to success

as a form of receptivity. In the first conflict, with Bob Ray Lemon,
Sailor loses because he wins through brutality. With the whining
punk at the Hurricane, Sailor wins temporarily by asserting himself within the context of the collective unconscious "power of E."
In his third battle, Sailor seems doomed by again seeking to win
through the illusions of "masculine" control, roaring a battle cry
in the feed store he and Peru are robbing. However, in his last and
telling battle, Sailor wins definitively by losing (control) and sub-
mitting to the redeeming power of the subconscious in the popular air.

The tough kids and the Good Witch teach Sailor his most important and truest lesson in life, reconnecting him with the reality
of his desires in a mapped terrain of false will and authentic energy
by successfully instructing him not to "turn away from love." At
this point, the film makes manifest another element of the border
between assertion and evolution, the border that our images tread
as cultural creations. When Sailor awakens, the willful artifice of
narrative closure is unmistakably marked upon him in the grotesque, exaggerated, comical swelling of a false nose, patently created by cosmetic alteration (see figure 14).

The nose is for us what Glinda is for Sailor, an overt cue that
narrative fiction is couched in a realistic-looking illusion. The closure of *Wild at Heart* maps the spectator's reality as that of a film
audience, a reality reflected in the complex terrain of the characters' multiple layers of reality. At the same time, there is a concur-
rent reality of the filmic illusion which identifies the spectator with
the corrupt will of the characters. The closure of *Wild at Heart*
stands as an indispensable part of the film story—a cultural construction—but one which must be careful to acknowledge that the
greater reality is the subconscious source from which cultural authority is derived.

"Had Enough?"

Near the end of the film, Sailor is twice
asked whether he's "had enough," first by
Bobby Peru and then by the leader of the gang. Both times, Sailor
affirms that he has, but there is a great difference between the two
affirmations. In the first instance, Peru seduces Sailor's will into
running riot, almost costing Sailor his life as well as Lula and his

child. In the second instance, Sailor surrenders his will and gains the world. In each of these two interrogations, the viewer's will is implicated differently.

When the question is first asked, Sailor is with Peru in a bar, reeling from too much beer and from Peru's insinuations that Lula has violated Sailor's privacy by revealing her pregnancy. When Sailor slams down his beer mug and barks, "Have now," in response to the question, he is reasserting his will over his circumstances—poverty, victimization by Marietta, and Lula's purported betrayal. His response signals that stock Hollywood moment when the hero gathers his resolve. However, the spectator's identification with the resolute Sailor, a familiar moment of seeming unity, brings both the viewer and Sailor to disaster. In asserting himself, Sailor has actually submitted to Peru's strategy to fulfill Marietta's contract on his life and finds himself in the middle of a robbery with an empty pistol, looking down the barrel of Peru's fully loaded sawed-off shotgun. By contrast, when the question is asked again, Sailor makes a fruitful decision in which the spectator is implicated in the opposite form of tension, that of associating pleasure and contentment with being stripped of will. In this most unusual mass-media moment, pleasure ensues after Sailor is knocked out by the kids and thus becomes *receptive* to Glinda. The viewer's pleasure in this moment comes partially from the dichotomy—our desire for the transparent reality of a happy ending is in tension with the unreality of the vision of Glinda and of Sailor's artificial swollen nose. There is also pleasure in our identification with Sailor's new mode of receptivity. Indeed, the implication of the spectator's presence in Sailor's new, subconscious understanding of the question is visually asserted. When the gangleader asks, "Had enough, asshole?" the question is addressed directly toward the camera, a position occupied by the invisible Sailor. This does not directly create the spectator as Sailor but does suggest a close relationship (see figure 15).

The first posing of the question makes the spectator uncomfortable with the entrenched mass-media, infantile fantasy of

15. Had enough?: a question for both Sailor and the audience.

omnipotence that is routinely gratified by Hollywood's standard controlling hero. The second posing of the question seeks to make us as comfortable as we can possibly be with having had enough of that fantasy. Lynch's mapping of the border within the context of Hollywood genres and images in *Wild at Heart* leaves us at last in a position of quasi-pleasurable, quasi-disconcerted ir-resolution, hanging in mid-air like Glinda. To some extent, the film honors our feeling that we have had enough of our fas-cination with the counterproductive reassurances of popular culture, but it also honors our difficulty in getting beyond that easy gratification. Even the obligatory and pleasurable final em-brace ambiguously suggests both the con-ventional position of male-dominance/female-submission and a more mutual position of equality (see figure 16).[11]

At the very least, *Wild at Heart* compli-cates our response to such stereotypes. It mystifies the process of taking control and disassociates it from its conventional labeling as a manly and heroic process. At the most, it cancels the privileged place of control in films as the focus of admiration and the mark of maturity and effective-

16. Sailor and Lula cresting the waves of the collective unconscious.

ness. In *Wild at Heart*, Lynch suggests that ordinary life can pro-ceed only through the everyday miracle of meeting the Good Witch, but he cautions us that we must not confuse the finite shapes of icons with the fertile subconscious that makes the con-tinuous production of such images possible. Sailor's fake nose is thus the most crucial element of Lynchian reality in this happy ending. It is the reminder that we are dealing with a human form when we watch movies, that we must enjoy but not be seduced by their illusion of reality. Sailor is not a definitive revelation but rather a fiction. Similarly, Glinda is not a definitive image of salvation. Instead, through Sailor she points toward a narrative model of our survival by means of access to subconscious cultural energies.[12]

3

"The Magician Longs
to See"

TWIN PEAKS

Twin Peaks (1990–1991) is a bittersweet creation for David Lynch in which he came close to embodying in narrative the heroism of the seeker in its most quintessentially Lynchian form. With Dale Cooper, the Log Lady, and the Red Room, he discovered his most original mappings of the heterogeneous mysteries of life. However, the complications of the extensively collaborative nature of television production had a deleterious effect on the series he co-created with Mark Frost; thus, *Twin Peaks* is uneven. On the whole one of the most provocative, original achievements of American television, this series, nevertheless, contains a number of moments when it threatens to become little more than a conventional, if sardonic, adventure story.

Twin Peaks is a serial narrative chronicling the yearnings of a brilliant detective, FBI Special Agent Dale Cooper (Kyle MacLachlan), as he conducts an inquiry in a small Northwestern town. In the course of his search, he unearths complicated domestic dramas, civic corruption, and worlds beyond those ordinarily inhabited by the Federal Bureau of Investigation, but no ultimate solution to the brutal and mysterious murder of teenage beauty queen, Laura Palmer (Sheryl Lee). No matter what Cooper discovers, it points not toward a bottom line but to a border. This is an appropriate situation for Cooper, who, as an FBI operative, is a border-crossing specialist, called into action only when the circumstances of a crime, like Laura's death, involve the crossing of state boundaries.

Borders pervade Cooper's investigation in the town of Twin Peaks. The mystery of the edge is epitomized by the image of its local hotel, the Great Northern, situated at the brink of a sheer cliff. The outskirts of town contain Glastonbury Grove, a circle of sycamore trees that is the gateway to another plane of reality envisioned by Cooper in his dreams as a Red Room. Similarly, Cooper finds aid in his search for Laura's killer from people who negotiate the border. Primary among them is Margaret Lanterman, the Log Lady (Catherine Coulson), a local prophetess and an important conduit for Cooper between the logic of communal events and some larger powers.[1] Through her fingers, lightly pressed on the log she carries, she receives a form of meaning that comes through the wood (see figure 17). Unlike the logic-obsessed detectives of mass-media lore, Cooper receives what answer is possible to the enigma of Laura's death through dreams and visions, by crossing the very boundary between life and death and hearing the name of the murderer from the victim herself.

17. The Log Lady: probing the edges of ordinary communication.

Through Cooper, Laura, the Log Lady, and the Red Room, *Twin Peaks* evolves as a milieu in which the longing to see, which is the great longing of all detective fiction and certainly of *Twin Peaks,* ceases to depend on human control and moves toward involuntary transportation beyond ordinary limits into a Lynchian contact between logic and the subconscious. As the investigation proceeds, not only the clairvoyant Cooper but also the ordinary folk of the town—Cooper's local sidekick, Sheriff Harry S. Truman (Michael Ontkean); FBI pathologist Albert Rosenfield (Miguel Ferrer), whom Cooper brings into town; Harry's deputies Hawk (Michael Horse) and Andy Brennan (Harry Goaz); and Major Garland Briggs (Don Davis), a local Air Force officer looking into UFOs—find themselves staring past the limits of their rational understanding. Everyone here is a detective, even Laura's best friend Donna Hayward (Lara Flynn Boyle), the ordinary girl next door. In her own search for an answer to the mystery of Laura's death, Donna meets a young boy (Austin Lynch) who can make creamed corn appear and disappear, and Harold Smith (Lenny Von Dohlen), an *âme solitaire* whose strength inexplicably drains away if he tries to pass the boundary of his front door.

However, this unsurprising Lynchian detecting by means of losing logical control is strangely and unexpectedly joined by an abundance of surprisingly un-Lynchian distrust of the subconscious in the later episodes of *Twin Peaks*. Late in the series, we are introduced to Cooper's former FBI partner, Windom Earle (Kenneth Welsh), whose fall into insanity through his contact with extraterrestrial mysteries suggests a distinctly un-Lynchian attribution of peril to the crossing of the lines between imagination and logic. The same is true of the developments in the story of local power broker Ben Horne (Richard Beymer), who has sick fantasies that he is General Lee when his life slips out of his control.

More unsettling, as the series progresses, Cooper's sources of subconscious wisdom dry up. The Log Lady becomes less central, and would have been completely supplanted by Earle in Log-Lady drag if Lynch hadn't rewritten the final episode as he taped it. The mysteries of the Red Room are replaced by the purported mysteries of UFOs, a subject that bores Lynch.[2] Worse, Cooper's boundary crossing terminates in his possession by BOB, Laura's murderer and the demon he has been longing to see/understand. The denouement of Cooper's search is disappointingly typical of rationalist narrative demonstration that we must not stray beyond the kinds of investigations deemed "real" by social norms.

In *Twin Peaks*, as in *Wild at Heart*, Lynch is involved with a project that has the potential to affirm the capacity for action by means of a productive relaxation of the heroic will. But running through *Twin Peaks* like a fraying strand in a stout rope is an ambivalence about heterogeneity that is not present in *Wild at Heart*. The Lynchian sense of wonder that originally illuminates Cooper as he crosses borders acquires a taint of transgression that clings to his forays into the subconscious and bursts into full-blown pathology in the final frames of the series.

To understand *Twin Peaks* as a part of Lynch's history, we must understand how the transgressive elements in the series fit into a career dedicated to recalling us to what he sees as our natural path to reality through the subconscious. The answer is not to be found in speculation about a "darker" side to Lynch, for indeed the majority of transgressive elements in *Twin Peaks* do not reflect Lynch at all. Lynch had little interest in Windom Earle and was firmly op- posed to depicting any possession of Cooper by demonic forces. That the series ends with such an event is ironically attributable to Lynch's loss of control over the series—the control that he habitu- ally exercises in order to lose control. When Lynch moved away from *Twin Peaks* for a temporary but prolonged hiatus, the series was left under the control of his partner, Mark Frost. Although Frost is interested in mysticism and the subconscious, he under- stands them from the point of view of a rationalist and is basically an illusionist filmmaker, as we shall soon see. On his own, Frost began to imbue the series with the rationalist's wariness of the nonrational. When he got involved in his own projects—his film *Storyville* and his novel *The List of Seven*—the show became in- creasingly vulnerable to the traditional ideas about popular cul- ture held by the network, and it speedily descended further toward conventional illusionist realism.[3]

Little needs to be said about the problems inherent in the deci- sions made by commercial television hacks—whether they are writers, directors, or executives—for a series like *Twin Peaks* or for an artist like David Lynch. The problems posed by Mark Frost are another story, for Frost, who is not a hack, had initially seemed to share a kindred spirit with Lynch. A Lynch/Frost affinity did ex- ist to some extent early in the collaboration, as is visible in many places in the initial episodes. At the beginning of the series, Frost's knowledge of the classics and of the literature of mysticism worked brilliantly with Lynch's instincts for the reality attainable when human intelligence moves beyond language and cultural form.[4] However, even in the early episodes it was intermittently clear that Frost's language-based artistry led him in significantly different di- rections from those preferred by Lynch. For example, the soap opera watched by the citizens of Twin Peaks, *Invitation to Love*, was envisioned by Lynch, who is interested in the emotional tones and moods that characterize the soap-opera form, as a popular culture fictional universe parallel with that in the series town. As I understand Lynch's original thoughts about *Invitation to Love* (from him), it might have served a function similar to that of Glinda in *Wild at Heart* (see Chapter 2). Lynch thought that he and Frost were in agreement on this and was surprised to find that

Frost had created a clichéd mockery of the soap-opera form. Similarly, when Lynch and Frost talked about "strange doings in the woods," Frost came out with an "aliens plot," with which Lynch went along but which violated his basic faith that such woodland energies as he had in mind are not *alien* to human life but rather integral to it.[5]

Worst for Lynch was Frost's plotting of Cooper's fall into division at the end of the series, a narrative direction that can best be understood in the context of Frost's identification of Cooper with Sherlock Holmes, an identification not shared by Lynch. This identification is illuminated in Frost's novel, *The List of Seven*, a fantasy about the adventures of Arthur Conan Doyle with a strangely heroic man who became the model for Sherlock Holmes. Plainly, Frost's selection and characterization of Doyle as his hero in this novel reveals how intensely Frost identifies the longing to see as a form of piercing logic empowered to keep irrationality under necessary control. The novel depicts Doyle as a man committed to the difficult feat of "walking the line" between the irrational and the rational: "He [Doyle] knew that the path of human perfectibility—the path he aspired to walk—lay exactly on the midpoint between them" (p. 5). Frost's interface with Lynch in his focus on the border is clear here, but even more clear is the vast difference between the two men in their understanding of it. Crossing is not an option for Frost. In *The List of Seven*, crossing the line puts a human being in the kingdom of evil, in the grip of what Frost understands as the Dweller on the Threshold, a cosmic satanic force that appears to be what Frost sees as the irrational side of "the line." It is from this un-Lynchian construction of the border that Frost arrived at the necessity for Cooper, who repeatedly crossed what Frost identifies as "the line," to fall into the power of evil. Lynch's and Frost's separate visions of the aftermath of the possession is pertinent to our understanding of the chasm between their narrative instincts. Both intended to deliver Cooper; however, Frost would have restored him to rationality, while Lynch, as is clear from the final episode that he rewrote (to be discussed in detail below) intended to restore him to his access to the subconscious.

As is to be expected, Frost's wariness of what he sees as the perils of the subconscious is accompanied by a similar estrangement from feminine experience and a persistent characterization of women only in terms of how they impact on male experience and desire. In *The List of Seven,* male bonding is emphasized, and women exist intermittently as obstacles or helpmates. Similarly, after Lynch went on hiatus to work on *Wild at Heart,* Cooper, who in early *Twin Peaks* certainly has male pals but also makes strong connections with female wisdom, becomes isolated from feminine experience. Thus, Frost's script for the final episode included a last glimpse of neither the Log Lady nor Sarah Palmer (Grace Zabriskie), whose psychic abilities had also been of help to Cooper in his investigation. Frost focused almost exclusively on a Holmes/ Moriarty antagonism. With Cooper as the prototype of Holmes and Earle as a prototype of Moriarty in one form of an estranged older mentor, the series became a conventional saga of the father-son bond. Frost's last script only barely alluded to Cooper's most startling connection with subconscious knowledge through the feminine—Laura Palmer.[6]

These crucial distinctions between Frost and Lynch were not perceived by either of the partners while *Twin Peaks* was being taped, nor is it likely that it is now clear to them. However, their individually created works attest to this impasse, and that impasse accounts for the cross-purposes of many series elements and for the tug of war that took everyone by surprise in the final episode. When Lynch came back to *Twin Peaks,* a project for which he had initially had great relish, the return was not a happy one for him. The momentum of the show had turned against his initial creative impulse, a tide he could not stem until the final episode. Taking his last chance, he put Frost's written script aside and improvised with the cast to create a series finale that recaptured the initial faith in the human roots of vision and creativity in the energies beyond language, logic, and reason.[7] But there were only so many changes possible. Lynch had to make what he could of the demonic division of Dale Cooper, which contravenes all he believes about life (and narrative). His changes in the final show, to be discussed below, bring into the open the larger questions about the possibility of an overall unity to a show that was so pushed and pulled by many hands. However, these changes also create the conditions for an organic coherence despite the periodic glitches.

Most critics believe that Lynch and Frost took American television to its zenith with elements of *Twin Peaks,* but, so far, critics have had difficulty with the sum total of the elements of the series. Given the clash in the series between Lynch's faith in the subconscious and the feminine experience, and Frost's faith in reason and masculine will, this uncertainty is understandable. Nevertheless, there is coherence to the series as a whole. Despite some detours and a few dead ends, the show rejects Frost's definition of the nonrational as irrationality, the foe of the real. Ultimately, *Twin Peaks* associates the longing to see, in Lynchian fashion, with the bounty of the subconscious.[8]

Wrapped in Plasticity The initial impact of *Twin Peaks* on the television viewing public was to bring eternity into carnivalized conjunction with the local and the ordinary. The central event of the series, Laura's murder, reveals the presence in Twin Peaks and its environs of BOB, a terrifying energy that moves across the boundary between the ordinary and the cosmic. BOB interfaces with ordinary life in his comic yet frightening possession of Laura's father Leland Palmer (Ray Wise), the proverbial "man of the law" and "pillar of the community."[9] In order to solve this mystery, Cooper must confront the existence of BOB, a discovery for which neither super-sleuth technology nor complex Holmesian strategies will avail. Rather, Cooper depends on the unity of his mind and body, which results in a strong lifeline to the subconscious both through the flesh and in the spirit, an umbilicus from which all of his success comes. Because only this crossing of borders appears to present any hope in the struggle with the horrifying BOB, fear of the movement between ordinary events and dreams is at first virtually nonexistent in the series.

For the viewer, there is only wonder and delight in the heterogeneous, carnivalesque spectacle of Cooper identifying as exuberantly with the plasticity of his body and with his dreams as he does with the discourse of justice that makes him a proud FBI agent. All of the most crucial information regarding Laura's killer comes to him when he is humbly within the ordinary events of his body—in sleep or in visions that require no special atmosphere or invocation. At their most exotic, these visions occur when he is closely connected with his body because he is severely wounded by a gunshot; at their most transcendent, these visions find him surrendering mental control to learn from the corpse herself.

78

Initially in the series, the spectator is enthralled by the possibility of gaining knowledge in that Lynchian locus in which "The laws, prohibitions, and restrictions that determine the structure and order of ordinary, that is noncarnival, life are suspended" (Bakhtin p. 122)—i.e., in Cooper's dream voyages. These pilgrimages take him and us to a theater-like Red Room, a carnival setting, "the place for working out, in a concretely sensuous half-real and half-play-acted form, *a new mode of interrelationship between individuals*" (Bakhtin p. 123). In the Red Room, a Little Man introduces Cooper to a woman who is and is not Laura, who tells Cooper the name of her killer. The knowledge available in the subconscious location takes many episodes to be articulated by Cooper's waking mind.

The struggle to know the subconscious word means a ceding of the will to a strong mind-body connection. As he strives to approach his subconscious wisdom on the plane of ordinary reality, Cooper gains access to a giant who aids him in his search and comes during a moment when Cooper is seriously wounded. The focus in the scene is unorthodoxly on the pleasure of Cooper's unsought receptivity rather than on the dangers of being shot. Thus, the initial hallmark of *Twin Peaks* is the reality and satisfaction in the surrender of control, particularly in the final delivery of Laura's message to Cooper's conscious mind in a privileged moment of mind-body connection and one of a handful of moments that define the heroism of *Twin Peaks*. Far from being a stereotypical Holmesian figure, Cooper is an empath who releases us from the usual fits of logical mania and the cold, body-denying, woman-avoiding calculation that marks Doyle's sleuth.

Through Cooper, the spectator leaps without fear to identify with the urgency that the detective should consult with body, dreams, and feminine experience in order to see. Fear is identified with relying on the mind alone, a reliance which leads into the dead-end sterility of the laboratory that we see in the redoubtable FBI pathologist Albert. Albert reduces the body to inert elements that reveal little more than the mechanics of Laura's death and sometimes unproductive speculation about obvious criminal sources of violation with which Laura was involved—drugs and pornography. The real mystery is about ordinary life, the life of the home, and it is through intense mental collaboration with the body—Cooper's in-the-body dreams and visions, as well as the Log Lady's touch of the log—that Cooper is led to Leland Palmer. The wonders of the banal are also suggested in another way—the more destructive of the larger energies, capable of outrageous horrors, identify themselves within the construct of the community with the absurdly ordinary names of MIKE (Al Strobel) and BOB (Frank Silva).

The viewer's longing to cross boundaries with Cooper is focused on his narrative function, but it is supported in a significant way by a textural plasticity omnipresent in the series. Objects, sometimes but not always touched by Laura's death, take on a life of their own beyond their function in the plot, crossing narrative boundaries into an experience of the thing's energies. The twin peaks themselves identify the location of the series within the maternal body, a powerful site of subconscious energies. Similarly, the recurring images of the fir boughs undulating in the wind and of the cascading waterfall foaming on impact with its basin bring us into the mysteries of the air, as, in another way, does the swinging traffic light (Mark Frost's contribution, it should be noted). The mysteries are twofold. The natural images—the fir branches—provide the experience of the free energy beyond human control and its narratives; the manufactured object in the wind—the traffic light—creates a direct apprehension of energy under the pressure of cultural control. The nonrational desire stimulated by these crossings complements the desires stimulated by the crossings of Dale Cooper and enfolds every event of the town in a larger context that places them all on the border between narrative structure and emotion.

Within this context, Cooper's plot grounds the series in a seeker who probes the outer limits of his heroic role, while around him a variety of familiar stories become carnivalized and thus available to us in a new way. Stock roles in melodrama are, on the border, clichéd, sentimentally predictable "plot" events and, at the same time, touching mysteries of real emotion. An example is the mapping of the relationship between Laura's secret lover, James Hurley (James Marshall), and Laura's best friend, Donna Hayward. The wedge taken out of ordinary narrative is the complication introduced by Laura's memory and the appearance of Maddy Ferguson (Sheryl Lee), Laura's look-alike cousin. James and Donna are potentially clichéd ghost-story ingenues afraid of what lies hidden behind their passion. Guilt that they may be betraying Laura when they discover that they are in love after she dies is exacerbated by jealousy and uncanny desire when Maddy arrives on the scene. As herself, Maddy is only a mousy girl, but at unexpected times she exudes a great deal of Laura's sexuality as if some force were hidden inside her, eliciting old feelings from James. Treated as familiar, conventional linear narrative, the James-Donna love relationship would reconfirm the peril of what lies beyond ordinary limits in the subconscious. However, *Twin Peaks* tells this story of ordinary young love by placing it on the border of male and female social roles and those forces that make sexual attraction and love possible.

In early *Twin Peaks,* in true Lynchian spirit, the social roles of the lovers are troubling. The social construction of sexuality that Laura represents—the blue-eyed, blonde icon of desire—baffled her in life, as we learn from flashbacks, about why it should be so easy to make people love her. The power of surfaces, as opposed to what is inside, is played out as the clothes and things that Laura left behind transform sweet, awkward Maddy into an irresistible sex object. Laura, who exists in the post-Laura events predominantly as a photographic image of the formulaic homecoming queen, even impedes Donna's relationship with her own body. When she puts on Laura's sunglasses, Donna enters a fight with "the Laura effect" for possession of herself, as the socially trapped energy from the object transforms her behavior. Horribly, this cultural construction of sexuality is as fatal to Maddy as it was to her cousin—BOB re-enacts his seduction murder of Laura with her. It is also fatal to the romance between James and Donna, which cannot endure the pressures that the allure of the constructed stereotype places on real emotions. The role of Laura's glamor, a costumelike exoskeleton that crushed her, also immolates Maddy and divides Donna and James, imperiling the subconscious forces that bond them.

Spectator consciousness of those subconscious energies redeems all of the potential stereotypes in *Twin Peaks,* particularly the political relationships most forcefully represented by Ben Horne, the major power broker in Twin Peaks. Ben is saved from stereotypes of villainy by the free energies of his daughter and of his own body. Into Ben's ruthlessly acquired financial empire comes the irrepressible energy of the intriguingly obstreperous Audrey Horne (Sherilyn Fenn). She pops up exactly where she will reintroduce all the nonrational force that her father has willfully exiled from his financial empire. Knowing that Ben is desperate to keep the news of Laura's death from the Norwegian investors he is about to defraud, Audrey heads for their conference room and strikes a dejected pose, calling all of their eyes to her body. At the moment of inquiry about her mood, she spills all the lurid details of Laura's death. Exit the Norwegians. Similarly, Audrey pops up in Ben's brothel, without his knowledge, as a self-appointed helper for Agent Cooper, whose attention she wishes to capture by connecting his detective yearnings with herself. This time, she has no idea of her father's part in the situation; when Audrey applies for a job at "One-Eyed Jack's," she is only taking on her own detective role and searching for clues to Laura's death. Audrey impresses the madam at Jack's, Blackie (Victoria Catlin), securing a job when she ties a cherry stem into a pretzel-shaped knot using only her tongue. Here, Audrey's energy again benignly imperils Ben's antisocial activities, causing Ben to face how his compulsive desire for mastery has perverted his emotional life. His self-aggrandizing policy, as owner of Jack's, of having the first fling with the "new girls" leads him to an inadvertent attempt to commit incest with his own daughter. Only Audrey's cleverness and a timely interruption save him from actually mauling his own masked daughter in one of the garish bedrooms there at Jack's.

Ben's ruthlessness is also qualified by the saving grace of his own exuberant physicality, unusual in characters of his type in mass-media narrative. When he flings open the double doors of his office and appears in the room like an actor making a wildly gesticulated entrance, his link to his own subconscious vibrates in the spectator. We experience Ben both cognitively, according to his narrative role, and viscerally. When, late in the series, Catherine Martell (Piper Laurie)—his paramour and a female version of himself—tells him that despite all of his treachery she still loves him because he makes her "body hum," this unusual phrasing represents a series truth. What is fascinating about these power brokers is not their conventional strategies of compulsive acquisition, but rather the humanizing fact that their bodies *do* hum. Indeed,

these characters are only interesting when their bodies—and thus
their nonrational energies—are in play. Late in the series, when
Ben hallucinates that he is General Lee, he is used in a very un-
Lynchian way to define the subconscious as a place of illness to
which we retreat when we collapse. At this point, his story becomes boringly arch.

Similarly, Catherine Martell is only interesting when her connection to her exuberant subconscious is a part of her domineering relationship with her husband Pete (Jack Nance), whom she
mercilessly—and stereotypically—henpecks. Catherine's betrayal
of long-suffering Pete with Ben Horne because her desire for
power is greater than her commitment to her marriage vows is a
rather stale melodramatic convention, one which concentrates on
feminine will as precisely the *wrong* kind of will and which demonizes the strong woman. This convention is interesting only when
it is simultaneously present as a stereotype with elements that
supersede Catherine's attempts at control. This occurs principally
when, realizing that Ben has planned to murder her in a double
cross that will gratify *his* hunger for power, Catherine leaves town
and almost immediately reappears disguised as a Japanese business*man*, Mr. Tojamura, planning a complex revenge on her
treacherous former lover. This cross-dressing renders Catherine
her most attractive—and vital—not because of the revenge strata-
gem, which is minimally effective, but because of the light it sheds
on the mysterious endurance of her marriage to Pete.

The Martell marriage acquires a depth that it has lacked as
the familiar holding action between battle-axe wife and milque-
toast husband when Catherine, as Tojamura, runs into Pete in the
lounge of the Great Northern. Pete's neighborly efforts at conversation with this stranger are met with a laconic dismissal only too
reminiscent of his life with Catherine. But later, in the darkness of
their home, Tojamura appears to Pete, who morosely assumes that
Catherine, missing after a fire at the family-owned lumber mill,
is dead. While Pete is assembling his customary bedtime snack,
Tojamura startles him, moving into the light out of the darkness
and throwing "his" arms around Pete. "Mr." Tojamura's exclamation that since they met he has "felt a strange attraction" to Pete
causes Pete to drop the glass of milk, sending glass and liquid
flying as he unsuccessfully tries to fend off "Tojamura's" kiss, the

most heartfelt and enthusiastic affection Catherine has shown him in years. Pete's discovery that the rotund visitor from the East with lips pressed against his is actually his wife is a strange and wonderful moment that breaks open their clichéd plot with relief, embarrassment, anger, indignation, affection, intimacy, and laughter, conveyed simultaneously as only Jack Nance can do it. The complexity of the Martells' strange relationship is best captured in this heterogeneous moment, not as a mere eccentric ploy but because the co-presence of the material body has been so firmly established in *Twin Peaks* that this odd gender switch tells us about the bond between these two in a way that cannot be restated in words. We are left with traces of visceral understanding of why Catherine remains with Pete and why Pete will do anything for her.

In early *Twin Peaks*, music is used to underline the tension between the energy in the characters and the stereotypes that only seem to define them. So the music does not, in the usual way, classify the characters rigidly but instead becomes another meeting place between social constructs and the larger energies. With this highly original stroke, the complexity of the "fit" between character roles and character energy is underlined by the fluctuations of the music themes of the series; now seeming to point toward major, now toward minor, the musical motifs early in the series alter the conventions of movie music. While the traditional role of such music has always been to phrase the unspeakable, it has, through rigidly maintained harmonies, tended to create an illusion of "fit" between the unspoken and the conventions of narrative setting. In contrast, the music in the early *Twin Peaks* episodes heightens our sense of contradiction between narrative conventions and what is unspoken. The major-minor ambiguities in the early Lynch/Frost series establish moving across boundaries as a valid part of the series infrastructure, preparing us for non-transgressive movement of the characters across *their* fictional boundaries. (The music can be seen as a complement to some of the visuals which also establish boundary-crossing conventions for the *Twin Peaks* fictional universe—for example, the dissolves in the signature montage that move through the boundaries between robin, factory, machine, and waterfall.) [10]

But, of course, it is Cooper's narrative destiny regarding Laura's murder—the process by which the magician/detective's longing to

see is realized—that is central to the reality presented to the spectator. Without Cooper as the principal focus of mind-body heterogeneity in *Twin Peaks,* the ambiguously constructed music and
the transnarrative objects would not engage our emotions, and the
background stories might seem like a pastiche. Cooper grounds us
in a non-transgressive experience of the crossing of limits. In this,
he is joined and supported by his guide, the Log Lady, in authoriz-
ing the channeling of audience desire to seek reality in the simultaneous exercise of social skills and unchanneled energy.

Both Cooper and the Log Lady are intensely ethical and lovable
presences, and their boundary crossing is neither threatening nor
corrupt. They link effective values to the subconscious, function-
ing as reassuring custodians of a world in which decayed principles are most resolutely associated with characters whose desires
are most willfully employed in cultural power struggles. They create a security within the series when they reap the rewards of reality in crossing boundaries and relaxing rational control.

Cooper's visions are the main form of the heterogeneous mapping of knowledge, making their formal entry into *Twin Peaks* at
the end of the third episode with his dream of the Red Room. His
discovery of the Red Room, where words and subconscious energies coexist in all their heterogeneous contradictions, begins the
real progress in the investigation. Cooper's crucial dream occurs
in two parts. In the first part that prefaces the appearance of the
Red Room, Cooper first sees BOB and MIKE, and MIKE recites an
enigmatic poem:

In the darkness of future past
The magician longs to see
One chants out between two worlds:
FIRE
walk with me.[11]

In the second part of the dream, Cooper finds himself as an old
man in a borderlike "place between two worlds," the Red Room.
The Red Room is a large enclosure surrounded on all sides by bil-
lowing red drapes. Within the curtained area, there are only three
black art-deco upholstered chairs, a torch lamp, and a Grecian
white marble statue of a female nude; the floor beneath is tiled in
an Escher-like geometric pattern. In the dream, the aging Cooper

is seated in one of the chairs. Another is occupied by a Little Man (Michael J. Anderson)—three-and-a-half feet in height—wearing a red suit. The other chair is soon filled by a woman whom Cooper identifies from her pictures as Laura, although the Little Man insists it is her cousin. The Laura figure in the Red Room is dressed strangely in an evening gown much like a costume from a 1940s B picture—low-cut, black velvet, deeply slit. Laura and the Little Man gesture enigmatically, their words strange and thick on the tongue, an effect Lynch achieved by a double reversal—the actors spoke their lines backward, and then the film was reverse-projected.

Cooper receptively watches the Little Man dance to repetitive, rhythmic music with a cool blues melodic line played on a saxophone. He again plays the responsive role when, at the end of the dream, Laura rises, approaches him seductively, kisses him, and whispers in his ear. On waking, Cooper knows not only that the incomprehensible gestures of the Little Man are of major importance to his investigation, but also that Laura has told him the name of the murderer. Nevertheless, his conscious mind is not yet ready to receive the information.

MIKE's poem tells the story. Cooper and BOB are both out there on the border where reality is available, but Cooper yearns to see and BOB yearns to control, chanting "FIRE, walk with *me*" [emphasis added]. The rhyme tells us that the evil that Cooper is stalking deals with the egoistic determination of closed self that burns with a desire to *take charge.* In the Red Room, Cooper distinguishes himself from that evil by being a receptive intelligence.

To the show's credit, it represents nothing easy about going beyond the cultural self. Not only must one surrender to the larger forces to gain individual vision, one must also get beyond the selfish desire that all boundary crossing be in our own image. Cooper's capacity to open himself is tested in his relationships with Laura, who exists beyond the border separating life and death, and with the Log Lady, who crosses boundaries in a manner different from and potentially alienating to his own. When Cooper first meets the Log Lady, their differences alienate each from the other. Despite his own vision, he is baffled by the visionary style of another and is unable to accept her invitation to ask her log for the information that he seeks about Laura's death. Nor is her invitation offered in an open and relaxed spirit. Anticipating his rejection, she is curt in the overture, and, when he hesitates to speak to a log, she is dismissive.

Touch, Margaret's form of receptivity, and sight, Cooper's mode, bear the irreconcilable differences of the intimacy of touch and the distance required for sight. These have been theorized as basic gender differences that mark the war between the sexes, as well as the basis of the socialization of women as secondary persons.[12] However, in *Twin Peaks*, the heterogeneous meeting between such differences contains the rich possibilities of meaning. Cooper and the Log Lady become allies because of, not despite, their differences, but not without a struggle. As the investigation moves along, Cooper, Truman, Deputy Hawk, and Doc Hayward (Warren Frost) arrive at Margaret's cabin, mistaking it for a cabin crucial to the investigation of Laura's murder. Margaret bullies the men like an old-fashioned nanny, insisting that they take tea and sugar cookies with her before she reveals what her log "knows." She actually slaps Agent Cooper's hand for trying to take a cookie before the tea is served. The incommensurable blend of petty schoolmarm manners and the largesse of mystic wisdom makes Margaret who she is. However, by the time Cooper is closing in on Leland/BOB, just before this compound monster kills his niece Maddy, Margaret and Cooper have found their bond. Margaret comes to Cooper as a form of annunciation: "We do not know what will happen," she says as they exchange a world of empathetic foreshadowing. Even though the combined powers of Margaret and Cooper are not enough to prevent the death of Maddy, such moments bond the audience to the consolations of longing to see across human limitations in a world in which that desire is usually inactive.

Cooper's ability to learn to appreciate and cooperate with Margaret's difference complements his capacity for surrendering to his own visions. These two relaxations of the will link him with Laura and distinguish him as an unorthodox Special Agent. They make him a worthy antagonist for BOB and define both Cooper's heroism and BOB's villainy. Cooper values feminine experience, BOB devours it.

Where *Twin Peaks* maintains its heterogeneity it also alters the conventional structure of gender. Cooper's crucial receptivity envisions feminine wisdom as necessary to the seeker, while BOB's aggressive thrust defines as tragically problematic the unstoppable will usually portrayed as male heroism. Through the representation of Cooper, Margaret, and Laura on the one hand and BOB on the other, *Twin Peaks* significantly transforms the pervasive phallocentrism of American screen fiction.

Conventional Hollywood heroes tend to be phallic figures, configured in conformity with dominant Freudian psychology that implicates the bearer of the phallus as the one who can attain knowledge and power. Theoretically, this formulation excludes both women and women's ways of knowing as marginal in importance both in narrative and in life. Certainly, there are exceptions to this dominant tendency. There are, now and again, strong women "as good as men" in mass media. These women, however, are phallic in concept too, depicted in ways that make phallic power a matter not of the biological penis but an abstract sign of the force necessary to create and organize.[13] They are atypically willful and controlling; they can learn to fight (with the symbolic phallic weapon) or write (with the symbolic phallic writing implement) so as to make them resemble the approved hero. These women are not associated with anything feminine like receptivity. With regard to both the male and female "hero," Lynch sees an imbalanced priority on aggression and control in knowing—or seeing. By contrast, in *Twin Peaks* the dominance of phallic power is represented by BOB, the annihilator of meaning. Receptivity is a value in this context, gaining a real place for women and a transformed relationship between the seeker and the feminine. Reality in *Twin Peaks* is dependent on a heterogeneous balancing of phallic force with feminine, labial receptivity.

Margaret's log visions, Cooper's dream visions, and Laura's part in Cooper's subconscious all map their power through references to the equilibrium of the phallic and the labial. Margaret's habitual cradling of her log in her arms, the phallic shape empowered by and empowering the maternal wisdom, is an icon of the necessary combination of the irreconcilable differences of feminine and phallic power in the making of meaning. The phallus is enigmatically present in the image of the log, but it is Margaret's receptivity that creates the conduit to the plane of mundane events. This balance also characterizes Cooper's subconscious, as we see in the composition of his dream destination, the Red Room. The Red Room is more blatant about the gendered aspects of the narrative. As a space in which the ordinary appearances that mask the sexual energies at the core of our values and priorities are made strange, the Red Room engages us in revealing carnivalizations. There, the balances of logos and the body occur in shapes that overtly remind us of the male phallus and the double-lipped form of female genitalia.

In Cooper's subconscious dream state, the slit in dream-Laura's dress creates the two lips of the female labia and points to her genitals while the low neckline of the dress emphasizes the twin peaks of female anatomy. In concert with Laura, the Little Man—a small, wiggling, dancing, rosy figure—has clear phallic associations, even in being called "the Little Man." To make those associations clearer, the Little Man of Cooper's dream frequently undu-

18. The Little Man as a phallic presence.

lates in front of a marble female nude such that his head is often framed with the statue's crotch behind it (see figure 18). (The statue's genital identity is emphasized by her hand, which both covers and points to her crotch.) These comic sexual images, in which sex organs speak, involve speech that is materially distorted and gesture that is untranslatable into logos. Even Lynch cannot "say" what each gesture means. Translation is not key here in any case; what matters is that, in seeking knowledge, Cooper must immerse himself in plasticity in tension with logos, that is, in the tension between the masculine and feminine.

In conventional detective mysteries, the logical construct dissolves the enigma of the body, and the masculine principle—phallic control sublimated into assaultive force—creates the desired order. However, in *Twin Peaks,* the Red Room as a site of discovery and meaning resembles the crime site in ordinary detective stories—places in which discourse is not in charge. In the Red Room, discourse and materiality are equivalent forms of energy. In the Holmesian detective—that is, the conventional Hollywood and television detective—the scrutinizing eye and the phallus become one, suggesting that the detective's potency transcends the peril and chaos of the feminized body. By contrast, in the Red Room plasticity also speaks. There, Laura—a wild, frightening, and confusing body to the denizens of Twin Peaks—possesses the solution to her own murder and is willing and able to share it with Cooper. Unlike the femme fatale with whom the detective is usually confronted, Laura is neither a sexualized nor desexualized object. She

19. The Giant as a phallic presence.

is another subject. There is pleasure when Cooper gains knowledge through merging with her—she reveals her murderer as she kisses him—but the desire satisfied in this kiss is a compound of his desire to understand and her desire to communicate. Similarly, the merging of two subjects is suggested later, when we learn through a diary entry that Laura and Cooper have had identical dreams of the Red Room. Since Laura is not an object, she is not the conventional detective's nightmare of what his own body could become should he lose control but rather is the corollary of his need to understand his body.

Laura whispers the name of her murderer after being presented to Cooper by the phallic Little Man. Her voice, which Cooper at first cannot consciously recall, is made accessible to his waking understanding by another of his phallic helpers from beyond—the Giant (Carel Struycken), represented in an angle-up shot foregrounding his crotch, first appears to Cooper in a vision as the FBI agent lies on the floor of his hotel room, apparently bleeding to death (see figure 19). At this point, Cooper's will is in abeyance and he is completely receptive, a situation that is unexpectedly productive rather than threatening. Cooper's apparent quandary creates frustration in the spectator when, in his wounded state, he becomes dependent on the senile Old Waiter (Hank Worden), who for some reason is confused by Cooper's request for a doctor, makes comically irrelevant small talk, and leaves Cooper instead of helping him. But this frustrating delay turns to wonder when Cooper's wound makes him receptive to a first visit from the helpful Giant. The Giant gives Cooper a number of clues but, most importantly, is later the medium through which Cooper finally hears Laura's voice identify her father as the killer. This subconscious balance between the phallic and the labial leads to her father Leland's arrest on the mundane plane of reality.

A hiatus in what is conventionally considered male potency seems to be necessary in order for Cooper to cross a boundary and gain access to a part of himself that is impeded by the limitations of discourse. The Giant, markedly still, hands crossed firmly over his genital area, unmoving, slow, and a rich, masculine basso in his speech, is a pointedly masculine figure but gendered to represent a male image of potency that does not conform to the active/passive polarity of media culture. The two forms of phallic power in conventional screen fiction are the thrusting mind/eye and the thrusting fist or gun. The narrative difference of *Twin Peaks* in this respect is the deferral of that forward thrust, visually emphasized by the literal emptiness of the frame left by the open door to Cooper's room with its feminine implications. We wait and wait for it to be filled by that male strike force we have been trained to trust. Only after a long delay do Harry, Hawk, and Andy burst in, guns uselessly drawn—how would they know that this is not a testosterone emergency?—filling the empty door frame with the usual rescuers. In comparison with the subconscious phallic power of the Giant, there is something diminished and foolish, but lovable and even helpful, in this conventional rescue—after all, Cooper does need to be taken to the doctor.

As Lynch develops, the place for women's wisdom is augmented. In *Twin Peaks,* Lynch certainly achieves a rich sense of the balance of male and female, with women's wisdom as the fundamental necessity of the male seeker. But Lynch does not achieve the kind of development of the secret-bearing protagonist that he reaches in *Wild at Heart,* and nowhere near what we will see in *Fire Walk with Me* (Chapter 7). In the latter film, Laura's is the central sensibility. In *Twin Peaks,* the Log Lady is external, though crucial, to the central events, like a guiding genius, and Laura is dead, her secret abundantly present in the narrative but effectively beyond the balances of culture and eternity.

Nevertheless, the usual guilts that are attached to women in popular culture do not pertain in *Twin Peaks*. BOB's relationship to Leland's body liberates the female body from the guilts with which convention automatically burdens it, and questions the conventional polarity which represents the male body as dependability incarnate and the female body as a threatening, shape-shifting lure for heroic masculine will. Initially in the series, not only is the seeker's will redefined, but bodily instability is re-envisioned as a symptom of a physical world too tightly constrained by phallocentrism rather than as a trait specific to women. Because he is possessed by BOB, Leland compulsively dances and sings, activity associated in him not with exuberance but with agony. Similarly, his hair turns white overnight. The mutability of his face—the sudden replacement of a beatific smile with the distortions of homicidal fury—results from his saturation with the energy of the self consumed by will, known in the series as BOB. This unrelieved phallic energy is marked by solipsism and murder.

Toward the end, when conventional phallocentrism abruptly takes over the series, everyone is in peril of dwindling into cliché. The town of Twin Peaks, suddenly not energized by its mammary setting, is narrated as a large chess board on which the action is completely defined by the competing logic of Dale Cooper and his Moriarty-like nemesis, Windom Earle. Within that dialogue, the female body, no longer a source of knowledge, reverts to its conventional role as an Oedipal trap for the male. James Hurley is betrayed by the stereotypical blonde femme fatale, Evelyn Marsh (Annette McCarthy). Worst of all, Cooper is led into Hell by a new love interest that was included in the end of the series, Annie Blackburn (Heather Graham), in the form of the stereotypical media icon of blonde desire that the original episodes had rejected as cliché in Laura's photograph. Only because Lynch strongly interceded to reroute the final episode did we return to a Cooper who, if he falls at the end of the series, does not do so because of the perils of the subconscious—stereotypically represented in terms of intimacy with women—but because of the failure of his original visionary ability to lose control and make contact with feminine experience.

When *Twin Peaks* veers into the conventions of illusionism, which pay homage to
the rationalist's faith in a phallic force and
properly directed will, the series loses its

sense of the benign subconscious and the affirming power of femininity. In the later episodes, the seeker regresses into a stereotypical hero. Proper reason directing Cooper's will becomes the heroic
focus of the action against the typical perverse will and reason
of the villain. The traditional conquest of Earle—not the desire to
see—becomes the desire of the series. Had things continued in
this manner, we would have completely lost Cooper as a mind-
body detective. But fortunately, Lynch was finally able to put this
deviation into willfulness in perspective as the cause of Cooper's
defeat in the final moments of the series—the crossing-over of
BOB's malevolent energies into Cooper. Thus, in the end, the series did not lose its foundation in heterogeneity.

When *Twin Peaks* was canceled, it was drifting, sustained by
the original actors who labored against increasingly self-conscious
dialogue, hackneyed casting of new characters, and emotional and
action-oriented storylines that occasionally sank to cult strategies
of parodying and commenting on itself. Gone was Audrey's original characterization as a young woman resistant to her father's
willful stratagems through her visceral spontaneity. Ruthless Ben
and verminous Jerry Horne (David Patrick Kelly) were suddenly
prancing around Twin Peaks as lovable buffoons. The carnival aspects of the initial episodes underwent a transformation in which
costume became a threat to our security rather than a carnivalized
border between the body and cultural forms. Worst of all, Cooper
was given a plot hinging on a formulaic romance with a clichéd,
flaxen-haired sweetheart that threatened to turn him into a stereotypical action hero. Adding insult to injury, he was outlandishly,
infuriatingly scripted to describe this central-casting ingenue as
the "most original human being" he had ever met.

Because Cooper's end-of-series "true love," Annie Blackburn, is
the spitting image of Caroline, Windom Earle's dead wife, the
stage is set for Earle and Cooper to re-enact the original scene of
their estrangement, a scene that is also a familiar and quite un-
Lynchian indictment of the role women play in subverting the
control men need over their lives. Cooper's final mission thus

becomes a formulaic struggle to take charge as he chases Earle—
and Annie, whom the villainous lunatic has abducted and threatens to kill. Why? The old story, of course. Our hero is threatened
by his previous closeness to father-figure Earle's wife, Caroline;
their once-upon-a-time, Oedipal, adulterous affair spawns an out-
break of "woman trouble" that drives Windom Earle to lose control. No longer a visionary journey across boundaries that embrace female energy, *Twin Peaks* comes perilously close to being a
conventional action story that yearns for male assertion of the will
to keep the boundaries intact and that fears female energy, here
stereotyped as a dangerous sexuality.

Lynch's sweeping revisions of the final script vaporize this trite
invasion of the banal into *Twin Peaks*. His emergency transfusion
forestalled a last episode in which, as scripted, when Cooper
crosses the boundaries to a beyond, he crosses into a world completely tyrannized by interminable oratory:

> You were such a dullard, Coopy, such an earnest, plodding, do-
> gooding Eagle Scout—it was all I could do sometimes to keep my-
> self from SHREDDING YOUR INTERNAL ORGANS OUT OF
> GENERAL PRINCIPLE! . . . Oh, I know all about those three "miss-
> ing years," Tibet and your pathetic eager-beaver globetrotting *quest*
> for enlightenment. In that one respect we aren't so radically differ-
> ent. Perhaps that's why I've tolerated you for as long as I did. Because
> I knew that, one day, you would prove useful. (Frost, *Twin Peaks*
> script for Episode 29 pp. 24–25)

Later, in a black and white abstraction of a doctor's office con-
flated with a throne room and located in Pittsburgh—site of
Cooper's first disastrous encounter with Earle's rage—Earle plays
Moriarty to Cooper by explaining what he has in store:

> This is the place of power. The other's a revolting mixture of milk-
> curdling sentimentality and bland acquiescence to the cosmic equiv-
> alent of good table manners. . . . Here's the deal, Dale. Throne room.
> Windom. Windom sits on throne. Windom king. Windom *happy*.
> Problem: Windom need to make deposit first. That's how it works.
> Windom can't make deposit all by himself. Windom *un*-happy. . . .
> Here's where the designers show their ingenuity. In return for
> the best seat in the house they want something in return. Guess

what: voluntarily offered, no strings attached, by its owner and oper-
ator . . . the soul of a good human being. (pp. 28–29)

In Frost's script, when Dale Cooper agrees to sacrifice his soul if
Earle will spare Annie, BOB, dressed as a dentist (of all things!),
kills and supplants Earle as the reigning speaker:

> [*To Cooper*] If you know what's good for you, and you do, don't
> move. [*Cooper doesn't*] The fool [Earle] broke the rules; it's really no
> good if you don't volunteer. Doesn't count if you're coerced. He'll
> have to be punished and he will be. . . . [*close to him*] Of course that
> doesn't mean we have to let you go. This is for *extracting* [referring
> to a large dental syringe]. (p. 30)

BOB's tactic of overwhelming Cooper linguistically à la Earle is a
disavowal of everything BOB has been in the series.

Lynch's taped show also addresses the fundamental wrongness
of a series finale, as Frost's script had constructed it, with no appearance of the Log Lady, the Little Man, or the Giant and scant
acknowledgment of the Red Room. There is a restored connection
with the Red Room and with the receptive feminine wisdom of the
Log Lady as part of Cooper's final act. She appears in the sheriff's
office—as Cooper foresees without benefit of verbal communication—with a talisman for him: a bottle of scorched engine oil, familiar to viewers as the odor that accompanies BOB. This present
reconnects the end of the series to the plastic elements of Cooper's
mind-body detecting by re-establishing this relationship and the
centrality of his relationship with BOB. In the taped show, the red
curtains are re-established as the hallmark of the large world; they
are what Harry sees as Dale enters and exits the gateway in the
grove, and they—not the black and white vision of Pittsburgh—
dominate the image of Cooper's experiences on the threshold of
the larger cosmos. Similarly, in Cooper's terminal encounter with
BOB, Earle's dialogue is reduced to two brief lines, a spoken total
of twelve words. BOB is once more a presence who articulates
himself predominantly with the subconscious sounds of speech—
the growl—and the plasticity of the body. Along with the restoration of such resonances on the body of the spectator comes a re-
emergence of sound in general and music specifically in the final
moments of the series.

There is no mention of music in Frost's script. But in the taped episode, Cooper is ushered into the Red Room with a song written by Lynch for the finale, sung by blues singer Jimmy Scott. The lyrics speak of Cooper's driving passion, his longing to see:

And I'll see you, and you'll see me
And I'll see you in the branches that blow
In the breeze, under the sycamore trees
I'll see you in the trees.

This melody tells of the treasure of the Red Room—a vision of the other through a balance of the cultural (that is, a musical and verbal construct) and the larger forces of nature. It is all there for Cooper, but he has lost the power. He has been scripted into the Red Room on a mission of the will—to conquer Earle and to save Annie. A reaction shot reveals Cooper, wooden, eyes wide open but unseeing as glimmers of piercing light blink through a darkness of the will that is the man's inner fog.

However, through Lynch's revision of the last episode, Cooper's loss becomes an affirmation of sorts. Although the magician who has longed to see falls from heterogeneity, audience *desire* for it is restored. In the final episode, we regain our desire to be a part of the Lynchian mysteries. How forlorn we are when Cooper can no longer serve as our conduit to larger worlds and the lessons of the Red Room no longer reach him. The Red Room continues to speak, but we no longer have him as our Virgil in this *commèdia*. The Old Waiter brings him a cup of coffee that is simultaneously potable liquid, a frozen solid, and oil sludge, but Cooper can no longer comprehend the border transformations of the subconscious. Laura as a charming, erotic woman is transformed by Cooper's fallen glance into a wounding, rapacious harpy. He is caught in a confusion between Annie and Caroline. He is thrown by Leland's declaration that he "did not kill anyone," a complex truth he once understood clearly.

The return of sustaining heterogeneity to the series heightens the pathos of the lost Cooper, whose fear empowers BOB to violate him. When Cooper and Annie mysteriously escape from the Red Room, Cooper is a doppelganger of his former self. He looks like the old Cooper, seeming to be more worried about Annie than himself after their mutually harrowing ordeal. Of Harry and Doc

Hayward he asks caringly, "How's Annie?" Like the Cooper who awakens from his dream of the Red Room with his hair standing on end, the doppelganger seems to show a heterogeneous connection to his body when he abruptly becomes intent on brushing his teeth after this latest adventure and disappears into the bathroom. This comic dislocation of a tense moment seems to announce Cooper's successful return to the mind-body connection. In fact, only surface appearances are preserved.

Lynch portrays Cooper's fall into the illusion of control as a descent into impotence. Once inside the bathroom, Cooper performs a ritual self-castration. He lifts the toothpaste tube, an object phallic in shape and, like the biological penis, full of a substance that can be expelled. This conflation of phallus and male organ is not visible, however, until Cooper takes the tube and demonically, futilely empties its contents into the sink. His meaningless exertion of control is more pointedly identified as a loss of manhood and potency when he looks into the mirror and sees not his own image but BOB's. Dashing his head against the mirror, cracking it and bloodying himself, Cooper asks in a pseudomincing tone, "How's Annie?" As he repeats the question several times, each repetition deepens the inflection of ridicule in a self-referential structure of language that points to its own emptiness. O the pity and fear of that final glance in the mirror. Comic and violent, it reveals the emptying of potency when the mind is trapped within the self-referential forms of culture. Cooper is marooned. However, the scene returns the (saddened) spectator to the initial desire for the integrity and wholeness of heterogeneity that was characteristic of the original episodes.

The last episode of *Twin Peaks* is Lynchian, despite former slippages and drifting; it leaves the spectator on the most complex side of the mysteries of logos and plasticity, even while the fallen angel Cooper is convulsed by energies constricted within a literal mind. The Red Room remains a possible site of vision, truth, and reality for the seeker. But if the final episode redeems our connection to the subconscious, at the same time it cannot reverse the un-Lynchian intimations built into Cooper's relationship with Earle that BOB is the greatest force in Twin Peaks. Earle's abduction of Annie has forced Cooper into a position in which BOB has overcome the heart of Lynchian heroism. This is not Lynch's "huge, big wonderful world." BOB's position at the end of the series violates Lynch's cosmology by representing the border as a portal of infection instead of as the porthole of reality. Frustration with this muddying of the *Twin Peaks* waters drove Lynch to narrate Laura's murder on his own in *Twin Peaks: Fire Walk with Me* (see Chapter 7). In that film, he completely removes the Frostian conception of BOB as the indomitable Dweller on the Threshold and once more represents the border between planes of reality as the home of redemption.

4

"Seeing Something That Was Always Hidden"

BLUE VELVET

Blue Velvet (1986) is David Lynch's breakthrough film. Jeffrey Beaumont, its protagonist, is his first completely developed Hollywood seeker-hero. In this film, by playing with very familiar, ordinarily bland and inoffensive popular culture conventions, Lynch begins to fully reveal the enduring potential energy and realism of a part of the Hollywood vocabulary that has seemed hopelessly clichéd.

In *Blue Velvet,* after Tom Beaumont (Jack Harvey) suffers a serious stroke, his son Jeffrey (Kyle MacLachlan) takes a temporary leave from college to return to his family in Lumberton. In fact, we meet Lumberton before we meet Jeffrey, in an initial montage of sunny images of garden flowers, white picket fences, and friendly firemen riding a shiny red fire truck. The film thus immediately locates us within mass media's infinitely imitable American hometown frequented by placid housewives in neat homes, polite high school students with straight white teeth, and fathers who are charged with holding it all together. But Lynch also makes changes in the customary picture. In the usual mediaville, daddy's control over his family is synonymous with light—civilization's bulwark against dark, alien evil. In contrast, in *Blue Velvet* Lynch reconfigures the relationship between father, family, communal order, and darkness. When the structure of the Beaumont family is shaken as the stricken father loses power, darkness becomes son Jeffrey's path to the knowledge that will make him an adult.

As Jeffrey returns from a hospital visit to his father, he comes upon a severed ear hidden in the grass of an uncultivated field and is immediately excited by the prospect of "seeing something that was always hidden." Even after he is enjoined by Detective Williams (George Dickerson)—a neighbor on the Lumberton police force—to leave everything to the authorities, he persists, ironically with the help of Williams's daughter, Sandy (Laura Dern), who is also curious about mysteries from which her father has excluded her.

The apparently gratuitous nature of Jeffrey's disobedience—there seems to be nothing at stake for him but idle curiosity—quickly plunges him into great danger. What is hidden may be fatal. His discoveries about the ear are made at the price of his involvement with criminals who are part of its mystery—Frank Booth (Dennis Hopper), a vicious drug dealer; Frank's deranged henchmen; and especially Frank's girlfriend, Dorothy Vallens (Isabella Rossellini), a singer in a seedy nightspot. But once known, Frank is clearly not the mystery Jeffrey craves. Jeffrey's attention veers away from the original case, virtually solved now by his knowledge that Frank has cut the ear off Dorothy's husband (Dick Green) and is now holding him and her little son hostage in order to extract perverse carnal favors from her. He too becomes interested in Dorothy's favors, the price of which is Frank's not inconsiderable wrath. To make matters more complex, as Jeffrey becomes Dorothy's secret lover, he synchronously pursues a romance with Sandy, the price of which may be Detective Williams's wrath.

However, everything leads beyond local mysteries to still larger vistas. Jeffrey's frightening adventures generate in him a series of dream visions that enable him to grow and develop into a manhood that empowers him to rid the police of a rogue cop, kill Frank, liberate Dorothy, and clear the way for his union with Sandy. In the tradition of the Lynchian seeker, Jeffrey's quest is possible because he lets forces beyond his reason possess him. In this way, *Blue Velvet* digs the foundation for the establishment of the seeker in both *Twin Peaks* and *Wild at Heart* (see Chapters 2 and 3). However, for Jeffrey, crime and transgressive behavior seem to be more conventionally implicated in his actions. His important dream visions are only possible after he has disobeyed Detective Williams and become a part (temporarily) of Frank's underworld. Thus, *Blue Velvet* would seem to significantly muddy the waters of Lynch's non-transgressive mapping of heterogeneity. In fact, it does not. The differences between *Blue Velvet* and the later movies, relative to transgressive impulses and the subconscious, disappear once we realize that the deviant behavior of Frank's world is nowhere equated by Lynch as the most significant part of the subconscious. Because Jeffrey's adventures on Frank Booth's turf are secret, we may mistake them for the crucial Lynchian involuntary mysteries. However, in *Blue Velvet* criminality is not part of the true beyond of rational logic; it is only hidden because "good" people don't allow themselves to see their own shadows.[1] Simply put, Jeffrey must cross Lincoln (Street?), which divides the two sides of Lumberton, to discover the secret analogy between Frank and Detective Williams as two parts of the same self-referential rational culture and thus go past its borders into vision.[2]

That step is not necessary in *Wild at Heart* or *Twin Peaks* because in those films a kind of social apartheid between the logical ideal self and the twisted logic of its shadow does not exist, as it does in Lumberton. *Blue Velvet* represents a less evolved narrative form in the Lynchian canon, in which Lynch has not yet learned to depict the interpenetration of the benign surface and malignant depths of an over-controlling rationality. In Lumberton, these qualities inhabit two sides of the tracks, and so each has a different reality problem. The "good" folk—in the style of Detective Williams—exhibit self-control and a subordination of their individual wills to the communal will, that is, the law. This is good, but it is not particularly real since the norms of behavior and "right" reason occur within the sphere of repressions so constraining that law-abiding behavior continually runs the risks of turning into a sterile solipsism. However, as for being "bad" in *Blue Velvet*—like Frank Booth—if it taps into the baser element in the subconscious, it is primarily just another mode of willful behavior in which perverse sexuality and violence determines another kind of solipsism.[3] It also endangers our connection to the real.

Jeffrey's visions distinguish him from *both* Frank and Williams. As a Lynchian seeker, he is after a manhood more expansive than that of police or criminals. His discovery of the severed ear is significant as a revelation of cultural limits placed on the incipient seeker by both law enforcement and outlaws. Initially, the compelling nature of his discovery is unclear, but ultimately we can see the severed ear as a sign of the mutilated manhood prevalent in society, a sign that Jeffrey must search for a renewed, whole masculine identity.

Like Jeffrey, if we are to reach beyond the flawed masculine identities of both the Lumberton detective and the Lumberton outlaw, we must also get beyond thinking of what is happening on the bad side of town as the essential mystery. Although the scenario played out by Jeffrey, Dorothy, and Frank would in the Freudian context be associated with the subconscious Oedipal drama, for Lynch, Jeffrey's desire for Dorothy and his seeming emulation of Frank's brutality with her takes Jeffrey on a journey that will demystify the Freudian narrative. Freud tells us that the unresolved Oedipus complex is a perversion of the individual psyche too closely associated with women, directed against a stabilizing social order of male-bonding hierarchies. However, Lynch is not a Freudian, and Frank's mutilation of the father and husband in *Blue Velvet* is not an attack of a "dangerous" individual subconscious against the culture. Rather, it reveals the problem of cultural definitions of masculinity—the maiming of a father and husband (Don Vallens) by a shadow father figure (Frank Booth) who is too willfully divorced from, not too much possessed by, subconscious feminine forces.

Frank's crime suggests a very different sexual pathology than the one in Freud's narrative. According to Freud, as we have used his work, an attack against the father is associated with an unmanning predicated on defective male bonding caused by too much familiarity with the mother, that is, too much attraction to women and their less logical, more subconscious forces. This feminization of the male in Oedipal pathology is strongly connected with castration, the Freudian labeling of the masculine anxiety of being womanish and failing to bond thoroughly enough with the father. In a Freudian context, the patricidal failure of male bonding attacks the capacity of men to take charge—always associated with the phallus. By contrast, the severing of Don Vallens's ear speaks of anything but an assault on phallic, "manly" domination. The ear has explicitly non-phallic, rather feminine, associations as a channel of receptivity. The mutilation in *Blue Velvet* is an assault on the masculine capacity for receptivity, or the male's likeness to women and his ability to know by losing control.

In maiming the legal father—Dorothy's husband, Don—Frank brings to the surface the secrets of a culture in which there is *too little similarity to women*. Frank is a Freudian, fearing too much similarity to women, but the spectator is overcome by the horror of too much dissimilarity to femininity in the secret criminal haunts of Lumberton, and of far too much control exerted over women. As Frank puts Dorothy through a sexual ritual of which he is in complete charge, she is like a bewildered soldier in a drill in which Frank's will is law; he is a shadow of, not the obverse of, the police.[4]

Frank's coercion of Dorothy is not Lynch's picture of the subconscious; it is merely a toxic form of control augmented by involuntary energy and is as constricting as the parameters of the "good" community. The bipolar organization of Lumberton, in which Lincoln divides the acceptable side of town from the unacceptable, is not the organization of the film. The division between the surface and depths of Lumberton is a false division created by its culture. The less savory side of the town, by being cut off from the respectable community, becomes a local habitation for the lower elements of the subconscious, the garbage, as Lynch puts it, from which we must protect ourselves. In connecting the fragments, completing a circuit as it were, Jeffrey gains access to the higher reaches of the subconscious—the "finer" part that liberates him for great secrets and to an undamaged masculinity, one that includes the capacity to receive as well as to assert. As with all of David Lynch's films, *Blue Velvet* is about "the will to lose one's will."[5] Jeffrey's seeking is rewarded with what lies beyond control and masculine aggression.

Jeffrey's achievement results in contact between the community and reality in the tangible form of his solution to the crime. And even though it may seem that the door to truth that he opens is closed by the end of the film, we will see that this kind of closure only applies in a limited way. *Blue Velvet* is limited in this sense because Lynch has not yet evolved a narrative by means of which he can imagine—as he triumphantly does in *Wild at Heart*—a heterogeneity that recreates the family out of the ashes of old crimes and willful repressions.

Jeffrey's visionary powers only exist in a brief interlude of enlarged perception when he distances himself from his place in the community. Though he has transcended his own fragmentation, the community remains a broken circuit, but one that, by the final credits, the spectator knows is full of potential. Thus, *Blue Velvet* suggests that in the cultural community there is only a brief time when reality is possible; ironically, that time is the one ordinarily demonized by the media—adolescence. The seeker-protagonist of Lynch's first original Hollywood narrative, on the border between being a teenager and a young adult, maps adolescence as a potential time of vision. Jeffrey is driven by his desires for the real not for the random, a reality from which the world of the fathers and mothers is cut off. His ultimate need to join that world is his limitation not his salvation.[6]

However, if *Blue Velvet* shows that Jeffrey's conquest of Frank makes very little social difference, Lynch is not counseling despair. For him, it is a matter of great hope that the human will is as limited as the social and anti-social structures it creates. If it does not rise to the sophistication and apocalyptic hope of *Wild at Heart*, *Blue Velvet* nevertheless has the freshness of the authentic beginning of an important development in cinema—Lynch's first full narrative rendering in Hollywood of the subconscious as our source of reality.

Wanting to Be a Bad Boy?

An understanding of Jeffrey's qualified journey to authenticity in *Blue Velvet* requires our understanding of the question Dorothy asks him in the middle of his penetration of the criminal enclave in Lumberton—does he wants to be a bad boy and do bad things? He doesn't answer this question, just as he doesn't clear up Sandy's earlier doubts about whether his desire to investigate the ear designates him as a detective or a pervert. He does not answer either question because he cannot. Within the discourse of a repressive and very limited community, the need for reality is inevitably confused with transgression.

Clarification of that muddle is the priority of this film. We begin to know the distinction between being bad and being real from the movie's beginning, which creates in us a Lynchian longing for the real even before we meet Jeffrey. The overwhelming sense of Lumberton's everyday reality as a carnivalized spectacle puts us in a mood to go beyond "the show" and impels us toward Jeffrey's adventure. This desire is immediately stimulated at the beginning of the film by the image of the white picket fence that suggests the fabricated aspects of the most ordinary limits of communal life. It is augmented by the sound track's use of the song "Blue Velvet," which sets the images into the context of performance even though what we see is very ordinary. (Later in the film, as we shall see, the performance of popular music will take on a more profound and complex meaning as it evokes not only surfaces but depths as well.) The lure of the real beyond the fence continues in the image of the fireman on his fire truck in this opening montage, more like the spectacle of a parade than an everyday action. These are not parodies of old films, as so many critics have suspected.[7] Rather, they are representations that emphasize the social construction of the forms of ordinary social life. Curiously, we believe in these forms as if they were real. It is as though Lumberton were, in the words of Bakhtin, "a pageant without footlights and without a division into performers and spectators"[8] (p. 122). The visibility of these contradictions breeds desire for realities greater than those of the flat and shallow forms of culture.

20. Tom Beaumont: watering the lawn as performance.

Even the circumstances of Tom Beaumont's stroke while he is watering his lawn contain elements of performance and spectacle. Beaumont's manipulation of the hose is oddly suave, his free hand hooked in the belt loops of his pants like a boy showing off by managing a convertible car with one hand. State-trooper sunglasses and a macho, wide-brimmed hat deepen the sense of Beaumont's role-playing (see figure 20). The impression is amplified when the hose twists and constricts the flow of water, and this is accompanied by a deep rumbling noise on the sound track that is more reminiscent of a machine going awry than of a mimetic "hose sound." Beaumont clutching his neck and falling to the ground is not immediately understood by every spectator as a stroke because it is not named and because it exists within the mysterious fascination of spectacle. Yet this is not in any way a representation of the disappearance of reality into media image, of which Fredric Jameson has accused Lynch in his scathing (totally mistaken) Marxist attack on *Blue Velvet.* Indeed, it is the reverse.

These opening images prevent our usual mistaking of the image for reality in popular films by reminding us of the constructed quality of representation in ordinary life. We are also reminded that there is a larger reality in the social carnival. With Beaumont's inability to organize the activity of lawn watering, energy surges through the film frame. The hose, dropped but still gushing, is no longer constructed spectacle but rather raw force, now at an angle that suggests a penis emerging from his trousers, now with a life of its own. More free energy appears when a baby wanders obliviously toward the fallen man and across his body, and a small dog leaps repeatedly for the stream of water flowing from the hose (see figure 21). Once Beaumont's domination of the frame has lapsed, we see into the activity in the grass, no longer a flat, solid green but a vast universe teeming with the energy of insects. There is something raw—real?—beyond image. We precede Jeffrey in sensing this.

21. Tom Beaumont: energy leaks out of a disrupted performance.

When we meet Jeffrey and join him on his visit to his father in the hospital, the spectacle of ordinary life continues. Tom is behind a curtain, which the nurse sweeps away when she presents Jeffrey to his father as if there were a staged presentation in progress. Beaumont's body is immobilized by a mechanism (invented by Lynch) that again evokes the constraints of the deliberate mechanisms of communal order. Later, after Jeffrey finds the ear and brings it to Williams, police procedure is performance too—a low-key, affectless but anxious, performance by Williams ("Yes, that's an ear") and the objective, unfeeling performance of the police pathologist ("I don't remember anything coming in minus an ear"). The police station sign and the town vista itself are like maquettes.

All of this contrasts with the immediacy and vitality of the scenes in which lapses of control make things happen. For example, Jeffrey finds the ear in a field gone to seed; in a moment of pure serendipity, his imagination is sparked in a place over which human volition has relinquished control. Sandy, who gives a direction to Jeffrey's desire to see, also comes to him in the guise of an accident, emerging out of the darkness outside the Williams house as if she were being created there for him out of a special light that comes from the fruitful Lynchian darkness. She brings with her the information about Dorothy that gives substance to his desire to seek and also, inevitable within such a controlled environment, to disobey. Sandy's appearance is, like the wild zone in which the ear is discovered, part of the representation of Jeffrey's receptivity that is the real contrast to the performative elements of the communal and, as we shall soon see, the willful behavior of the criminal orders.

BLUE
VELVET

When Jeffrey discovers Frank and Dorothy in Dorothy's apartment, the breakthrough is part of a continuous process of losing control. Dorothy finds him spying on her from her closet when he accidentally moves the hangers, and he loses further control of the situation as she begins the process of rape. At knifepoint, she forces him to strip and begins to make love to him. Frank's arrival at her apartment while Jeffrey is in a state of arousal intensifies Jeffrey's loss of control.

Jeffrey has carefully calculated his arrival at Dorothy's apartment, but it is his inadvertent fall into receptivity that marks the dynamic of this scene. Significantly, the darker side of being in control becomes visible once Jeffrey is out of control. Frank's brutal delusions of mastery are the insidious side of the pageant of communal order. Like the police, Frank's sense of being in control is delusional, as seen, for example, in his ritualistic requirement that the room be dark when he molests Dorothy. Frank's definition of "darkness" is significant. He reviles Dorothy for failing to make the room "dark," but his pronunciation of the ritualistic words "now it's dark" once she complies with his fantasy is a pure fabrication. Only some of the lights are turned off; one wall sconce and one votive candle remain lit. Because this "darkness" is only what Frank decrees is darkness, it is untenable to read this scene as anything other than a performance of will, just as we cannot associate his vile behavior with the absence of light. Rather, his perversity is associated with inappropriately taking charge. Frank's tenacious will-to-control is underlined by his initiation of his rape of Dorothy with the inhalation of gas from a plastic mask. The use of the gas is a mysterious gesture since we have no idea what kind of gas it is or why Frank is using it. But these literalisms are completely irrelevant. The crucial issue here is his tampering with one of the two most important involuntary human reflexes— the breath, which along with the blood is the basic involuntary energy of life. Frank creates sexual excitement by taking control of breathing.[9]

In contrast, the alternative to the spectacle and performances of Lumberton's surface and depths is the gift of the subconscious.

22–26. Frame Series #1: Jeffrey moves into the realm of the subconscious.

As Jeffrey emerges from the darkness outside of Dorothy's house, an intense white beam of light illuminates his head; a process of enlightenment is taking place that is not under his or the community's control. It comes to him in a series of images: an image of his father's head, distorted like a melting wax figure and accompanied by the equally melted sound of his father saying, "help her"; an angle-down image of Frank, crouching and roaring like a rabid animal; an image of a dark space lit only by a votive candle guttering in a rush of wind; a black screen over which Frank whispers, "now it's dark"; an intimate, extreme close-up of the red lips and white teeth through which Dorothy, upside down, implores Jeffrey to "hit me"; Frank striking out toward the camera (into a space shared by Jeffrey and the spectator); and a black screen over which an electronic shriek cuts, suddenly jolting Jeffrey from his dreams (see figures 22–26).

This montage is not a rebus, which creates significance only after it has been translated into linguistic syntax. Indeed, words cannot bear the burden of Jeffrey's discovery.[10] He is putting together pieces concerning perceptions of masculinity that cohere, as they do not in Lumberton. The "good" father's imperative for proper action—"help her"—is a function of the incapacitated father, not the phallic media guardian. The "bad" father's solipsistic action is the phallic will accompanied by the burning fire that makes the air into a holocaust. It is also the distortion of Dorothy's sigh of pleasure that vibrates the air involuntarily into a masochistic response.

The insufficiency of language as it is commonly used in this context is made clearer when Jeffrey attempts to report to Sandy what he has found. As they sit parked in her car in front of a church, serenaded by numbingly conventional strains played by the church organ, his equally conventional rundown of facts omits almost everything of significance. He can relate nothing more than

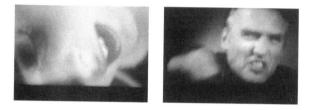

a censored account of his night at Dorothy's, emptied by his actual inability to articulate his vision and leaving him to vague agonies: "Why are there people like Frank? Why is there so much trouble in the world?" The real question he cannot ask, the question that is forming in his subconscious, is, "What is the connection between these people, this trouble, and me?"

Sandy attempts to console Jeffrey by retelling a comforting dream that she had on the day she met him. In her dream, the world is dark and loveless until a swarm of robins arrives and brings (blinding) light and love to the troubled earth. She counsels him to wait until the robins arrive. Her simple rebus-reading of dreams is certainly reductive. Its oversimplicity is emphasized by the organ music on the sound track, which is nothing more than the most banal exercise of chord progressions. Nevertheless, her innocent optimism is derived from something beyond her waking mind, and it does conceive of a relationship between what she can see and what she can't see, even if she does domesticate this wisdom. Simple as it is, Sandy's dream is a kind of Lynchian narrative. Narrative always reduces the dream on which it is based. However, the validity of the dream in the Lynchian concept of reality gives Sandy's inexperienced attempt at narrative a kind of legitimacy, for it gives Jeffrey a sense of hope that is necessary but not sufficient for his journey. It is a fledgling Lynchian representation of the importance of the ease with which the feminine sensibility has access to the dream and the subconscious, and how important this is for the masculine sensibility. Sandy's access to dreams is more true and important for Lynch than the details of her explication.

In contrast, the empty language of the police and of the criminals—unleavened by the dream—is in a permanent state of collapsing in on itself. The outlaw version of Detective Williams's affectless, tautological "Yes, Jeffrey, that's an ear," is Frank's tautological vortex of self-parodying logic when he catches Dorothy and Jeffrey after a tryst. Darkly surveying them, he asks, "Who is this fuck?" To Dorothy's lame attempt at presenting Jeffrey as a neighborhood friend, Frank replies, "Oh, you're from the neighborhood. You're a neighbor. . . . Hey, do you want to go for a ride?" When he talks at Jeffrey here, he burlesques the reassuring gestures of the "Good Joe." Jeffrey tries to keep the performance going with a polite but terrified, "No thanks." However, in the ensuing conversation, Frank aggressively bends language to his purposes until its logical syntax turns into the spasms of his will:

Frank: "No thanks?" What does that mean?
Jeffrey: I don't want to go.
Frank: Go where?
Jeffrey: I don't want to go for a ride.
Frank: A ride! Hell, that's a good idea. [*Smiling, placid, as though affably accommodating Jeffrey's desires*] Okay. Let's go.

Language is nothing but construct here, blowing in both the cold wind of the sterile communal will and the hot wind of the outlaw's volcanic will.

In order to attain his vision, Jeffrey must see a larger picture of the cultural evasions of reality. His misbehavior, then, is a function in *Blue Velvet* of his valid resistance to the emptiness of language and culture in general in their most barren incarnations. He is led to Dorothy by accident and by a positive fascination of an allure beyond his will in an early Lynchian vision of the collective unconscious in popular culture. Dorothy comes to Jeffrey from a space in which the fragments of divided community are joined, a place that is always magic in the Lynchian universe—the popular stage.

The spectacle on the stage of the Slow Club when Dorothy sings is a construction of glamor that transcends its almost laughable artificiality and makes accessible to ordinary people (i.e., a mass audience) another level of reality. Offstage, Dorothy is almost frumpy. Onstage, in the blue light, raised beyond the reductions of ordinary life by the kernel of the collective nonrational in popular love songs, she touches the subconscious authenticity of desire.

The fetish aspects of Dorothy's glamor—the erotics of the will—are represented humorously. The comedy of fetish is intentional, as is clear not only from the film itself but also from what Isabella Rossellini has said about her fascination with how Lynch used her beauty for comic effects.[11] Indeed, Lynch covers the extremely beautiful Rossellini with absurdly exaggerated "glamor" make-up, featuring lurid tones of lipstick and silly-looking patches of blue on her eyelids and red on her cheeks. To literally top this effect, a long, dark, curly wig comes perilously close to being a fright wig. During her performances at the Slow Club, where she is billed as "the Blue Lady," she wears a cheaply made, revealing, black evening gown in the style of 1940s singers, which becomes romantic spectacle through the music and light that surrounds her. Her fascination for Jeffrey—and the spectator?—derives from the potent Lynchian tension between the artificial conventions of the temptress and the underlying visceral nature of the actress's sensual, motherly, full-breasted body, soft voice, and liquid eyes. Dorothy clearly becomes a flashpoint for the conflict between the paraphernalia of glamor and the body's energy in the blue light of the nightclub stage, where mass-media flimflam and the subconscious are brought together in their disunity so that a real energy makes a brief appearance within the social context.

In representing popular culture as an access to reality, Lynch makes us aware of the balance between absurdity and magic in this part of the community. Generally speaking, in Lumberton this kind of balance is impossible; divisions are characterized on the surfaces and in the depths of the town by the imbalances of phallocentric aggression. It is the sickness of culture. The much-remarked-upon line that Dorothy mysteriously says to Jeffrey after the first time they have sex, "Now you have put your disease in me," and which she later echoes when she tells Sandy that Jeffrey has "put his disease" in her, has been steadfastly misinterpreted as meaning the disease of sadomasochism. On one level, the disease in Dorothy is, as is clear from an earlier draft of the film, the actual sperm from intercourse.[12] But on another level, it is Dorothy's internalization of self-loathing from a phallocentric society that in both its overt and covert manifestations values masculine will and reviles, or at least represses, feminine receptivity. Unless Jeffrey can go beyond social definitions of behavior—legal or criminal—he too will be forced to hit women for sexual gratification (Frank) or not touch them at all (Detective Williams). In searching as he does, Jeffrey does not want to be a bad boy; he is refusing the transmission of the kind of fathering and manhood that cuts culture off from the feminine and thus from an important aspect of the real.

You're Like Me?: The Non-reproduction of Fathering in Lumberton

Lynch casts his vision of Jeffrey's pilgrimage to manhood in terms of his release from fetishism, which is the ritualistic drama of the disavowal of women and reality in the same gesture.[13] In *Blue Velvet* Lynch portrays fetishism as the paradigmatic reality problem—the disease?—of a phallocentric, will-driven culture. His critique of gendered imbalances is implicit in the narrative development of Jeffrey's reality, that is, his new manhood, as he distances himself from the fetishistic denial of femininity in both Williams and Frank. The film, unlike the town, values the openness of feminine energy in Dorothy and Sandy and devalues the conventional association between masculinity and control by closely associating male domination with abuse and fetishization.

Jeffrey's actual father, Tom, is most productive as a mentor for Jeffrey when he loses control, while Detective Williams, in his increasing attempt to assert the control of the law, is paradoxically ever more ineffective and frightening (to be explored below). Jeffrey finds his release from the control of the "good" fathers by traveling into the outlaw fragment of Lumberton. But he must then find a way to free himself from the compulsions of manhood as an assertion of the will as it is defined in the doppelganger side of the community. Indeed, it is Jeffrey's departure from the lessons of all of the fathers, that is, his unique evolution of a more real masculinity—in Lynchian terms—that combines assertion and receptivity and takes him beyond the heroic and into seeking. Jeffrey's discovery of the severed ear is his introduction to Lynchian knowledge of the mutilation of men. To avoid this mutilation, he must overcome the lessons of the fathers which make masculinity the foundation of everything, including the cultural image of women. This imbalance fosters not only a constricted version of ordinary life, but, even worse, a substitution of projections of the masculine will for dreams.

Male control of everyday life is innocuous enough on the surface of Lumberton that passes for ordinary reality; but once Jeffrey sees the underside of masculine dominance, he encounters its most awful secret—the replacement of the larger realities of the dream with shallow fantasy that is no more than a whim of the will. The representation of this ultimate form of Lynchian horror is the mysterious Ben (Dean Stockwell)—misguidedly stigmatized by Robin Wood as a homophobic element in *Blue Velvet* (p. 48). Indeed, Ben is another form of the severed ear, a more pointed revelation of masculine alienation from femininity and the subconscious. He is the reduction of the feminine to a masculine performance of softness and receptivity, admired by Frank as much as he loathes not only women but also what is humanly open and sympathetic. Ben wears a glamor drag similar in artifice to Dorothy's but one that thinly covers the violence of a thug (see figure 27). (Ben, after all, indulges himself in casual brutality that resonates of Frank.)

27. Ben is a masculine projection of the feminine.

Only as Ben's masculine performance of mannerisms does Frank value femininity. Indeed, Ben's performance of femininity is the only thing that Frank does admire or respect. He lauds Ben as "one suave fuck" for his elaborately mimed manners, while he savages Dorothy for her softness: "Don't say please, shithead." Even Jeffrey's receptive masculinity is contemptible to Frank—a softness Frank identifies with being a "pussy." When Frank forces Jeffrey to pay tribute to Ben in a "toast," the meaning he gives Jeffrey's capitulation is full of the implications of homosexual violation, which does not implicate gay life but rather heterosexual obsession with domination. "I can get him to do anything I want," Frank says smirkingly to Ben. Ben is the object of Frank's affections precisely because there is nothing really feminine—or open—about him.

Ben is the keeper of the dream only in Frank's terms, a base form of fantasy that is constructed, sterile, and toxic—one totally opposite the Lynchian dream. It is a phallocentric fantasy, a poor excuse for the dream, as we see when Frank compulsively puts a tape of Roy Orbison's "In Dreams"—which Frank tellingly refers to as "candy-colored clown"—in the tape recorder at Ben's.[14] Ben obliges by lipsynching it for him, holding a worklight as a micro-

28. Ben's reduced form of illumination.

phone, which casts an eerie glow on him as he silently moves his lips and the voice of Roy Orbison flows from the machine. The extraordinary power of the image of Ben lipsynching "In dreams I walk with you; in dreams I talk with you" is its revelation of the pathetic reduction of dreams within this context. Frank is agitated from the depths of his being by a totally fabricated experience. Ben might say with Shakespeare's Iago, "I am not what I am." His performance is the icon of non-being—a man who makes the gestures of femininity, and who opens his mouth and does not sing. The rapture to which it moves Frank represents Frank's profound alienation from the real and from the dream, a pairing that is the core of the Lynchian narrative; for Lynch, realists are by definition dreamers. Ben's performance could not contrast more strongly with Jeffrey's dream visions. In his visionary life Jeffrey is flooded with light and sound from somewhere beyond the immediate social context (whether "bad" or "good"). Ben, however, carries his own reduced form of illumination as a sign of the impoverishment of energy in his performance (see figure 28).[15]

Lynch has called the scene at Ben's the eye-of-the-duck scene. That it takes place over a bar called "This Is It!" is a wonderfully ironic confirmation of its significance. This is the scene, therefore, without which the film cannot be brought to a close, according to Lynch's definition of the "duck eye" (see Chapter 1). Here, Jeffrey, despite Frank's belief that he has him under control, moves away from the noxious fantasies of the outlaw will and toward the dream. Significantly, it is not what Jeffrey *sees* at Ben's—which is nothing but confusion—but what he *hears* that determines the rest of the film. He has been scheming to *see* something secret, but it is finally receptivity—hearing—that brings him to where he needs to be. He hears the voices of Dorothy and her child from behind a closed door—a high-pitched child's complaint and Dorothy's agonized cry, "No, momma loves you"—and the whispers of Frank and Ben carrying on a drug trade with a corrupt policeman named Gordon, Detective Williams's partner. On a narrative level, this gives Jeffrey the ammunition he needs to "break" the case. On a visionary level, the experience opens his ears to what has really been hidden from him—that which we are always the last to see, ourselves. Where before he had possessed a naive perception of Lumberton, through learning about Gordon, Jeffrey intuits his town anew. Where he had pitied Dorothy but still played the game of controlling her, through hearing her talking to her son, Jeffrey becomes open to a full empathy with her.

The scene at Ben's is both a prologue to the violation of Jeffrey and the beginning of his spiritual growth. The song Ben lipsynchs inspires the aroused Frank to drive Jeffrey, Dorothy, his henchman, and a woman one of them has picked up at Ben's to Meadow Lane, a sodden industrial wasteland which belies its name. There, Frank tells Jeffrey, "You're like me," kisses him while wearing Dorothy's lipstick, and beats him. Frank's thuggish donning of female glamor parallels Ben's; the lighting at Meadow Lane has echoes of the lighting during the lipsync. Both are performances, carrying a reduced and circumscripted form of energy, and visually representing a psychology of maimed masculinity arising from depleted identification with boundless female energy.[16]

But Frank cannot absorb Jeffrey into his perverse fantasies in which vulnerable femininity disappears into a series of stereotypical gestures and the masculine will engulfs everything. This scene is not about jealousy but about Frank's hatred of women—and reality—as is apparent in what he says to Jeffrey as he prepares to beat him to a pulp: "Don't be a good neighbor to her . . . [or] I'll send you straight to Hell, fucker." The core of Frank's existence is the transformation of the energy of love into an energy of abuse. Kindness and affection are forms of accessibility that are not options for him, as he all but says when he threatens Jeffrey with a love letter: "You know what a love letter is? It's a bullet from a fuckin' gun, fucker." The phallic aggression that takes the place of receptivity and mutuality in this image needs no comment. Further, it is the castration threat hidden in a phallocentric, control-driven society—be like me or I'll kill you. Frank covets Jeffrey's identity. "In dreams you're mine, all the time. Forever in dreams," says Frank.

However, Frank knows nothing about dreams in the Lynchian sense. He is, indeed, a Lynchian atrocity—a dreamless man—but, as the aftermath of this scene shows, he is not as strong as the real-

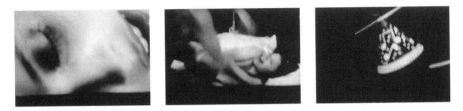

29–34. Frame Series #2: The subconscious moves Jeffrey into a higher form of knowledge.

ity he tries to shout down. For Frank does not define Jeffrey's dreams. Before Meadow Lane, Jeffrey's father *as an incapacitated patient* and Dorothy speak to him in dreams, and Frank attacks Jeffrey's dreams with an assaultive blow. After Meadow Lane, Jeffrey cries because of a second crucial montage. In this montage the nonverbal, dreaming part of his mind ranges over a series of images concerning Dorothy, her love for her son, and his own violent sexual relationship with her. The essence of this series is its ability to touch Jeffrey in a meaningful way that transcends logic and thus the discredited logic of his (and our?) dysfunctional, fragmented community. His subconscious ranges over images of the votive candle guttering in the wind, reminiscent of his accidental discovery of the Frank/Dorothy liaison; of the hat once worn by, and the door behind which Dorothy finds, Donny, her yet-to-be-seen son; and of Jeffrey's violent sexual foreplay with Dorothy and her orgasmically parted lips (see figures 29–34). The montage is all we (and Jeffrey) can know of the path by which he arrives at a new kind of manhood, an arrival marked by tears of remorse, not for having broken social rules but for having bought into Frank-like fantasies. The path Jeffrey takes in the montage brings him to what no man in his community can teach him—to recognize with compassion Dorothy's suffering and self-loathing. In this recognition, he is—in significant part, if not totally—delivered from the compulsions of his own outlaw will to use her and is truly "in dreams," that is to say, beyond the addictive mirages of control fantasies.

After Meadow Lane, Jeffrey reincorporates himself into communal order, but as he does, we understand more clearly the interchangeability of the "good" and "bad" men. Not only Williams's partner Gordon but Williams too looks different to us. It is not simply that we, briefly, are unsure whether he too is corrupt and

conspiring with his police colleague. We see a dangerous Frank-like ferocity in him that we have not seen before, a ferocity about *and toward* his daughter. The possibility that Sandy may know what Jeffrey knows enrages Williams. Although Jeffrey lies to reassure him that Sandy has had no part in his sleuthing, once Williams is alone with Sandy, his attitude toward her bears such a sinister aspect that we know if Williams—is there a pun on "will" here?—ever went on a rampage he would resemble Frank in his attitude toward women.

Similarly, Mike (Ken Stovitz), Sandy's jilted boyfriend, is now resonant of Frank when Mike takes action against Jeffrey for "stealing" Sandy from him. As she and Jeffrey return home from a party, Mike and his buddies—whom Jeffrey initially fears are Frank and company—ambush the couple. When Sandy tries to intercede, Mike shouts and points at her in an unambiguously Frank-like manner. However, his outlaw impersonation collapses when evidence of Frank's brutality surfaces in the scene. Dorothy, naked and covered with bruises, has been deposited by Frank on Jeffrey's doorstep as a warning. When she moves into the light on Jeffrey's darkened porch, Mike is too much of the "good" community to persist. But the likeness is now visible. What manifests itself in repression in the good part of the community is quickly convertible to sadistic aggression.

Sandy and Dorothy have more in common than erotic activity with Jeffrey. They both benefit from his refusal to accept the instruction on becoming a man that he receives from both "good" and "bad" men, which is to fear, disregard, or brutalize the feminine. *Blue Velvet* shows us a seeker who evades the futility of both attitudes. Jeffrey is not going to be like Frank *or* Detective Williams. By the end of the film, he has arrived at a point at which he must stop Frank, but not by depending on or acting like Williams. Instead, he triumphs over Frank through the heroic masculinity of the seeker that uses the strength of receptivity.

Jeffrey tricks Frank with a strategy that has the stamp of femininity on it. Jeffrey plays to Frank's belief that Jeffrey is "a pussy," and he achieves that victory appropriately through manipulating the channel that Frank has cut off for Don Vallens—the ears. Frank unwittingly has Jeffrey trapped in Dorothy's apartment. Knowing that Frank has a police radio, Jeffrey calls for help to Detective Williams on a police transmitter. He gives an exact description of his location—Dorothy's bedroom—but then hides again in her closet, this time for a different purpose. Frank is completely ensnared by Jeffrey's trick because of his skewed view of reality. As he heads into Dorothy's bedroom where Jeffrey supposedly is, he has all the power gestures of the fetishized outlaw will—the blue velvet robe (especially the sash that he uses so prominently in his sadistic rituals), the gun, and the private air supply—and all the contempt for what seems to him to be the vulnerable Jeffrey. "Pretty, pretty," Frank calls in a falsetto voice as he stalks the boy. Frank is fatally mistaken; action based on receptivity is strength. Jeffrey makes the point with a bullet between Frank's eyes.

Giving Us the Bird: The Mysteries of the Air

Although Lumberton is as fragmented at the end of the film as it was at the beginning, something important has changed. In shooting Frank, Jeffrey retains his connection to "normal" male will. However, in another way he has forged a new manhood that is the hope and pleasure of the conclusion of *Blue Velvet*. This new manhood shows itself in the tone and quality of his love relationship with Sandy, which was not a reality before the narrative began. This is a different kind of male-female relationship than BLUE any we have previously seen in the film. On the "bad" side of Lum- VELVET berton, we have seen only abuse and sadism, on the good side, sterile distance. We never actually see either the Williamses or the Beaumonts as couples—we merely know that these people are institutionally joined in wedlock; at the end, the men are out in the yard at the barbecue and the women are talking in the living room. In contrast to the gender segregation of the older generation at the end of the film, Sandy and Jeffrey are an integrated couple. Happily ever after?

Well ——. Few people who see the film can escape a nagging reservation in the final scene. The future for Sandy and Jeffrey in a "good" but not completely real fragment of the community is marked by the mechanical-looking robin that appears to them and seems to suggest that her dream-come-true is bogus. The discordant note of the robin here has bothered critics almost as much as the sudden appearance of Glinda at the end of *Wild at Heart,* and it is equally misunderstood. The mechanical robin is often misread as a burlesque of Jeffrey and Sandy's contentment, which it is only in so far as it reminds us, like Sailor's nose and Glinda at the end of *Wild at Heart,* that we are watching a movie.[17]

At the same time, the robin also reminds us of the Lynchian mysteries of the air that mark most of his films. These mysteries suggest the wonder of reality in the way that the air already fills space and yet there is also room for the culture that human beings create (see Chapter 1). We see this mystery in the rising and falling of drapes in Dorothy's apartment, to which the film cuts during Jeffrey's assignations with her. This image reminds us of what is hidden and revealed by constructed forms. Similarly, when Jeffrey brings himself to hit Dorothy so as to have sex with her, the screen bursts into flame. This is one of the early uses of the image of fire that Lynch later resorts to extensively in his *Twin Peaks* narratives and in *Wild At Heart.* Seeing air, usually invisible, is always part of Lynch's strategy to relativize the artifacts of human will that are conventionally visible. Narrative is, in this way, also a balance of free energies and willful actions.

The mystery of the robin, then, caps a series of mysteries associated with the air—and the subconscious. Not the least of these is electricity, one of the most interesting and basic of the Lynchian mysteries of the air, important as far back as his pre-Hollywood *Eraserhead* (see Chapter 6). The mystery of electricity pervades Jeffrey's return to Dorothy's apartment at the end of the film. With the police pursuing Frank, there is seemingly no reason for Jeffrey to involve himself further, but an important part of his new manhood is a new, unexploitative sympathy for Dorothy. Because of that sympathy, he goes to her place to try to help Don as she has asked him to. What he sees there makes him decide to leave all of this to the police. But that vision and the decision that arises from it cannot be understood in the terms of conventional illusionist realism. Certainly it is logical for Jeffrey to defer to the police.

35. Jeffrey sees what Frank has done to living energy.

Don is dead—his wound from the severed ear gaping, the blue velvet sash in his mouth—as is Gordon, the turncoat policeman, whose head has been mutilated by an electric drill. But perhaps logic is not motivating Jeffrey. This is not just an ordinary scene of carnage. Gordon, through dead, is standing. And nearby two oddly important objects are emphasized—an illuminated two-bulb lamp and a broken television set (see figure 35).

Although Jeffrey encounters seemingly bizarre sights in Dorothy's apartment, the vista is organic to the film, strongly suggesting what transformations have been proposed by it to the spectator and also to Jeffrey. The images raise the spectator and perhaps Jeffrey to that Lynchian angle of vision that makes visible, and visually "speakable," the point of view of the subconscious toward which Jeffrey has been progressing.[18] The upright position of the dead Gordon, and the broken electrical appliances speak of disturbances of energy, central to preconscious reality rather than of life as it is rationally understood. From the latter perspective, a broken television refers us to practical considerations. The visionary thrust of *Blue Velvet* has primed us for a more poetic vision that renders it and all the other images in the room a testimony to the ravages of the will on the flow of energies, as inflicted by Frank. In this way, Frank's perversion of life forces is not condemned through a simple moral protest but by means of a more cosmic indictment. Ideally, at this point in the film the viewer is now prepared to see the scene in this way. And if we don't actually know how conscious Jeffrey is of the changes wrought in him by his experiences, we do see in this scene of carnage a contrast between Jeffrey's *actions* now that he has a newfound visionary access and those that he planned out at the beginning of the film, when he was inclined exclusively to willful behavior.

Lynch very clearly shows in the scene at Dorothy's that it is only the accident of Frank's arrival that designates Jeffrey as the person who must dispatch him—not Jeffrey's desire for a confrontation. Vision is very strong as Jeffrey's adventure ends; his defeat of Frank is the will to lose will, and so he does. The end of Frank is also the

end of the police in Jeffrey's life as they fade into the background of the "crime scene." The spectator's focus is directed toward a foreground surge of brilliant energy beginning in the light bouncing off Sandy's pale blonde hair and enveloping her and Jeffrey as they embrace.

36. Jeffrey and Sandy: a new gender configuration in Lumberton.

However, even though Jeffrey and Sandy have found a flash of uncorrupted bliss, the events of their lives can never occur within the energy of light, evocative of some eternity beyond culture. Life also means human forms. Hence the equivocal nature of the robin that appears to them at the happy ending of the film (see figure 36). The robin is mechanical but also a bridge to something larger. Like the film in which it appears, the robin is a constructed thing, clearly a purposeful fabrication of human consciousness; yet, also like the film, at the same time the robin evokes and perhaps taps into the

37. Robin and insect: as above, so below.

involuntary bounty of the subconscious, that is, as it alludes to Sandy's dream.

The end of the film combines a conventional closing note with a narrative rupture. Since Sandy and Jeffrey do not notice anything disillusioning about the bird, this moment with its special Lynchian pleasures belongs to the spectator. We are gratified by the fulfilled desires of the harmonious happy ending, but also by an acknowledgment of the reality that narrative closure is always to some degree an artificial, somewhat violent (hence the allusion to the robin as predator) bounding of the flow of real energies. Further, and more importantly, the robin and the insect encapsulate a vision of an interconnection between above (air, bird) and below (ground, insect), making visible one of Lynch's favorite mystical truths—"As above, so below." This is a point at which culture and energy are briefly revealed in balance (see figure 37). Robin and insect at this moment constitute and make visible a Lynchian, asymmetrical balance of human and eternal forces. This is also Lynch's homage to Jeffrey's achievement in accessing the larger order, making that and not the police issues crucial in Lumberton.

5

"The Stream Flows, the Wind Blows"

DUNE
THE ELEPHANT MAN

Lynch's first two Hollywood assignments, *Dune* (1984) and *The Elephant Man* (1980), are drawn from conventional linear narratives—a novel and a documented history. Because each story was assigned to Lynch in a rationally ordered form, each put its own set of obstacles in the way of his narrative sense. In each case, he made more concessions to the rational/linguistic structure of the narrative than he had made before or has ever made since. Therefore, I am assuming in the following commentary on these films that these are in some ways anomalous Lynch films, much influenced by the conventional parameters of his assignments. This is not to say that in these first two films there is anything cynical, perfunctory, or subservient about his work. Rather, we see in *Dune* and *The Elephant Man* a profoundly earnest Lynch trying to work out a path by which he might take his mass-media film assignments, within the constraints of his employment, toward the border at which cultural form melds into subconscious energy.

Dune: "The Stream Flows?"

Dune is the only Lynch film about which there is valid general agreement that it doesn't work.[1] It is a difficult film to discuss because it is full of beautiful, inventive images and narrative strategies that may appear to be pure effect in the context in which they are placed but which resurface in Lynch's later films to become the foundation of effective storytelling. Worse, discussion of *Dune* is impeded by the lack of a definitive cut. A distended version shown on television—embellished by extensive voice-over commentary and many scenes added "for clarity"—is a distortion of what is sold on videotape and shown in movie theaters as "the director's cut." However, this "director's cut" may be a distortion of a rumored, undistributed version that may exist (I have no evidence for or against) and may more closely reflect Lynch's preferences. Given the duress under which he composed this film, uncharacteristic of anything else he has ever made, it is appropriate to wonder if there really exists a film of *Dune* directed by David Lynch. Because "the director's cut" is popularly known as a Lynch film, and because Lynch has never denied his authorship of it to me—or to anyone I am aware of—I consider it in this study. However, since the textual problems are quite real, the following commentary is probably most valuable for the insight it provides into Lynch's relationship to the commercial mass media.

For all its fantasy-laden interplanetary settings and futuristic technology, the plot of *Dune* is impossibly un-Lynchian in nature. Unfolding the struggle of the Kwisatz Haderach—the Savior of the Known Universe—*Dune* chronicles a conventional rebellion in the struggle of hero Paul Atreides (Kyle MacLachlan) against an unjust social authority. In Lynch's movie, and even in Frank Herbert's novel on which the film is based, Paul himself is potentially a Lynchian hero since he develops his sense of identity through dream visions. There is an entirely Lynchian project in a possible film of *Dune* which *could have* pitted Paul's receptivity to inspiration against the aggressions of both his allies—the family Atreides and the Fremen population native to the planet Dune—and his primary antagonists—the forces of the Empire, which combine Emperor Shaddam IV (Jose Ferrer), the Space Navigators' Guild, and the House of Harkonnen. However, in the film Lynch was constrained to make, *Dune* falters because he could not muster any real enthusiasm for *conquering* the "known universe," regardless of the rationale.

A hero's mandated conquest of the "known universe" does not leave enough room for the fundamental receptivity of the Lynchian seeker or a secret-bearing protagonist. The Lynchian seeker and secret cannot rejoice in the victory of an administrator of a closed system, which is what Paul becomes in Herbert's novel. Certainly, Lynch did not sabotage *Dune* intentionally; that kind of behavior is not in his character, but neither is it in his character to deny what he is as a filmmaker. The totality of *Dune* articulates his frustration, falling between the director's validation of Paul's vision—his lack of control—and the centrality he was forced to give to the crowning of Paul as the rightful *ruler* of the "known universe."

The plot of *Dune* confronts Paul and his family with the obligatory obstacles over which only a determined hero can lead them. The battleground is Dune, a seemingly barren desert planet. Barren though it may be, Dune is the center of the Empire because it is the only source of "spice," the foundation of the "known universe" of the future, used as both a mind-altering drug and a replacement for fuel. To this planet Emperor Shaddam IV lures the noble Atreides from their watery planet Caladan to supervise the mining of the spice. He uses the pretext that the evil Harkonnen have mismanaged the planet and are being replaced. However, unknown to Duke Leto (Jürgen Prochnow)—Paul's father—the Harkonnen, the Emperor, and the Space Navigators, who control the distribution of the spice, are in collusion against the Atreides, whose upright nature threatens their corrupt power.

Once the Atreides are on Dune, the Emperor plans to kill them and support the return of the Harkonnen to Dune by force. Under orders from the Space Navigators, Shaddam will have Paul killed first, since Paul is suspected of being the Kwisatz Haderach, who the prophecies say is destined to oust the Emperor. But Paul's visionary power, inherited from his mother, forewarns him of the Emperor's machinations and also enables him to make himself the master of the mammoth sandworms of Dune, which tunnel the planet and produce the mysterious spice. His power over the worms is the sign that he is the messiah; the worms are also his means of taking power since they can overwhelm any military might that the Empire can muster. In addition, he has a strange skill with sound, another blessing from his mother, that helps him to lead the Fremen, the repressed natives of Dune, to a successful victory over the evil forces. In the final scene, Paul stands in the place of the Emperor. Much of this is a lot of fun, but the plot insists that we also revel in Paul's mastery, and we don't. We don't really care at all because Lynch's profound sense that the will-to-control leads to absurdity as well as to harm led him to represent the delusional structure of *Dune*'s "known universe."

Lynch has never been moved to imbue the *"known* universe" with a value that can inspire legitimate desire. From the first image of the film, the lessons of Bacon, Pollock, and Hopper led Lynch to represent the known universe as a grandiose concept (see Chapter 1).[2] Consequently, his *Dune* begins by representing its grandiosity through an absurd image of a woman's face, that of Princess Irulan (Virginia Madsen), daughter of Shaddam IV, dominating the stars (see figure 38). (In contrast, even in the pop-cult television series *Star Trek*, noted for immensely grandiloquent protagonists, the stars always dwarf human technology and heroes.) Irulan is there to give the audience an overview of the history of 10,191, the year in which the film unfolds. She intends to be authoritative, but her dignity is comically undermined by a fadeout "double take" in which she decorously disappears and abruptly fades back in briefly with a kind of "oops" effect.

38. Irulan defines the comic arrogance of the "known universe."

Silly her, she has "forgotten" one detail— unfortunately, the one most crucial to the "known plot." She needs to introduce the spice, a substance found exclusively on the planet Dune; spice is the most important economic, political, and spiritual part of the known universe.

Lynch's use of Irulan anticipates his use of the white fence, flowers, and fireman in *Blue Velvet*. She immediately reminds us of the futility of control, even the filmmaker's control over the film's fantasy. The comedy of her grandiosity depletes the force of narrative structure. To further weaken the notion of narrative and heroic control, she instantly disappears as the voice of the narrative. In the initial scene of the film, she is banished from her father's throne room as the first important plot event is about to occur. Later, her voice exists only infrequently, conveying information that often makes us wonder why she bothered. At the end of the film, she is visible as a bewildered, overdressed supernumerary.

After Irulan, it is difficult to have an illusionist stake in the action, and the narrative continues to ridicule the putative prize. The Emperor makes matters worse as he talks to the Navigator like a bad actor from a bad play. (Shaddam in this way prefigures the bombastic character of Frank Booth, as discussed above in Chapter 4.) The comical appearance of the Navigator also helps to undermine the conventional aspects of the plot—he resembles a bloated, pockmarked goldfish and travels in an enclosed glass structure that resembles an aquarium in which the medium is orange gas instead of water. This odd fish of a Navigator burlesques his august position further when, after inciting Shaddam to murder Paul Atreides, he leaves with the words, "I never said this; I was not here." There is nothing very lofty or even real about the structure of the known universe.

The ineffectuality of the structure of authority in *Dune* is further suggested by the attire of the Emperor's court and its architectural design and decoration, which are a riot of styles, historical periods, and resonances. The look of *Dune* is bewilderingly carnivalized. The monumental gold set is full of the grandiosity of early communist monolithic design, as well as the scale of massive Egyptian temples conflated with gilded oriental splendor (see figure 39). A throne in the center engulfs the Emperor. The effect is both ornate and shallow, as if a full-sized cathedral were constructed of thin metallic plate.

39. The carnivalized look of the Empire.

In these halls, which suggest the confusion and indeterminacy of human ideas, characters mill around aimlessly like guests at a themeless costume party. The Emperor sports a uniform that combines the bourgeois style of a business suit with the cut and decoration of a Tsar's uniform and the black and silver colors of a Nazi officer. The veiled, bejeweled, overdressed women affect the frontal baldness of the otherwise copiously maned women of Flemish paintings. Their clothing is a conflation of women's dress from the great Flemish canvases, from the Spanish infanta's court, and from the Elizabethan court. To add a further carnivalesque quality to the proceedings, leashed pug dogs—animals strongly associated with ladies' laps, not high adventure—appear in the throne room and reappear later, cuddled by warriors on battlefields. This texture is entirely Lynch's creation, having no precedent in the novel or indeed in futuristic films, which have very distinct conventions that govern how things will look: spandex; cellophane-like materials; minimalist glass, steel, and formica decor; neutral colors; and *no* pugs. The brilliantly gilded halls of the Emperor, the lush velvet and wools, and the exuberantly ornate irruption of mixed resonances of ancient and early modern history all destabilize the spectator's confidence in linear rationality. All of this anticipates the carnival road-life of the desperately out-of-control, controlled society that Sailor and Lula meet in *Wild at Heart.*

Lynch also uses heterogeneous mapping in creating his version of the villainous Harkonnens. Their

40. Harkonnen mutilation.

planet, Giedi Prime, is, in hindsight, the home of the mutilated masculinity as it is more powerfully defined in *Blue Velvet.* Lynch used the image of the severed ear in his next film after developing that image and others like it in *Dune.* The Harkonnen world is predominantly characterized by the maiming of the senses as portals of entry—ears are sewn up and eyes are covered with impenetrable mesh (see figure 40). Hearts are put under political control by the insertion of a heart plug in all of the planet's inhabitants. The organic appears primarily as lumps of tissue in drains waiting to be flushed, or as an upside-down cow in a sling on which midgets are performing some unknown work. Sensual pleasure on this planet derives from the degeneration of the vitality of the natural body—the draining of blood and the caressing and consumption of diseased tissues. It is a planet diseased by a lack of receptivity. Again in hindsight, we can see the first appearance of the line from *Blue Velvet,* "Now you have put your disease in me," in the diseased skin of the leader of the Harkonnen family, the Baron (Kenneth McMillan). The Baron's doctor (Leonardo Cimino) attends him continually, draining the clusters of swollen eruptions on his face and cooing about the beauty and pleasure of the Baron's disease: "You are so beautiful, my Baron. Your skin, love to me. Your diseases lovingly cared for, for all eternity."

The portrait of the Harkonnen homeland suggests that all of

their cruelty culminates in nothing more than an illusion of order. On this sensory-deprived planet, Harkonnen mastery for its own sake is epitomized by the intimidating buoyancy of the Baron, so swollen with the greed of self-involvement that he appears to dominate the air. However, this seeming domination of the most incontrovertible force of nature has application only within the confines of his own culture in which he can swoop upon and attack the helpless citizens of Giedi Prime. Ultimately, his escape from gravity becomes a sign of his nothingness, a weightlessness that bears him to oblivion at the end of the film.

The presentation of the Emperor and the Harkonnens is absolutely Lynchian, compatible with his sense of the tyranny of cultural forms. In that respect, *Dune* is an early draft of what later became Lynch's characteristic visualization of social repression in carnivalized images. In contrast, there is a strained effort, against Lynch's grain, to validate heroic control in the "good" Paul, because Lynch doesn't believe in the benefits of that kind of control. Thus the revenge story in *Dune*—Paul's mission to avenge his father's murder by the Harkonnen—and his succession to the authority of Shaddam never really engage us. Audience detachment is particularly obvious when we, the spectators, are confronted with conventional attempts to encourage us to identify with Paul as the kind of hero who can and must assert command to effect revenge and to seize control from the villains. On Caladan, Paul demonstrates immense control of his body and an impressive capacity to best an opponent when he defeats a frightening mechanical training device through his aggressive amplification of sound waves. Later, after his family has moved to Dune, he single-handedly halts in midair the progress of a hunter-seeker—a tiny guided missile used to murder individuals—before it kills an innocent Fremen woman. He also kills a Harkonnen soldier menacing his mother, woos and wins the daughter of the Fremen chieftain, and conquers and rides the train-sized worms of Dune. In the obligatory penultimate clash of hero and villain, he defeats in hand-to-hand combat a young, revoltingly villainous Harkonnen champion, Feyd-Rautha (Sting).

Yet our passion is never engaged more than momentarily by Paul's display of conventional derring-do. He seems less a hero we have been trained to love than someone who is dressed up and playing cowboy. This is particularly true when he rides the worms that he has mastered, giddy with the rapture of the deed as if asking, "Did I really do this?" (see figure 41). The fight with Feyd-Rautha gives us another example of the stalemated quality of the film. This duel is in many ways a conventional display of heroic force and is the final obligatory test of the dominating hero who will assume control. But indeed, Paul wins by abrogating his will. He escapes Feyd's poison blade by bending "like a reed in the wind." And although he commits a particularly aggressive violation of Feyd's corpse with the power of sound, the victory is immediately followed by a belittling comic exclamation from one of Paul's Fremen associates (Everett McGill), who pronounces Paul's name in a humorous tone that makes it sound as if he is saying, "Whoa, what a guy."

41. Paul role-playing as "worm conqueror."

This is not the moment of Hollywood exultation of the will because the will is not what makes Lynch rejoice. If we care at all about Paul, we do so not because of his plot-necessary skills at asserting himself in a purposeful manner but because of his skill at what really interests Lynch—the journey into the subconscious. With this element of *Dune,* Lynch is at home. And because this journey is connected with the women in his life, Paul's relationship with women is thus rendered with more fluidity and interest than his stilted relationships with his father and other male-bonded buddies. His father, Duke Leto, tells him with overripe authority, "The sleeper must awaken." But Paul's subconscious awakens through his bond with his mother.[3]

For Lynch, the passion of Paul's story is in his subconscious life, represented by his four waking dreams in the narrative of *Dune.* In these visions, Lynch begins to evolve a montage technique for putting the spectator in touch with the protagonist's extra-narrative energies, a technique he later employs in *Blue Velvet* and *Twin Peaks.* Unlike the interior montages in his subsequent films, these, because of the heavy hand of the plot on the film, are more like rebus images to be decoded than like the later, more visceral visions. However, the dreams constitute the core of *Dune* and suggest what the film might have been had Lynch not been constrained to do a conventional treatment of Paul's destiny. Each dream marks a major transition toward a Lynchian messianic identity and thus implicates the messiah not as one who controls but as one who can open himself. But even more startling, given that Lynch is working in a narrative tradition that tends to assert the Freudian definition of masculinity—that is, a hero cut loose from feminine associations and traits in order to bring the film to closure—the waking dreams bring Paul closer to his larger identity as they bring him *closer* to feminine experience.[4]

This is particularly true of his third waking dream. After Paul and his mother have crashed in the desert, he has a vision of the inside of his mother's womb, which tells him that she is pregnant with his sister. His vision of the fleshy, red-orange, moist, pulsating fetus is the annunciation not only of the birth of Alia but also of his own rebirth. That the prelude to Paul's rebirth is this intimate knowledge of his mother's womb is the most compelling aspect of Lynch's *Dune*. This is an important step in Lynch's evolution toward narrative that depends on a representation of the feminine as a major force in the larger aspects of human life beyond the self-defining, self-absorbed paternal world of cultural construct. Paul's dream visions build on the maternal force of the visionary elements Lynch explored in *The Elephant Man* (to be discussed below) and anticipate the feminine aspects of vision in *Twin Peaks* (Chapter 3), *Wild at Heart* (Chapter 2), and *Fire Walk with Me* (Chapter 7).

Indeed, the fourth dream, in which the "sleeper awakens," results from Paul's imitation of his mother's actions. To become the Bene Gesserit Mother of the Fremen, Lady Jessica (Francesca Annis) has had to drink the Water of Life, a poison distilled by the worms of Dune which her body must covert to a benign visionary stimulant so that she can take her ritual place. When Paul drinks the Water of Life, he accomplishes what no man has before, a process which dilates his inner and outer eyes and causes the worms of Dune to encircle him and stand at attention. In the process of converting the Water of Life, Paul transcends the rebus of his earlier images and makes both an internal and external voyage in which his capacity for vision expands beyond the boundaries of the known universe.

Paul's awakening is represented as a bonding between him, his mother, and his sister. At the point of his conversion of the Water of Life, a drop of blood trickles from his eye, and Lady Jessica and Alia (Alicia Roanne Witt) undergo a sympathetic seizure, their mouths dripping with blood. Scrambling all of Hollywood's gender constructs, the allusion to menstruation in the bloody-mouthed women attaches itself to Paul's bleeding eye—the mouth and the eye are conventional displacements of female and male genitalia respectively. The cultural silence about menstruation in narrative representations typically has been presumed to be an aspect of the link between castration and menstruation in masculine fantasies. Such a connection haunts this scene, but it is strongly balanced with much more positive suggestions about Paul's empathy with feminine experience.

In the dominant mass-media culture, and in the conventional mass-media narrative, everything about women suggests a dangerous nothingness which imperils the phallocentric definition of reality. From a phallocentric perspective, the phallus is "something" while the female genitalia mark the spaces where a biological version of the phallus should be, rendering the female genitalia "nothingness." In that context, the menstrual blood is a confirmation of the threat of nothingness, the sign that a castration has taken place. All of this is reversed in *Dune*. In *Dune*, the phallocentric construct of reality is clearly represented by the linear messianic plot which Lynch mocks inadvertently. Lynch's imagination is stirred precisely by those "feminine" energies usually suppressed in heroic tales. For example, where space is usually a void between cultures, in *Dune* it is not. Rather it is a somewhere else represented by a warm, bubbling, orange, feminized beyond, full of the sparks of energy. What lies beyond power and bureaucracy is pervasively both important and associated with femininity, in the feminine process of transmuting the poison of the Water of Life into a saving liquid and by the feminine mysteries of the power of sound which Lynch took directly from Herbert's novel. In fact, Lynch went beyond Herbert by representing the mysterious Dune worms as quasi-feminine.

There is nothing in the book to suggest the distinctively feminine aspects of the worms as Lynch has drawn them. These aspects cast a feminine light on Paul's most powerful allies in his quest. Standing tall or roaring through the deserts of Dune and giving off lightninglike bolts reminiscent of the weapon of choice of the father gods, the representation of the worms alludes to all of the conventional constructs of phallic power except in one startling detail. Lynch's representation of the worms shows them also with cavernous, hairy *insides* which allude to female genitalia, again suggesting that interiority is "something," something quite compatible with the phallic element of life, indeed its complement. Thus, both the Water of Life scene—in which the savior patterns himself on the maternal example—and the hairy interiors of Lynch's Dune worms diverge from Herbert's rather conventional phallocentric images. These differences join the problem of Herbert's willful hero in provoking a stalemate between Herbert's story and Lynch's vision, particularly when the plot calls for the worms to be war machines, a narrative exigency that fights the balance between masculinity and femininity in the Lynchian image.

The same is true of the function of sound in *Dune,* which is strikingly like femininity since it is neither nothingness nor something in conventional understanding.[5] In both the novel and the film, sound takes on unusual, Lynchian importance and is associated with femininity; sound management is the "weirding way" of an order of witches, the Bene Gesserit sisters. However, sound in the film loses its potential power because, like the worms, it is forced into an un-Lynchian position in which what is essentially strong due to its receptivity is represented as the essence of aggression.

In *Dune,* sound is used to subdue, a process that for Lynch is a perversion of the portal of the real. In a most un-Lynchian way, the plot of *Dune* seeks to discriminate justified from unjustified invasion through the ears. "The voice," a guttural, irresistible use of speech cultivated by the Bene Gesserit, is truer and more potent in Paul, his mother, and his sister than when the Bene Gesserit sisterhood compromises it for the purposes of the Emperor. At the beginning of the film, "the voice" is used to subdue Paul by the most powerful of the Bene Gesserit, Reverend Mother Gaius Helen Mohiam (Sian Phillips), the truthsayer to the Emperor. Using "the voice," the Reverend Mother forces Paul to submit to a test that normally kills boys to whom it is given. By the end of the film, Paul and his sister Alia reduce her to silence with their "truer voices."

Nevertheless, because Lynch is so sensitive to the power of sound, he fascinates us with his use of the "the voice" in the film and sometimes dramatizes sound so successfully that it assumes momentary Lynchian force, even though it is always tied to the heroic strategies of the plot. In one of the most successful scenes, Paul uses "the voice" for the first time to liberate his mother's voice after treachery has destroyed the Atreides government on Dune. Here, Paul and his mother, Jessica, are bound in a helicopter-like vehicle while the two Harkonnen pilots threaten to rape her before his eyes, prior to abandoning them to be eaten by the giant sandworms. Since Jessica is gagged to prevent her from using her weirding ways, Paul summons up the power of his own voice to command one of the Harkonnens to remove her gag. Once the gag is off, she uses her more mature powers to lead the Harkonnens to their self-destruction. This scene is much more fascinating for its sound design than for its depiction of the heroism of the "good guys." Similarly, the scene in which Paul teaches the Fremen the weirding ways, although certainly designed for future aggression, contains Lynch's delight in the process of representing the unexpected power of thin air—sound—over the seeming solidity of rock. Paul encourages the Fremen to hit, cut, and yell at a black obelisk—reminiscent of the recurring mysterious image in Stanley Kubrick's *2001: A Space Odyssey.* The scene has real buoyancy, which is missing from the unsuccessful, uninvolving war scenes in which sound becomes deadly as it is used to defeat the Empire.

In *Dune,* Lynch was ambushed by the enduring power of the most sterile conventions of Hollywood heroism and storytelling. Although he was forced to overtly observe these conventions, he could not compel himself (or be compelled) to submit that part of himself that he has never tried to control. Thus, he was brought to an impasse in making *Dune.* This conflict is not that wonderful Lynchian mystery in which structure and energy assume a divided wholeness that is his vision of reality. Rather, it is the director's ninety-percent solution taking with one hand what he gave with the other.

In contrast with *Dune, The Elephant Man,* the story of the much-exploited John Merrick and Lynch's first Hollywood assignment, presented more opportunities than dead ends for his instincts. Indeed, *The Elephant Man* presented an extremely felicitous entrance into Hollywood for Lynch, with its Hollywood passion for the underdog and its undercutting of the value of heroic assertion. Frederick Treves, Merrick's would-be rescuer, cannot save him, and for this reason Bernard Pomerance, who dramatized Merrick's story for the stage, found an occasion for cynicism; he bemoaned the absence of the triumph of the "good" heroic will.[6] In contrast, Lynch offers the audience a testament of faith and hope in the failure of the will; he offers a corrective to the distortions and repressions of the society that literally excluded and figuratively killed Merrick.

The Elephant Man: "The Wind Blows!"

The story of John Merrick, born with such a severe congenital deformity that he was condemned to a life as a freak, has been taken from the papers of his doctor, Sir Frederick Treves, and from the work of Michael Howell and Peter Ford, two contemporaneous medical historians who, using Victorian diaries and medical records, flesh out Treves's portrait. What preoccupies the historians about this story is, predictably, the use of Merrick's life to argue for a need for better technology and government. What preoccupies Lynch about Merrick's situation, also predictably, is the suffering caused him by the exclusive standards of his society. In Lynch's hands, *The Elephant Man* becomes as much the story of the terrible limitations placed by "normal" society on the "normal" doctor, Frederick Treves (Anthony Hopkins), who finds and desires to rescue John Merrick (John Hurt), as it is the story of the limitations that culture places on the freak.

Through the narrowness of Treves's good intentions, Lynch questions the imbalances of, the rigidities of, and the lack of sensitivity to the part of reality beyond those of the known universe, Victorian style. As we have come to expect from our explorations of his later works, here in *The Elephant Man* he represents the beyond of society's logic in terms of the feminine. With *The Elephant Man,* we can see, because it is there from the beginning of his Hollywood career, how integral the transformation of gender definitions is to Lynch's narrative vision of reality.

Merrick's freakishness is in the deformation of his body. Beyond that, it also exists in his identification with his mother—his father is barely mentioned in the film—an identification that makes him that ordinarily most suspect of media characters, a man overly attached to the maternal. Yet the plot of *The Elephant Man* is a means by which we cross beyond initial, ordinary reservations about Merrick. He is the first of that category of Lynch's most Lynchian Hollywood characters, the secret-bearing character. This figure, whose nature cannot be accommodated by culture, shows us all that secret part of ourselves. Frequently, this secret-bearing protagonist is a woman; here, Merrick is associated with femininity, which in Lynchian fashion does not compromise his masculine standing in the film. Merrick's intimacy with femininity is represented not only through his powerful feelings for his mother but also when, in the story, he is treated as a passive spectacle in the way women are.[7] (There will be a full discussion of Merrick and femininity below.) Nevertheless, the film characterizes Merrick with a firmly established masculine identity—we are bluntly told that, whatever else may be damaged on his body, his genitals are perfectly normal. Moreover, the major plot action of the film—and the greatest representation of Merrick's value—is the effect he has on his supposed savior, Dr. Treves, whose identity as a man is opened and enriched by his friendship with the purported freak. By ordinary standards of society, Merrick needs to be rescued by the good doctor. But by the standards of the film, it is the good doctor who needs Merrick. Treves is an emotionally repressed, constrained man who agonizes over whether he is a good or a bad person until he is released from the logic of socially imposed value by the feelings for Merrick that he develops *and expresses.*[8]

Lynch's inversion of the relative worth of normal and marginal male identity is his solution to the central narrative problem posed for him in the history of John Merrick. Lynch does not believe in the concept of normality as it is glorified in medical accounts of Merrick any more than he believes in the concept of messianic heroism as it is narrated in Frank Herbert's *Dune*. For this reason, Lynch had to solve the problem not only of the patronizing medical attitudes toward Merrick, but of Merrick's own rejection of his difference expressed in his probable suicide at the age of twenty-seven as he tried to sleep like "normal" people. Evidence of his suicide is not conclusive but is likely since he was found dead while sleeping in a prone position, one that he knew to avoid since the weight of his distended head meant that lying prone would stop his breathing. Because the province of the Lynchian hero is ordinarily sleep and dreams, the historical accounts of Merrick's death posed special narrative problems for Lynch.

Lynch solved his problems by creating a film that, as we shall see, miniaturizes Victorian England against a larger reality of the freer flow of energy, like air, such that Merrick's biological problems almost seem social rather than natural. His death suggests at once the tyranny of the "normal" and a simultaneous freedom from it in a greater reality beyond the idealized Victorian framework. Toward this end, Lynch created an expository section of the film in which, as in *Dune,* the audience is impressed with realities beyond the limitations of narrative control before it is brought into the limits of the scientific world of Treves. The opening of *The Elephant Man* is a means of giving the spectator a real vantage point, in the Lynchian

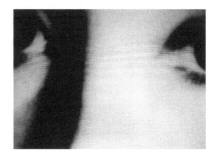

42. Merrick's mother: unbounded maternal energies.

sense, from which to experience the reductiveness of Treves's rational logic.

The initial image of the film is a mysterious, extreme close-up of the top third of a dark-eyed woman's face (Phoebe Nicholls), exactly what a young baby sees of its mother's face (see figure 42). In this opening image, which imbues the audience with the primary mysteries of maternity, origins, and birth, narrative content exists but as another element in a composition that also consists of light and sound. Only later will narrative become the dominant element that it usually is in Hollywood movies. In other words, the initial contact between spectator and *The Elephant Man* maps a heterogeneous relationship to narrative. The film begins as an enigmatic, porous, maternal texture into which the masculine narrative will intrude as a smaller, more rational, but ultimately troubling, representation.

In the opening frames, Lynch leads us to experience the struggle in filmic representations between the flatness of the bound image and the stirring of the senses. The baby's vision of the mother's eyes and forehead is discontinuously juxtaposed with the image of a framed, miniature portrait of a dark-eyed shadowy female face, which is succeeded by a flat image of a woman's head appearing in unbound space like a conventional filmed close-up. The clash between bound and unbound images creates an identification in the spectator with the process of film imagery that precedes any identification with a protagonist and any pure objectification of what is looked at.

To further complicate our conventional relationship with the film's narrative, Lynch next shows us the apocryphal story of the Elephant Man's birth in discontinuous images from diverse angles of vision. Over the final unbound image of the maternal face a lap dissolve of a procession of elephants appears moving from left to right. These images too remind us that we are dealing with human forms when the image freezes, leaving the rump of a large elephant and the head of a smaller elephant—certainly coded as a mother and child—with one superimposed over each of the eyes of the mother's head (see figure 43). To remind us that we are spectators, Lynch then executes multiple changes in the audience's perspective of these images; the elephants move toward the audience after which we see the woman stomped by the elephants both from her perspective up at them and from their perspective down at her. These initial frames place the audience in its only relationship in the film that is truly different from that of the looking involved in a freak show, the dominant metaphor of the film. In many ways, *The Elephant Man* roots the spectator in these frames to suggest that inhumanity is a false habit of seeing.

43. Merrick's mother: the presence of energies beyond social forms.

These first frames create a visceral relationship between the audience and the film that will haunt the structured narrative of Treves's ensuing quest to free Merrick, whom we first meet as a horribly exploited public display. The alternative flowing, empathic mode of seeing, which precedes "normal" modes of objectification in this film, becomes the call to reality about what is missing from the lives of both Merrick and Treves. The moving eye of the initial frames is always there in the depths of the narrative that follows, a silent contrast to the abusive tendency in the society portrayed by the story to turn "the other" into an object. The mode of looking to which we are first introduced silently abides to bring into bold relief the habitual Victorian domination/submission patterns that doom both Merrick and Treves in different ways.

The entrance of a conventional plot into this film is a highly visible event, a situation that contrasts with the usual operation of the plot as the invisible organizer of the movie experience. In this context, the ordinarily user-friendly plot becomes an invasive presence that appears to eclipse the earlier, freer kind of vision with a dominance/submission pattern of objectifying people that is not only at the heart of the plot conflict but also a troubling, reflexive model of how *The Elephant Man*'s audience is likely to regard the film's characters. The conventional plot action begins explosively as Dr. Frederick Treves is searching for the "Elephant Man" at the freak tent of a carnival. A rising jet of flame and a whirling circle of black and white forms force their way onto the screen, illuminating for the spectator a quest undertaken by the quiet, formally dressed, top-hatted Treves. The drive with which the narrative erupts into the unbound elements at the beginning of the film represents Lynch's sense of the violence of linear narrative. This sense of invasion is strengthened by the ambience of transgressive behavior that permeates Treves's first actions. He walks into a curtained corridor marked "No Entry," continues through a carnival sideshow, past a fetus in alcohol billed as "the fruit of original sin," and past giggling crowds viewing standard freak spectacles. The elements of the socially normative and the deformation of the carnival collide in front of us; we cross the border between these with Treves, the utterly composed conventional hero with whom we can identify for reassurance.

At the end of the dank corridor is the Elephant Man, a forbidden sight behind a curtain, presumably much more bizarre than what we have already seen and beyond what can be tolerated by society. A policeman bars the way, seemingly a solid boundary between Treves and the "forbidden" sight as well as between the film's audience and the Elephant Man. However, this putative solidity is belied by the existence of a mere curtain as the barrier to the unseen, a curtain that is soon drawn, becoming a Lynchian suggestion, as in *Dune*, of the illusory, fragile quality of the boundaries of the known universe. The beginning of the narrative plot suggests we are heading beyond limits because of our identification with the quester, Treves.

Although trespass of social limits is suggested in this sequence, this is not a film about sin. Lynch is interested in secret correspondences between parts of society that at first glance appear utterly different. He emphasizes the commonalities between the science

44. The scientific form of freak-gazing.

that Treves champions as he strives to free Merrick and the comedy and violence of the freak exhibit. When Treves first meets Merrick in a fetid dungeonlike enclosure, the barker, Bytes (Freddie Jones), draws back the curtain, bullying Merrick to reveal himself to the crowd. The same process occurs in Treves's exhibition of Merrick to a scientific group, a demonstration which echoes the drawing and closing of curtains and the commands issued by both Bytes and Treves to "turn around" and "stand up."

Science and carnival have different styles of diminishing Merrick's humanity. Picking him out of the darkness by means of the firelight of gas lamps, the sideshow preserves the mystery of the body, and thus its visceral substance, but reduces him to property which Bytes claims to own. By contrast, intense light attends the medical inspection of Merrick, light which reduces his body to a shadow. The first image in the scene in which Treves presents him to the gaze of science is of the spotlight that is to be trained on his body. It is a bright, burning point in the frame. When Treves introduces him, a curtain is drawn revealing Merrick to the assembled doctors but not to the film's audience. We are moved to a perspective behind the curtained enclosure in which Merrick stands; we can see only the shadow he casts in the spotlight through the backdrop of the enclosure (see figure 44).

Although science and carnival equate in many crucial ways, Treves and Bytes do not in the most important way—as individu-

als. Lynchian narrative, as we have seen, marks its heroic characters by the degree to which they are impatient with and move beyond the constraints of cultural forms. Treves is, in contrast with
Bytes, heroic with all of the attendant ideals and limitations that
heroism implies for Lynch. Bytes is his doppelganger. Treves's ex-
cellence and Bytes's shadowlike distortions are depicted in terms
of Treves's capacity for going beyond his role and Bytes's total
incapacity for such expansiveness. We see the necessity for this
journey in a representation of the medical community in *The Elephant Man* that is, in its way, as crude and grotesque as that of the
midway.

The hospital in *The Elephant Man* is comical and violent in its
pretensions of being the sum total of human knowledge. Here,
Lynch is helped in representing its violence and comedy by history. The Victorian version of medicine is ridiculous from the vantage of hindsight. When Treves is operating on the victim of an
industrial accident, the body of the patient lies open on the operating table in a completely unsterile environment. Orderlies and
doctors in ordinary street clothes attend the body, which is held
still by a system of ropes creating a context of force and absurdity
not unlike that of a torture chamber or a sideshow. Practicing a
medicine innocent of the use of sterilization, Treves coughs into
the incision, and an unwashed street urchin is admitted into the
operating room bearing a message for him.

Lynch's film conveys a vision in which the rigid, limited theoretical order of the hospital establishes norms that open up spaces for
care while tying up bodies and penning up emotions. What gives
Treves the calm consideration to come to Merrick's aid also pres-
surizes explosive energies that victimize Merrick. The chaos of
what medical science cannot address in the human condition is
represented by the blind spot of the hospital's daytime staff to what
the building becomes at night when it is the preserve of a cruel and
ignorant night porter (Michael Elphick), who makes a few extra
shillings by using Merrick's hospital room as a sideshow tent.

The carnival elements in *The Elephant Man* are relatively muted
as compared with those of the later films but nevertheless are very
pointed in their depiction of the backside of what passes for social
order. The doppelganger effect of model Victorian life and its
shadow is, as in *Blue Velvet,* rendered with a clear division between

the two, offering an elementary Lynchian depiction of the carnivalesque relationship between social order and social disorder. By day in his room at the hospital, Merrick increasingly becomes a pet of good Victorian society with its elaborate etiquette and decorum; by night, the violent carnivalesque release from this decorum renders him a scapegoat at the mercy of the night porter. Why does he fail to protest his treatment as a lapdog by good society while he rails against the mob's treatment of him as an animal? This question is not answered as obviously as it might seem and is the crux of Merrick's tragedy.

The nighttime of institutional order reveals what is under the nervous visits of good society through the night porter's forays to Merrick's room. What is given by day is taken by night when the daily repressions are released. The cruelty reaches its zenith concurrently with the pinnacle of social charity. The night porter invades Merrick's rooms with a leering mob immediately after Merrick has been granted a permanent home in his rooms at the hospital at the request of Queen Victoria. The hospital board, Princess Alexandra (Helen Ryan)—as Victoria's emissary—and Treves raise in Merrick the fantasy of acceptance; the night porter rips it away. Worst of all, the nighttime of the hospital contains the opening for Merrick's return to the bad old days at the sideshow. For Bytes hides among the revelers that the night porter brings to Merrick's room. After they leave, he kidnaps Merrick.

45. Lynch working with John Hurt on the scene in which Merrick saves himself from an angry crowd.

Only the other freaks at the carnival in continental Europe to which Bytes spirits Merrick have real compassion for Merrick's suffering and help him to escape. But what is there for him in normal society? Making his way back to Treves, he must save himself from an angry crowd of normal people that wrongly thinks he has molested a little girl. Although Merrick is now capable of roaring at the savage hordes of normality, "I am not an animal! I am a human being!" we soon see how impossible that kind of affirmation will be to maintain (see figure 45).

When Merrick is kidnapped, the night porter becomes the same

kind of wake-up call for Treves that Frank Booth was for Jeffrey
Beaumont. However, Treves, in a film bound by a belief in historical fact, achieves less visionary growth than did the protagonist of
Blue Velvet. Nevertheless, his loss of Merrick shocks Treves out of
his clinical manner. When Merrick returns to him just before
Merrick dies, Treves has a moment of pure feeling, embracing him
in joy at the return. If Merrick has come a long way, so has Treves.
However, this embrace is only a fleeting release for them from
both the prison of scientific order and its grotesque carnivalesque
mirror image. It is only a sign of what might be possible if their
lives were not so constrained by closed forms. The film frame
of this moment tells the story (see fig-
ure 46). Treves and Merrick are still po-
liced by cultural limitations, and that will
turn out to be fatal, as we shall see.

Cultural patterns of objectification are
not as deadly in the form of police and
doctors as they are in their most cloying
and insidious form—the Victorian ideal
of love and beauty. The most terrible barrier for Merrick lies in society's corruption of what Lynch has shown in his later
films to be the conduits to vision for the

46. Social limits to the understanding
between Merrick and Treves.

hero—female wisdom and the collective unconscious of popular
culture. In *The Elephant Man*, Lynch suggests that the deadliest
aspect of Merrick's situation is Victorian culture's treatment of
women and its popular entertainment. Both have been embalmed
in such idealized sweetness that they can no longer access the reality of energies beyond society.

The sympathetic women of sensibility and cultivation—Frederick Treves's wife, Ann (Hannah Gordon), and Mrs. Madge Kendal
(Anne Bancroft)—inadvertently do Merrick more harm than
good. And "feminized" popular culture, in the form of a pantomime which Merrick attends as a treat organized by his good
friends, virtually buries him. Suffocated by sweetness, Merrick
does not even know enough about this form of abuse to protest it. We shall soon discuss the pantomime as the final straw
for Merrick's tenuous grasp on reality, but understanding of this
paradox will benefit greatly from a general discussion of Victorian

distortions of femininity. To do this we must first distinguish Ann and Mrs. Kendal—respectively a middle-class chatelaine and a socially prominent actress who shower Merrick with affection—from the uncultivated women who behave toward Merrick with the revulsion that the spectator expects.

The women at the carnival freak show faint and flutter upon viewing the Elephant Man, as do nurses in the hospital and the women who are brought for erotic purposes by the patrons of the night porter. The lack of acceptance—revulsion—is dramatized unequivocally as a part of the limits of socialized behavior, which later changes for the nurses when they sentimentalize Merrick. The change in the nurses' attitude seems positive; however, we are led to understand that it parallels Merrick's acceptance as a social mascot and has a very perilous aspect.

The major drama of Merrick's relationship with women concerns the ambiguous representation of the social acceptance that cultivated women make possible for him and that leads directly to his suicide. In hindsight, we can see that, respecting the Victorian environment in which the story takes place, Lynch represents the feminine in a manner different from that of his previous or subsequent films. He portrays Victorian society's fatal social co-opting of femininity into the idealization and domestication of feminine energy. Meaning no harm, Ann and Mrs. Kendal offer Merrick a very seductive kind of objectification against which he cannot defend himself as he can against the loathing and fear of lower-class women. They introduce him to the saccharine idealization of emotions that creates idols to which he is eventually willing to immolate himself.

When Treves brings Merrick home for tea, Merrick is overcome by the sweet idealization of parents and children of which the Treves home, and Ann Treves in particular, reeks. Ann can barely stand to look at him, but they find common ground when he rhapsodizes over pictures of the Treves children and over the nobility of her parents' appearance in the photographs on the living room mantel. Similarly, Ann is startled and impressed by the beauty of the miniature of his mother which he carries around with him. This warm domestic scene has sinister undertones, as Merrick is quite taken by a scenario of "perfect" normality from which he must always be excluded.

The seduction is even more insidious when Mrs. Kendal beguiles him with the idealized romance of the theater. She performs *Romeo and Juliet* with poor Merrick, which he reads from a volume of Shakespeare she has brought for him. What delusion can be more cruel than the one Mrs. Kendal passes off on him as she, responding to his naive intensity when they read, tells him that he is not an elephant man, but Romeo? But he isn't Romeo, as the image of his enchanted face clearly shows.[9]

Ultimately, *The Elephant Man* shows us a rationally structured culture in which its "bright" side is even more lethal than its dark side. The idealizations of a sentimentalized popular culture are devastatingly seductive invitations to self-loathing of our secret incommensurabilities with normality, which in Merrick's case are exposed for all to see. The fatal ramification of that seduction is represented by the eye-of-the-duck scene. Ostensibly peripheral to the plot, it is the moment when Merrick is terminally overwhelmed by the passion to objectify, a passion with which he cannot possibly coexist and which kills him.

47. Merrick immolates himself before a poisonous fantasy of the mother-child relationship.

Merrick's visits with Ann Treves and Madge Kendal lead directly to his experience as a dazzled spectator at the holiday pantomime of *Puss in Boots,* a performance dedicated to him by Mrs. Kendal. He goes home delirious with joy and longing to repeat the experience, as he tells Treves. Repeat it he does in spirit, as he deliberately gets into bed in a prone position. In imitation of the idealized pantomime and the sentimental picture on his wall of a *normal* sleeping child, he lies down in his bed looking at a traditional, sentimental tintype of his mother (see figure 47). The sweetness of the day has been deadly.

If we examine the images of what Merrick saw at the theater, we can understand both what motivated him to commit a "beautiful" suicide and why Lynch later developed a technique of using disruptive comic images at the end of his films. The fantasy ballet is the kind of narrative Lynch loathes, one that produces hallucinations not reality. It is an unrelentingly delusional portrait of Victorian England, which Lynch has previously shown us in all its industrial grime. Our perspective on Merrick's perspective on the pantomime is rendered when Lynch shows us Merrick's face superimposed over the dizzyingly sweet spectacle (see figure 48). The ominous undertones of his passionate enjoyment of the play are conveyed to us in two ways. First, Lynch's composition of the image suggests the play has gone to Merrick's head only. His joy requires him to be cut off from the troublesome reality of his body. Second, the proscenium is represented with a pronounced and elaborate border, as if Merrick were captured within the frame.

48. Merrick engulfed by the sweet poison of the pantomime.

Now seemingly one of the normal public, and a spectator at last, Merrick identifies against his own humanity when he rapturously takes pleasure in the removal of the ogre from the sugar-candy kingdom. Spun sugar has lured him to turn against his own difference.[10] Through its sweet poison, the pantomime eclipses, as no Bytes or night porter ever could, the life-giving tension that Merrick represents, that which has made him so precious to Mrs. Kendal and to Ann and Frederick Treves.

In so using Merrick's trip to the theater as an insight into his mysterious death, Lynch makes the most pivotal part of his first Hollywood assignment turn on a tension between his vision of reality in popular narrative and that in illusionist narrative. He has identified the scene of Merrick at the pantomime as the eye-of-the-duck scene in *The Elephant Man,* a scene unconnected to the plot but necessary to bring the narrative to a point of closure (see Chapter 1). Indeed, it is Lynch's first Hollywood use of this kind of scene, the crucial moment when the protagonist is either seduced into the closed system or can see its limits, either a moment of visionary empowerment or of absorption into the hollow false faith of the bounded cultural system. In his later, more highly developed *Wild at Heart,* Sailor is released by a goofy, patently artificial glamor of popular culture. Here, Merrick enters into a *liebestod,* a death rapture, seduced by false faith that does not allow for that double vision.

However, there is release. Although Merrick is caught in the coils of the pernicious illusion, the spectator is not. We whirl from his death through the open window and toward the great sky, beyond the miniaturized culture forcefully represented in both the play and the completed maquette of the cathedral and into the vastness of unbounded space. The maternal voice of the silent image from the beginning of the film—an unbound maternal energy that contrasts with the framed maternal face that accompanies Merrick's suicide—tells us that "Nothing will die." The final frames reawaken the tension between form and energy that guarantees actuality. As a palliative to the tragedy of the limits set up voluntarily by culture, the female voice speaks encouragingly of the involuntary and the boundless when she tells us that the stream will flow, the wind will blow, the cloud will fleet, and the heart will beat. The image fades to the by-now-familiar Lynchian flash of white light, the representation of the moment of pure transparency of meaning.

Lynch's return to the maternal at the end of *The Elephant Man* transcends the women within the plot as a force both of the cultural form and simultaneously beyond narrative representation. Thus, although Victorian society has maimed female power, he leaves the audience with a womanly bridge to the authentic, maternal femininity in its largest, most potent form as both alpha and omega. It does not take us back to the reassurances of childhood as the pantomime does, but outward to the knowledge that there is more. In his use of the cosmic maternal at the beginning and end of *The Elephant Man*, Lynch does not look back to a golden, uterine world—that is, the fantasy world of false faith. He looks forward toward the possibility that we have seen him embrace in more detail in his later films—of some complex union of cultural limits with the irritations and promise of excluded energies.

6

"Please Remember, You Are Dealing with a Human Form"

**SIX MEN
GETTING SICK**

ERASERHEAD

THE GRANDMOTHER

THE ALPHABET

Lynch's first four filmworks—*Six Men Getting Sick* (1967), *The Alphabet* (1967), *The Grandmother* (1970), and *Eraserhead* (1976)—exhibit his most naked, unmediated interest in moving pictures. Strikingly, when he was working unambiguously outside of the popular culture arena and had no commercial constraints upon him, he chose to use narrative forms—an observation about his student films so simple and obvious that it is never remarked upon. All those who ponder the effects of commercialism on Lynch as an artist ought to consider that in his early work he is what he is later, a narrative filmmaker who wishes to tell stories without falling into illusionist realism.

If there is a purity about Lynch's pre-Hollywood films that we will never see again, that is because of the nature of beginnings. The esteem in which these first films are held is justified, but to regard these early works as the standard by which the later films should be judged is only to partake of the sterile worship of youth in America. There is certainly an implicit excitement in these early pristine ventures. However, part of this excitement involves their role as the foundation for Lynch's later, much more complex ventures into Hollywood.[1] The purity of *Eraserhead* and the student films gave Lynch the narrative language that he used later in the mass media.

In the early films, Lynch goes back to origins—the origins of form in the little meaning factory of the human mind and the origins of energy in the primal soup of matter. This is a primitive heterogeneity in all its strangeness (inherent differences and disruptions), uncomplicated by familiar daily appearances and the conventions of the media with which Lynch later chose to work. This strangeness has been available only intermittently within popular culture, but it has been increasingly present since young filmmakers saw Lynch's first full-length film. The seismic energy in his own later films derives from his struggles back toward these origins from within the Hollywood purview. Thus, it is true in some ways that Lynch's films are most productively read against the primitive beginnings that we see in his student films.

ERASER-
HEAD
and
Other
Early
Films

However, when I say that Lynch is straining toward the early purity of his work, I do not mean to imply any inferiority in his mass-media films. On the contrary, I mean that in pushing Hollywood conventions toward the energy of his early work he displays a powerful sense that drawing clear lines between high and low culture works against the representation of reality. His struggle is to pull together the language of David Lynch the Hollywood director and David Lynch the painter. This accounts for the great latitude for the subconscious to reform rational narrative in his films.

The Alphabet, The Grandmother, Eraserhead, and even *Six Men Getting Sick* illustrate Lynch's fascination with a world in which the widespread, passionate demand for the closed structure of the story is just as real as the strong, unbound truths of the energy of the subconscious and the random. The special quality of his love of narrative, like his declared love for the 1950s, is a fascination with the finite as a conception of which only human beings are capable and which marks our collision/cooperation with nature and our special place in the cosmos. This intense interest, while gratified by painting, to which Lynch retains a fervent commitment, is even more gratified by the collision of movement with the finite structure that takes place in cinematic narrative.

Six Men Getting Sick, Lynch's first foray into the narrative of moving images, is a telling transition from painting to film as he makes the process of vomiting a Lynchian paradigm of the narrative structure. Vomiting is a brilliant image of the unstoppable narrative compulsion, proceeding relentlessly from the beginning, through the middle, to an end. At the same time, it is a completely involuntary process. To make an art object out of this process is to fuse nature and culture, which is what Lynch is after as a creator. As a cinematic narrative, *Six Men* is a unique mixed-media creation, a sculpture that consists of a screen made of white resins on which Lynch has raised in an asymmetrical composition three faces of men in the process of distress and openmouthed purgation. One other man is depicted in a flat image on the screen. Another figure is represented on a tape loop that plays continuously, superimposing a "neverending" filmic image of the process of regurgitation over the figures on the screen (see figures 49–51). If we check the numbers, this brings us to a possible "five men."

49–51. *Six Men Getting Sick:* three angles on the screen from Lynch's first filmic project.

Perhaps the "sixth man" is the spectator, and the title is a humorous comment on viewer engagement and identification.

Six Men is an elegant stripping away of accidental surfaces to the basic process of narrative in all its humor and violence. The presentation of vomiting as art is funny in its incongruity and also in its reduction of the desire to control life through human systems—here art—to the point of absurdity. Nevertheless, at the same time *Six Men* is a genuinely wonderful collision of the static forms of control with the plasticity of the flux of movement. This "moving" sculpture creates a tension between the flat and the three-dimensional. The typically inert, but here expressive, screen meets with and adds dimension to the endlessly repetitive movement of the flat, filmic image as the tape loop brings the moving image to the point that the static sculptural image has occupied all along. In this film/sculpture, there is a moment when outside and inside, beginning and ending, are conflated, a moment that questions all recipes for narrative movement—the moment of regurgitation. What process other than disgorging can better simultaneously represent the lack of control and the culmination of a discrete pattern?

Six Men Getting Sick is a helpful paradigm for Lynch's narrative sense. It does not take the logical route of directly reassuring us that what is beyond control is orderly. Rather, it takes an oblique path; it presents us with a humorous example of our own myopia on the subject. It represents a process abhorrent to most people, but one that reveals the tidelike orderliness within it and that renders absurd in a most unexpected way the ordinary equation between being overwhelmed and disorder.

Eraserhead

The dynamic of *Six Men* is the dynamic of the narrative and plastic movement of *Eraserhead*. In *Eraserhead*, matter emerges from the mouth of Henry Spencer (Jack Nance), the young protagonist of the film. Volition plays no part here. Henry does not will this eruption. The matter itself exhibits no will. Volition enters the film later in the narrative when the matter becomes part of an internal and external chain of events. At the beginning of the film, an elongated fetuslike mass of tissue, articulated only by a headlike shape and a tail-like extension of matter, comes out of Henry's mouth (see figure 52). When Henry next sees it, it has been articulated so that it has acquired a social label—the characters call it a baby—and a stronger anthropomorphic resemblance. However, despite the imprimatur of language that it carries, it bears only a superficial resemblance to a baby. It cries, coos, eats, gets sick; it is completely dependent. But it lacks the integrity of a natural body; it is all head, eyes, mouth, and stomach. Crucially, in lacking ears it lacks any suggestion of receptivity and thus the subconscious that is so germane to Lynch's understanding of humanity. Lacking a bone structure and covered only by a mucous membrane, not by skin, it also lacks the characteristics of a real form in the Lynchian sense— that is, the tension between the rigidity of form and the border at which there is an interchange between interior and exterior energies. This "baby" is the essence of illusionist reality—there is something there, but it is actually formless, held together only by the word and a bandagelike swaddling.[2] It is an ironic representation *not* in that it is the new life of the infant but rather the preclusion of new life by a social will.

Henry becomes trapped by that labeled mass of matter, bound to it day and night, his only sense of freedom sparked by a dancing lady in his radiator who is simultaneously real and a dream. The enigmatic lady is an early form of the transformative feminine energy that appears later in Glinda in *Wild at Heart* (see Chapter 2). Like Glinda, she has a goofy charm. Like Glinda, she is associated with the liberating energy of popular culture, appearing as a music hall dancer. However, the metaphor here is not initially the freedom of the air but the energy at the heart of the machine. Henry gains access to that energy when, driven beyond endurance by the frustration of being trapped in the gears of the social machine of relationships, he tears into the "baby" with scissors, making manifest its actuality as a mass of unformed matter and setting in

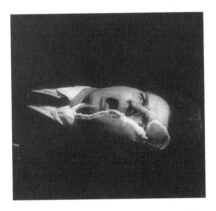

52. The mysterious inception of the "baby."

motion a flow of force that sweeps him as on a flood of air out of the limits of his daily life. Henry's sudden release is an involuntary process—as unintentional as vomiting and not much prettier. The freedom of the air is paradoxically his once he destroys the label on the matter and discovers himself in a virtually unlimited, billowy, radiant limbo, in which he finds a contented moment with the dancing lady.

The film challenges the spectators to deal with profound narrative issues as they view the story.[3] The narrative depends on the conflict between the audience's perception of the barely formed matter (its resemblance to a sperm defines it as the potential for actual form not as its realization) and the characters' beliefs that they are dealing with a baby. Because we have seen the so-called baby emerge from Henry's mouth as elementary matter and energy, we understand the hollowness of what the characters try to make of it when it becomes a part of Henry's external life. But we also see the power of these empty assertions. Mary X (Charlotte Stewart), a girl with whom Henry has a painfully awkward romantic attachment, and her family, the X family, create a narrative made only of empty forms when they treat the unformed matter as Mary and Henry's baby and thus as the basis of a forced marriage for him. Both Mary and Henry are marooned by the marriage in a dark, threadbare, one-room apartment. Thus, the

ERASER-
HEAD
and
Other
Early
Films

capricious labeling of energy and matter has created a Chinese box of self-referential forms within which people are immured. One of the most startling visceral images of this incarceration is that of Mary through the bars of the bed's footboard, ambiguously struggling with these metal bars. Though her actions have a bizarre superficial appearance, she is actually doing nothing more mysterious than pulling a suitcase from under the bed, driven by sleeplessness to go back to her mother. The driven quality of her motion, however, implies that she cannot control her flight and suggests the baser level of the involuntary. The same kind of frustration propels Henry to make another kind of departure, into a world of real dreams not of delusional fantasies. (As we have seen, in Lynch's later films the difference is a crucial one—that between the truth and a further alienation from reality.) Thus, we will see Henry's breakthrough to the real as we chart his involuntary progress.

The narrative of *Eraserhead* is itself the process of the creation of narrative. This is represented as a complex relationship between human will—primarily the tyranny of words—and the involuntary processes. The mass of animate tissue that emerges from Henry through no plan of his own draws responses from the characters that they would give to a baby only because of what it is called. The compulsions of labeling are the binding force of the narrative; the releasing energy of the narrative derives from the involuntary processes that propel Mary X and Henry to freedom from these constraints. The film, however, is not about Mary but about Henry and his liberation from "dark and troubling thoughts," as Lynch described Henry's situation to me.

Eraserhead presents the subconscious as a corrective to what is "dark and troubling." However absurd the lady in the radiator may appear, Henry's union with her is the gift of his subconscious and a means of contact with reality that is obscured by the threatening narrative growing around him. We can better understand *Eraserhead* if we interpret it with the help of Lynch's phrase "dark and troubling thoughts" in the context of the narrative sense he demonstrates in his later films and in the context of his early influences. On that basis, we must conclude that he is referring to the dark cloud of linguistic forms that shadows important parts of Henry's reality. Indeed, the narrative structure of *Eraserhead* describes the double nature that is so exciting to Lynch. On one hand, it is a limiting, even oppressive, form. But on the other hand, it mysteriously and paradoxically contains within itself a form of energy—embodied in the dancing lady—that produces freedom from within its confines.

The first seven minutes of *Eraserhead* produce the rest of the film. Henry begins the film in a pre-narrative limbo with no time-space coordinates to anchor him in a plot structure. Neither floating nor still, his body moves in a nebulous greyness. The sound track, a low wind sound layered subtly with the chug and banging of machine pistons, creates a sonic space different from, but intersecting with, visual space.[4] The motion of Henry's prone frame is neither mechanically regular, as is conceptual movement proposed by Newtonian principles, nor is it unstable like a machine gone wrong. Instead, like the motion proposed by chaos theory, it tantalizingly suggests an order under what appears to be random flux.[5] Behind Henry's head, "the planet," a small globe the size and texture of an orange, occupies a fixed point in the frame. This planet is Lynch's means of representing the reality of the socialized man's interior life. Henry's planet is a little interior factory which Lynch speaks of as the source and processing mechanism of that limited kind of rational construct that is culturally understood as meaning.[6] The factory has many characteristics similar to the male organ, producing the spermlike capacity for form, which we later see come to a ghastly pseudofruition in the womb of cultural linguistic syntax.

When Henry moves out of the frame, the camera inexorably approaches the planet as the wind rushes with greater intensity and the industrial noises grow louder. The interior of the planet is opaquely grey, pocked and craterous, and filled with open and closed forms not recognizable as objects but rather as the basic building blocks of the structure of objects. In the barely lit interior of the planet, there is a room resembling a long-forgotten attic. Here, seated motionless by a window opening onto darkness and in front of three rusty gear shifts, there is a barechested, muscular man (Jack Fisk).

Cutting away from the planet's interior, the camera reveals Henry, as before, but now opening his mouth as if to yell, though no sound is emitted. Instead, a creature—describable as wormlike or spermlike—emerges from within his mouth. It briefly lies in the frame in a position parallel with Henry's. The mottled man in the planet moves in a slow, robotlike fashion and shifts a creaky gear. The spermlike creature then quickly and smoothly moves out of the frame like a monorail departing a station. The impassive gear-shifter performs two more mechanical manipulations. The first switch of a lever opens the shell of the planet to a brightly lit, liquid space into which the spermlike creature plunges to an accompanying sound of bubbling and splashing. The second shift of a gear opens the planet's shell to a space full of white light and expectant buzz, which washes out the film frame. Henry has produced what will be the kernel of this narrative. In its purity, the creature is reabsorbed into the white, unlimited transparency of eternity, but in the external world it will become the material of bondage.

The X family, primarily Mother X (Jeanne Bates), turns this matter into a baby and then a marriage. We see this coercion of Henry as a part of a larger modus operandi that is typical of the X family and also of the industrial city in which Henry and the Xs live. Their emotionally sterile mode of behavior is externalized in the physical appearance of Henry's "normal" world, a claustrophobic maze characterized by streets of industrial refuse and slag heaps and by the apartment house in which he lives. Within the confines of the houses in this world, there are long, dark hallways, which are only putatively illuminated by sconces and lamps that are incapable of shedding more than the most localized pinpoints of light. The walls in this industrial city sharply delineate the boundaries of rooms and buildings, but their orderliness is undermined by the bits of matter that erupt randomly within the confines, gathering, for example, at the base of the radiator and punctuating the walls. There is no "normal" order within—Henry's dresser alogically contains a two-quart saucepan full of water and a photograph of his girlfriend Mary torn into two pieces, one of her head and one of her torso, that can never make a whole. Henry's home suggests the degeneration of energy and matter into nonform and non-function within what is accepted as the social order.

The X home is similar with its solid walls and its sparsely placed lamps, breaking but not illuminating the darkness and silence. Bodies here are rigid as though constrained. The X family sits stiffly in the lighted places in the room, suggesting that rigor mortis is a process of the living that becomes progressively extreme with the years. Thus, Mary X is the most fluid, Mother X and Father X (Allen Joseph) are in advanced stages of inflexibility, and Grandmother X (Jean Lange) is completely immobile. Mother X includes Grandmother in family life by lighting a cigarette and placing it between the older woman's gums, where it remains as a smoking stick. Mother tosses the salad by shoving the spoons into Grandmother's hands and manipulating her completely impassive arms. Father X's face is stiff with a forced smile, and his left arm is completely without feeling. Mother X uses a completely deadpan voice to pummel Henry with questions. The conversation of this constipated group is interrupted regularly by the release of chaotic energy—when Mary and Mother X each have seizures—and by the resounding noise of the one natural relationship in this place, a mother dog and many suckling puppies.

At the X family dinner, the main course is "man-made chickens," which have much the same relationship to food as the labeled matter has to a baby. The baby and the chicken are parallel representations of forced meaning. As Father X emotionally bullies Henry into a funny/horrific encounter with one of the chickens, so Mother X bullies him into marrying Mary. The comedy and violence of culture and nature in human society is distilled by Henry's attempt to carve one of the man-made minichickens. Although the matter on the plate looks superficially like a chicken, it is in fact a mass of unformed material. The first chicken he approaches with the knife begins to move and then expels a trickle of blood which balloons into a large, bloody bubble through an unmistakably vaginal aperture. The more culture tries to dominate form, the more powerfully matter and energy beyond control assert themselves. Needless to say, Henry cannot carve, and no one can eat this manufactured bird.

A similar process takes place when Mother X uses this dinner to insist that there is a baby—Mary is not sure—and so there must be a marriage. As Mother X bullies Henry, we again see the involuntary chaos of energy within cultural pseudoforms. She flies at him as she demands that he marry Mary, kissing him on the neck with vampiric persistence and thus causing Mary to whine and cry and Henry's nose to bleed. As Henry tries to absorb the demands being placed on him, the lights in the living room suddenly go out.

Henry and Mary's marriage creates a strange but familiar matrimonial scene—Mary feeding the "baby" and Henry returning to the apartment, seemingly from work. However, although the "baby" is cooing, spitting, and doing all the things that babies do when they eat, it is not cute and rosy but skinless, boneless, and wormlike. Similarly, Henry's return home in the conventional position of the father at the end of the working day is rendered problematic by his previous response to one of Mother X's questions, saying that he is on hiatus from his job as a printer at LaPelle's factory. That is, what he does when he is not home is mysterious, since we know he has no job. This adds to the sense of aimless behavior in the industrial city.

Narrative structure is open at every seam, and only the willpower of the spectator could force it to seem closed, but the film scrambles the stock reaction. The desire for conventional narrative is ordinarily bound to identification with such a desire on the part of the hero. However, Henry's desire moves away from the world of will. He is oppressed and confused by the X family, his marriage, and the "baby" through which he has been drawn into the parameters of this leaky social order. Desire arises beyond the ineffectual but repressive boundaries and beneath the pocked, permeable surfaces of orderly existence. He yearns for a loose-living, beautiful, dark woman across the hall, just out of his reach, and for a perky, reassuring blonde who dances within the recesses of his radiator behind its soldered metal frame.

Henry gets his chance to escape the clutches of imposed social authority when Mary leaves him, although at first her exit seemingly makes matters even worse. Now with no one to help him, he is more overwhelmed than ever by the responsibility of taking care of the constantly demanding "baby." However, contrary to his expectations, things improve. Sensual touch now becomes available as a form of release and contentment where they were not an option in the "marriage." Despite the implication of previous intimacies, in the actual film Mary and Henry do not touch, and their relationship never rises above a strained exchange of glances. However, in the dark of the night after Mary departs, the woman across the hall (Judith Anna Roberts) arrives asking to spend the night. "I'm locked out of my apartment," she whispers seductively, "and it's so late."

Their murky sexual encounter leads indirectly to Henry's sudden passage through the metal of the radiator onto a brightly lit stage deep within its recesses where he is equally moved by the touch of the "woman in the radiator" (Laurel Near). She is blonde and chubby and wears white dancing shoes and a white cocktail dress, circa 1956, which emphasizes her considerably rounded hips. The dancing blonde also offers a touch, and this precipitates a still more visionary encounter for Henry—a dream vision. In this vision, Lynch situates the image that obsessed him and from which the film grew—the taking of "a core sample of the eraser in his [Henry's] brain."[7]

Henry's encounter with the sensuous neighbor indicates that his adultery is located outside of the phantom forms of marriage and family through its nonverbal and involuntary quality. Henry does not seek the dark lady. Instead she emerges from darkness with her unspoken invitation in the manner of those gifts that Lynch sees in the fertile unknown. This vision refuses to recognize the Judeo-Christian association of darkness with evil and sin, or even of adultery with deviant behavior.[8] In Henry's life, adultery is a resistance to an absurd imprisonment. Nevertheless, it is certainly not glamorized in the titillating terms of forbidden fruit. There is a comic return to the origins of energy and plasticity in this act when Lynch replaces Henry's bed with a milky wading pool into which Henry and the neighbor sink as they kiss until all that remains on top is a clump of floating hair, the neighbor's abundant tresses. And even that yields to a screen washed with waves of white water. There is again no effort made here to idealize this coupling with twining limbs and coded romantic images. Rather, the brief dissolution of all structures of representation—in *Eraserhead* these forms always feign totality in their absurd incompleteness—is the reward of gratified desire.

But the brief release afforded by the neighbor is ultimately thwarted by the "baby." During her visit, Henry desperately tries to hide its presence, but after the dissolution comes the return and the neighbor's disgusted apprehension of the presence of this visible mark of Henry's bondage. By contrast, the lady in the radiator offers a more enduring solution. She prefigures Henry's deconstruction of the "baby" at the climax of *Eraserhead* when she squashes material and energy back into matter before any narrative can coerce these building blocks of reality into a constricting chain of events. The ever-smiling, dancing blonde wordlessly reassures Henry that there is a way to keep those spermlike creatures from growing into burdens, as she dances on them with a conspiratorial giggle.

When Henry enters the interior of the radiator, he finds that it is a little carnivalized world full of the music of which there are only intimations in the industrial city. It is a space in which theatrical form meets and merges with non-theatrical life such that there is no hard line between the two—a blurring of the boundaries that is urged when Henry meets the dancer for the first time by stepping across the line of footlights. The dancer's performance and Henry's viewing continue, but there is also involvement between the two. The performance becomes an invitation to touch, and at that joining of hands an electric shock of bright white light again washes image from the screen. The white flash of transparency—and satisfaction—is associated with touch not with the word.

Lynch never identified the eye-of-the-duck scene in *Eraserhead* for me, but I infer that it occurs during this scene, most importantly when Henry touches the dancer. Here, the protagonist comes to the place of hope in which matter can be released from its stultifying social label. Henry's vision, stimulated by the dancer's touch, takes a narrative shape—the narrative of how form may be made but also erased.

The process of erasure temporarily represented by Henry's dalliance with the neighbor, and more powerful and available when he touches the dancing lady, is an essential element in *Eraserhead*. It is the part of reality missing in the industrial city, a part that must always be in tension with the assertive processes of the cultural will if we are to live fully and humanly. At the lady's touch, Henry is able to see past the factory in his brain. In a series of images after Henry reaches for the lady, we see the man in the planet as an internal pressure on Henry to lose the vision of the lady, leaving empty space where she had been. However, the energy she stimulates in him with her touch is too strong. Henry is afraid again, but now he is afraid that he has lost his chance at paradise; he is in the process of being swept beyond reductive constraints.

As the prelude to his release, Henry loses his head in his central vision of the pencil factory. The release is not immediate because, before he can really be released from the pseudoforms of the industrial city, he must get past the "baby." But the vision manifestly reveals that the process by which matter is narrated as the confining baby is internal to Henry as well as an external compulsion from the X family. When Henry's head falls off, the baby pops up through his shirt collar. As the internalization of social labels, this interior "baby" is an impediment to the fulfillment Henry seeks. However, the fallen head bodes well. When, in Henry's vision, a child obtains the head instead of an old man who also reaches for it, the fluidity of childhood is associated with the decapitation. Further, when the child takes Henry's head to a pencil factory, a core sample of his brain produces a pencil, a perfect Lynchian image of redemption. The pencil that emerges from Henry's brain reassures us that the human mind is a tool for creating both open and closed form since it can both impose a mark on paper and take it away. Once the head is no longer on top (in charge), it can attain reality and significance.

This Lynchian truth is underscored by the ultimate image of Henry's vision of the pencil factory—a luminous pattern of eraser dust in the air. When a man in the pencil factory—a much more complex place than the factory in the planet—erases the pencil mark that he has made to test the product and brushes the eraser dust away, the erased mark enters space as a magical form. This compelling image suggests the dancing, asymmetrical form of the magnetic field, and the eraser dust permits us to see the energy all around us disguised by rigid, manufactured forms.

That vision precedes and precipitates Henry's attack on the "baby." Once the vision has passed and he is back in the industrial city, he takes a more aggressive stance toward his desire for release, intentionally seeking the woman across the hall. But this leads nowhere. The ersatz "baby" cannot be circumvented by an escape to shady ladies; it must be destroyed or it will always block him. The sultry neighbor, as it happens, is a prostitute, unavailable to him now not only because she is otherwise engaged with another (very sinister and seedy) client, but because she is disgusted by Henry's relationship to the "baby." As Henry looks at her imploringly, or perhaps with disappointment, she returns his look with a rejecting stare, seeing the "baby's" head sticking through Henry's collar where his head should be, as in the vision.

Henry, sensing what his neighbor sees, secures scissors, cuts the swaddling of the cooing "baby," and pierces its innards with scissor points. The innards erupt in a torrent of foamlike substance, releasing all of the flowing and still-unshaped matter that has been trapped inside this primitive shape. At the same time, the energy that has been channeled within the city walls to the absurd, almost useless lights goes wild. All of the electric sockets and appliances in the room begin to spark, blink, and buzz. The repressed energy of the air breaks out (see figures 53 and 54).

ERASER-
HEAD
and
Other
Early
Films

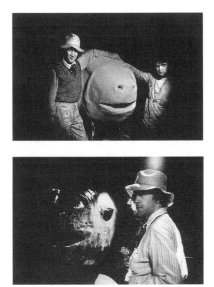

In the stunning frame that has become the signature of this film, Henry, now beyond the confines of the room, appears backlit against an illuminated space in which the magnetic pattern of the eraser dust of his vision is reiterated, his trademark hair shining and erect (see figure 55). All of the energy in the walls has been rechanneled into Henry. With this receptiveness to the energy in the universe, his reductive internal factory breaks into pieces, and the man at the gears is supplanted by the eraser in Henry's brain. The man is in great agony; this is a painful crossing of the borders between the micro-order of culture and the macro-order of the larger universe. Lynch has consistently represented the pain of cultural limits in just this way, as an affliction that comes from the machine of cultural meaning, not from any dangers on the more cosmic plane of existence.

53–54. Lynch uses a large model of the baby to create effects during Henry's liberation.

Nevertheless, the terrible suffering does not work here—or anywhere in Lynch's film—to re-enforce limits as it might. Pain is logically thought to cause a negative tropism. One has only to think of the social engineering produced in Aldous Huxley's *Brave New World* when the underclass babies are trained to avoid the diversions of culture—so they can be work-force drones—by shock therapy much like the electric upheaval Henry undergoes. However, Lynch does not believe in the power of society to accomplish that kind of dehumanization. Henry is *unable* to further countenance the constraints. The forces of free energy may hurt at first, but at last they liberate him. Free of labeled matter, Henry emerges into a limitless, light-filled, cloudy white heaven in which he can have the full satisfaction of the touch of the blonde dancer from the radiator. She moves into an embrace with him in this billowy paradise for a moment of complete gratification.

55. Henry's apocalyptic moment of liberation.

Here at last is a balance of the limits of narrative and the boundlessness of light—the outlines of the embracing forms of Henry and the dancer are completely visible but made translucent by the white radiance. His contentment is a terminal moment that presents itself to the spectator's desire as a world of free matter, that is, not random chaos but the inherent form of the universe beyond what human beings have conceived and built. The end of *Eraserhead* represents the two incommensurable regimes of energy and structure together, never to be harmonized but sometimes in a blinding flash to be balanced. We have narrative closure, but only as a result of having broken free from the narrative structure.

Lynch uses the label of "baby" for the repellent wormlike creature to represent what he perceives as the sickening sentimentality of our commitment to unreal illusionist realism (see the commentary on *The Elephant Man* in Chapter 5). Its spermlike shape is an important part of the erotics and gender representations in *Eraserhead*. The stuff of our limitation is almost literally rendered as potential for masculine creativity that is stifled by its isolation from femininity in the form of free energy, the subconscious, and the maternal. In contrast, as Henry frees himself from this mutilated masculinity—by refusing to sentimentalize it any longer—Lynch maps the interconnection of the male and the female.

In *Eraserhead*, Lynch assumes the conflation of phallic and vaginal images and energies as a given. Indeed, Henry's subjectivity is represented in a way that recalls the association between femininity and the Lynchian secret-bearing protagonist. Femininity is present not only in female characters but also in vaginal (as opposed to phallic) images when Henry produces through his mouth the spermlike form that the social order will transform into a shackle it calls a baby. Similarly, Henry's head is represented as a vaginal site after his vision of the eraser in the brain. Images associate his subconscious with vaginal openness, for example, through the cut to him in his room in the industrial city after the pencil factory vision. At first we see what look like knees which separate to reveal his head, also revealing that they are actually his elbows. The dreaming head between the elbow/knees is thus given a feminine, vaginal resonance.

This conflation does nothing to imperil Henry's masculine identity; rather it represents sexuality in terms distinctly different from those of the domination/submission modes of mainstream representation, which are always related to the construction of sexuality into a power relationship identified as marriage. Through Mary and Henry's marriage, Lynch preserves the relationship between domination/submission and marriage in *Eraserhead*, but he represents it as devoid not only of the seductive glamor with which it is embellished in Hollywood but of any sexual energy at all. In the industrial city, voyeurism takes the place of touching. Henry and Mary never touch, rarely do the Xs touch, no one ever touches the "baby." In contrast, the rhetoric of *Eraserhead* enters into a dialogue with voyeurism by rendering the visual elements of the "love scenes" either murky (as between Henry and the neighbor), carnivalized (as in the vaudevillian setting of the dancing blonde), or unrepresentable within the confines of constructed image (as when sexuality dissolves the image into water or disseminates it into light).

Thus, the originality with which Lynch treats gender in his later films is here in embryonic form. Henry Spencer is bedeviled by women whose active desires have been closed by the social structure—Mary and Mother X—and helped by women who remain open—the neighbor and, to a greater extent, the dancing blonde. In *Eraserhead*, female desire is an orifice in the imagined totalities of social order but a welcome one nevertheless, one that protects rather than imperils the thrust of male desire. The relationship between femininity and origins in *Eraserhead* suggests a context within which women are not relegated to the presocial incubator of culture. Indeed, the metaphor of the baby as an oppressive relationship between construct and matter is the crisis of humanity that the blonde dancer precludes. The dancer with her ovarian face both crushes and opens the masculine potential in the sperm-like matter, as does the biological ovary. The old parable that the seed must die in order to live resonates, if in completely unexpected form, in this image. The dancer's playful desire to dispatch the matter by action rather than to label it suggests a possible identity for women that is coequal with masculine identity, not secondary to it. The image of the dancer thus becomes one of Lynch's earliest representations of femininity as a joyous, active principle—not the dread-producing nothingness that provokes the fear of castration. Indeed, if we absorb the full implications of the ovarian dancer, we find she embodies a hopeful contrast to the women in the industrial city. Unlike the repressed women of the X family and the promiscuous neighbor, the dancer represents a feminine energy that prohibits castration.[9]

In the pairing of Henry and the dancer at the end of the film, the tensions between logic and matter—culture and energy—are balanced for a moment of satisfaction. Given that this is a movie, there is a narrative aspect to the final images—that is, "language or something like language" is present—but it is no longer warping matter as in the phenomenon of "the baby," the insignia of the process of forced generation that is routine in the industrial city. Rather, narrative becomes cloudlike, and then pure light, incorporating air and electricity, two of Lynch's favorite images of living form. In giving Henry a way out of the constrictive boundaries of ordinary life, his union with the dancer becomes a return to origins, or as much of a return as is possible for humankind, the Lynchian rendezvous with form as perceived by the subconscious, evoked here and ever after in Lynch's works in the location of the bed and in the experiences of dreams/visions and culturally unprocessed erotic touch.

In this way, Lynch not only averts the fears of castration anxiety but also the fears of some feminists that any anchoring of reality in origins by its very nature marginalizes women. Luce Irigaray is particularly vocal in asserting that when origins are irrevocably maternal—as they indeed are in Lynch's films—this relegates women to a position as the passive anchor of men who then proceed to build the culture.[10] But in Lynch's representation of maternal origins, feminine energy is as active as the logic of culture in creating meaning.

ERASER-
HEAD
and
Other
Early
Films

The Grandmother and *The Alphabet*

This excavation of origins in *Eraserhead* is good preparation for exploring the central preoccupation of Lynch's short student films, which serve in some ways as preliminary sketches for *Eraserhead.* The availability of these very early works is fortunate for those interested in Lynch's filmic art. They permit us to trace some part of the development of Lynch's complex use of narrative form. Almost studies for *Eraserhead,* these two films play with the images of the bed, touch, darkness, and the function of dreams in stories about our human negotiations of the forms we create and then experience as our limits. In *The Grandmother,* the immediately preceding film, Lynch experiments with the image of decapitation, used in *Eraserhead,* to narrate a child's attempt to palliate the blows of social order with a kind of erasure. *The Alphabet,* a briefer and more elementary narrative, also depicts a child distressed by cultural constructs; here, the child's sleep is disturbed by "language or something like language."

The Grandmother's version of the relationship between the involuntary/subconscious and conventional narrative form is more primitive than *Eraserhead*'s but much more complex than *Six Men*'s. In *The Grandmother,* a little boy (Richard White), confused and terrified by his mother and father, hears a whistling sound in his attic. Upon investigation, he discovers that the sound is emitted from a bag of large podlike seeds. When he comes upon the precise pod making the sound, he plants it in a mound of earth that he transports from outside to a bed in the attic. His tender care for the seedling is rewarded by a harvest of a fully formed and clothed grandmother (Peggy Lynch during the "birth process," then Dorothy McGinnis). The grandmother loves and comforts the boy and teaches him to touch gently as a matter of physical contact free of the stresses of social power relations. This differs from the rough touch of his parents (Virginia Maitland and Robert Chadwick), which is always coercive and directed toward his socialization. But all too soon the grandmother dies. The culmination of the boy's mourning is the replacement of his head by the same kind of pod as that from which the grandmother emerged.

The Grandmother concerns what is missing from the social order, as *Eraserhead* does, but in a more conventional narrative structure. Its child protagonist is traditionally purposeful and willfully active while Henry Spencer is responsive and receptive. During the course of the film, the child learns to be a seeker, one who finds by losing the will-to-control at the end of the film. The initial seed is the kind of discovery made by Lynch's seekers. The germination of the seed into a large pod comes about because of the child's assiduous determination to grow whatever is in it. However, the attic is an image of the subconscious in its representation as a space to which his parents cannot follow him since it is accessible to him alone through a dark passageway above the living quarters. Further, although the narrative has a controlling hero, his forward movement is continually broken by a mixture of animated and live-action sequences which open the film past his control. Even the live-action sequences are disrupted by irrational appearances. Although *The Grandmother* is filmed in color, periodically the mother and father appear in kabuki/clown white make-up; the boy appears this way throughout the film. The family home consists of ordinary household objects, like a bed and a table and chairs, but against a surrounding darkness that doesn't resemble the usual representation of domestic space.

Unlike in *Eraserhead*, where Lynch had begun to experiment with darkness layered by many thicknesses and intensities of greys and blacks that bleed into visible objects, the darkness here is a uniform, pristine, patent-leather blackness, and the objects stand out against it crisply and distinctly, another way in which Lynch reminds viewers that they are looking at constructed forms with no organic relationship to reality. The initial set of animated sequences depicts the separate births of the mother and father as full-grown, clothed adults emerging from vertical channels in the earth. Their sexual conjunction to give birth to the boy is a highly stylized representation of the two of them, still fully clothed, intertwining above a third channel in the soil through which the child, aged 11 or 12, emerges wearing a formal black suit and a white shirt. As in *Eraserhead*, birth is re-envisioned within the social structure as the coercion of new energy by cultural forms.

The life of this family is a series of brutal repressions of the involuntary processes by imposed behavior. This is the center of the boy's relationship with his father as represented in the paternal pummeling he repeatedly endures for wetting his bed. The father habitually rushes into the boy's room seeking the telltale yellow stain, after which he throttles the boy. The mother threatens an imposed emotionality that the boy experiences as another adventure in being shaken and throttled. Moreover, *The Grandmother* shows the medium of this tyranny to be a dysfunctional language which never goes beyond the level of brutish, partially formed, monosyllabic sound bites. Poorly formed explosions of "C'mon!"—an all-purpose, unvarying command to submit to the parental will—is the only thing approaching synchronized dialogue in the film.

In contrast, in the secret attic room the grandmother, emanating from some larger source than the cultural will of the family, is wonderfully productive and never abusive. The pleasure and satisfaction of the secret room issues from the natural, unmanufactured body—the smile and the touch. When the grandmother first initiates the boy into touching that is unconstructed by the socialization process, it is mutual and erotic—the two kiss on the lips, and the screen is washed out by liquid in the form of falling rain.[11] The erotic aspects of the child's relationship to a grandmother he grows in the attic is a study for Henry Spencer's erotic relationship to the blonde dancer he mysteriously discovers inside his radiator. However, there is an unsettling, incestuous flavor to this earlier escape.

In *The Grandmother,* apparently for the last time, Lynch uses animation to represent the world of inner fantasy. Animated sequences reveal the boy's revenge fantasy of quasi-mechanical, quasi-natural devices for cutting his parents in two and blowing them to pieces. As part of his release in the fantasy, his urine, free from rebuke, overflows the bed into a pool into which the boy imagines plunging and frolicking. The child's extreme fantasies of complete freedom are part of a dualistic landscape in the film in which there is a clean division between social constraint and the free, involuntary processes. There is a more simplistic dualistic edge to this film than to Lynch's more mature cinema.

Yet this film does suggest that within the terms of the child's either-or vision, contentment cannot be gained. Life is not a choice between society and freedom, and the grandmother cannot remain a perpetual Edenic alternative. One day, abruptly, she dies. In the grieving aftermath that follows, the boy is suddenly filled with an energy that moves him about involuntarily. Suddenly his head is replaced by a superimposed image of a formation of earth and woody roots resembling the one from which the grandmother emerged. The boy's experience constructing the grandmother has led not to an enduring construct but to a different kind of head. The pod-head suggests the mind as a channel for energies beyond reason, enduring access to involuntary processes and energy—a far, far better thing in the world of Lynch's cinematic art.

The Grandmother is not *Good Times on Our Street,* the "happy family" primer from which Lynch learned to read and which he remembers for its evocation of the idyllic family of the 1950s.[12] Yet surely the film is about David Lynch's experience of the seductive platitudes of that text and may perhaps serve as a possible model for understanding what he means when he says he loves the 1950s. The clarity of those clichés enables Lynch to use them to create narrative evidence of the simultaneous power and limits of what human beings create and impose on the free fear of natural energy. The family in *The Grandmother* is imagined against a background of *Good Times on Our Street*—it is very much a contrast to the sentimental idealization of the family in old-fashioned primers. The lyrical joys of the grandmother herself are representative of a more authentic happiness. The primitive forms of the animation suggest the constructed forms of punishing parental authority are artificial and limited.

Lynch's first student film, *The Alphabet,* contains his initial statement of the tensions between construct and what lies beyond it. *The Alphabet* is a brief, quite direct caution about human forms. It was made in close collaboration with his wife Peggy, who, by both of their accounts, provided him with much of the material from which he formed this short film. The only live actor in the film, she also provided the film's premise. On a visit to a relative, she had shared a bedroom with her six-year-old niece. Entering the room to sleep, she discovered her niece reciting the alphabet in her sleep and frantically tossing about. Lynch was intrigued by this anecdote and decided to make a film inspired by it. The film, however, is in no way a simple recreation of a homey event; the child's distress is rendered in epic terms. Lynch began his career in filmmaking by interpreting the invasion of a child's sleep by the linear structure of the alphabet in the context of the most advanced thinking in art and linguistics. We can see the germ of the idea for the "baby" of *Eraserhead* here in his depiction of the original "*A*" of the alphabet as a birth that generates a terrible imposition on the human subconscious. Like *Eraserhead, The Alphabet* is also a film that proceeds by revealing the process of creating narrative.

The film, predominantly black and white splashed with deliberate swatches of color, combines animation and live action. The live-action portion features a sheet-swathed figure (Peggy Lynch)—the child—in a bed that dominates the center frame position, its white sheets glowing in a black setting. The head and arms of the child, who is otherwise covered by the sheet, are kabuki white, punctuated by dark flowing hair and clownlike painting of features on the face. On the sound track, in nonsynchronous accompaniment, a childish voice sings "The Alphabet Song." At first it is tentative; "*A-B-C*" is the extent of its progress through the twenty-six letters. Finally, the voice proceeds from *A* to *Z* and ends with the request to "Tell me what you think of me." The process by which the entire sequence is finally enunciated is ostensibly a narrative triumph for the child, but it is accompanied by the visible physical distress of the on-screen figure which breaks out in spots, on the sheet as well as on the body, flails frantically among the enshrouding folds of the sheets, and in the last frame bleeds explosively from the mouth.

The intercut animations depict letters that are sentimentalized and amusing in a "cute" way. They jump, they pop; the initial series of "*a*'s" are small and cry like babies while an overripe male voice tells us, "The alphabet is surely fun." But when the alphabet is poured into a cartoon representation of a body, suggesting a cubist representation of a human figure that oscillates between seeming masculine and seeming feminine, the body hemorrhages.

An afflicted live-action body in the bed parallels the afflicted

ERASER-
HEAD
and
Other
Early
Films

cartoon figure. A frame of the cartoon figure gasping in distress is juxtaposed with the live figure gasping in a similar distress. The body of the girl in the bed is contorted as she reaches for physical manifestations of the letters that appear in every quadrant of the screen even though she is required to deliver them in a linear form. When she completes the series, it is clear that she has succeeded in a social sense: "Now I've done my ABCs. Tell me what you think of me." But this is not a happy ending. The conclusion depicts an assault on her by a torrent of energy, an effusion of blood through her mouth, and a sudden rush of wind. Her induction into social order—the alphabet—wounds something in her that we cannot see. Later in Lynch's films, that exclusion will find articulation in the part of Henry Spencer that his society excludes, and in John Merrick as a freak. In an even more evolved form, the secret appears again in Laura Palmer, first in *Twin Peaks* as a dead body possessing the answer sought by the police, and then in *Fire Walk with Me* as the truth behind the cultural stereotype of desire (see Chapter 7).

The humor and violence of the later Lynch are present in the comic violence of the letters and the linear order to which the child is being "normalized." But there is a humorous direct address to the spectator defying normality. The juxtaposition between the live-action pictures of the child and the animation is interrupted by an extreme close-up of a nose and, under it, red lips which have the only synchronous line of dialogue in the film: "Please remember, you are dealing with a human form." The "nose" is a false extrusion that has been fastened onto Peggy Lynch's chin, presenting the spectacle of upside-down lips and a right-side-up nose. In this moment when the spectators are brought into the point of view of the film, they are simultaneously addressed through intellect and affect, by means of a tension between the two. The words tell us in a comparatively direct manner that culturally derived forms cannot contain either the human sensibility or the whole of reality. The frame image carnivalizes the rational coding of the perception of the human face.[13] The tension between the humorous visual and the direct address dissolves the spectator's conditioning to stock perceptions and reactions.

Like *Six Men, The Alphabet* seeks narrative in the circumstances of everyday life—vomiting and learning the alphabet. Form is alphabetical and intrudes upon us. Form is plastic and wells up from within us. Conflict is inevitable. Narrative is everywhere. Resolved closure is impossible. Rather, narrative is the representation of dynamic tensions in specific material situations with specific cultural forms. Remembering that we are dealing with human forms is a matter of survival. We need to be aware of what we control and what we don't control to understand the human condition.

ERASER-
HEAD
and
Other
Early
Films

We can also see gender implications in a new relationship to form in this early work and in *Six Men*. They all suggest the role of receptivity in masculine desire. In addition, in *The Alphabet* the feminine subject, so notably missing in most Hollywood films, becomes a possibility in the Lynch film. The female subject in this short film, split between the desire for an imposed linearity and her conjunction with her materiality, will later be more completely and richly represented in Laura and Lula. Significantly, the female body, even in this early Lynchian narrative, is in evidence not as the conventional disturbance of ordinary life but as an endangered energy imperiled by social logic.

Already in *The Alphabet*, we can see that control issues have always been a part of Lynch's filmic art. Even here, the spectator is neither bonded to nor distanced from the central figure by the narrative doubling of the protagonist's control with the control of the camera. Indeed, the camera is not a controlling eye but one that to a large extent yields before the opacity of materiality. In the Lynch film, *control* of the gaze does not stabilize the narrative.

With *The Alphabet*, Lynch begins defining a career-long struggle to avail himself of the power of the full double helix of meaning—the force of materiality disrupted but not diminished by powerful Hollywood discourse, and the power of Hollywood discourse disrupted but not diminished by the force of materiality and subconscious energy. He rescues the difference—the otherness of plasticity—through the creation of the energy with which it may meet the camera's gaze. The stylized features of the figure in the bed and the prominence of the bed itself make it impossible for these objects to become mere transparent elements in a narrative progression. Yet the power of the alphabet and the narrative linearity it iconizes endure. Lynch does not harmonize these elements—irresistible discourse meets immovable materiality. We can almost hear the wind blowing through the interstices of our brains. *Six Men Getting Sick, The Alphabet, The Grandmother,* and *Eraserhead* thrive on the tensions inherent in all of conventional Hollywood narrative strategies; rather than solving, resolving, or dissolving those tensions, these works make irresolution a rich source of narrative power. Clearly distinct from the classic Hollywood films that solve the tensions, from the newer Hollywood films that play them out but resolve them, and from cult films that dissolve them through hyperexaggeration and parody, Lynch's earliest narrative films reject both harmony and dissonance for balance. They innocently dismiss the need to deal with audience expectation of conventional narrative representation.

This innocence made early enthusiasts imagine Lynch going on to becoming a subversive, fringe filmmaker. But David Lynch did not because he could not.[14] He was not born to subvert, to oppose, to satirize, or to mock. The closed systems of Hollywood were a challenge to Lynch the artist looking to draw balance from imbalance. The innocence of the early work did not yield to jaded experience but rather to a higher form of innocence, one achieved as a transformation of the reductiveness of closed narrative.

7

"If You Are Falling in Space"

TWIN PEAKS: FIRE WALK WITH ME

The issue of origins that played such a conspicuous role in Lynch's earliest films resurfaces with much of the initial daring and singularity in *Twin Peaks: Fire Walk with Me,* his personal rejoinder to the problems of collaboration that television presented to his Twin Peaks mythology. To date, *Fire Walk with Me* has been widely misconstrued as a botched continuation of the adventures of Dale Cooper despite Lynch's best efforts to preclude that error by situating the film in the time just before Cooper's arrival in Twin Peaks. Even Lynch's dramatized rejection of the power of the detectives in the first thirty minutes has not been understood by enough of the audience as a cue to shift *away* from the detective sensibility that unified the televised narrative through Dale Cooper. Yet the prequel to the series clearly points away from him to Laura—in a successful, if harrowing, narrative representation of the origins of *Twin Peaks* events, the time when Laura becomes capable of acting as the secret-bearing sensibility that guides Cooper after he arrives in the television series.

Through its visual and dramatic evocation of the failure of the detective machine to fire up during a pre–Laura Palmer mystery, *Fire* evokes the existence of an as-yet-unknown antecedent to Cooper's genius. Thus, the momentum of the film moves from the hero that much of the audience has learned to love toward his origins, that is, to the enigmatic Laura, the secret-bearer.[1] *Fire Walk with Me* begins with a group of FBI agents playing serious detective games as they attempt in vain to make sense of the murder of

Teresa Banks (Pamela Gidley), a seventeen-year-old drifter. Surprising and confusing many who saw it, the film actively distances us from identification with the FBI sleuths at the beginning of the movie. In this way, the story implicitly makes the point that it must progress with no customary heroic hand to shield or avenge either Teresa Banks or Laura Palmer (Sheryl Lee), the beautiful Twin Peaks homecoming queen. Both women are murdered with impunity by Laura's father, Leland Palmer (Ray Wise), who is possessed by the demon BOB (Frank Silva). With Banks's death, Special Agent Dale Cooper (Kyle MacLachlan) intuits a pattern at work in the universe but admits resignedly that there is nothing to be done—by him—for the moment.

When the film plunges us into the life of Laura Palmer, surprisingly we are liberated from the limitations of the would-be rescuers. Again overturning expectations, Lynch reveals that this will be a very different kind of journey from the one on television. This journey concerns Laura's passage through the multiple planes of the real and its lessons for her and us about life, death, and the depths and boundlessness of reality. In *Twin Peaks*, Laura teaches Cooper how to solve the mystery of her death and plays a major role in his boundary crossings; in *Fire*, through a mysterious negotiation of time and an involvement in her transformation, we see what she had to become before she could be what she is to Cooper in *Twin Peaks*.

Laura's passage, the central event of *Fire*, begins with her situation in ordinary reality and takes us more deeply into the heart of her mystery, which only pulsates on the surfaces of *Twin Peaks*. She is the quintessential Lynchian enigma, for she herself is the meeting place of socially constructed form and the larger energies. Superficially, Laura is the standard of ordinary life—blonde, blue-eyed, and beautiful; she is, theoretically, just as Lynch has described her, "the classic American girl." But her very synchronicity with the portrait of the perfect girl—daddy's princess—afflicts her. Her living energies are as alienated as were those of the freak John Merrick, although for exactly the opposite reason. She is cut off from culture as well as from reality by being the cultural image of desire. Trapped within the stereotype, she lives an alienated life, peering frantically at the world through her desirable shell.

Lynch is swimming upstream with this film. The mystery of the alienated is the mystery of the asymmetry of culture and nature, the mystery of the chimera of labels that he examined in *Eraser-head*. The bad fit between labels and life so terrifies us that we endlessly repeat stories that falsely reassure us that the social is also the real. But the secret of the alienated is at the core of our greatest fear and suffering, and the urgent need to confront it validates the risks that Lynch takes here. *Fire Walk with Me* braves our nameless anxieties of slipping and sliding through the cracks in a man-made world (that *we* didn't make) by braving the perils of inviting us to actually *identify with* one particular kind of radically problematic protagonist—a woman and an incest victim. Like John Merrick, whose body slides out of the reassuring image of "normal" anatomy, the body of a woman seems to set off alarm bells that bodily parts may slide away, and the female incest victim presents for men the spectre of an even more horrible slippage—castration by direct violation.

For that reason, with the exception of incest narratives in daytime television soap opera, those few incest stories that have reached the mass media firmly displace audience identification away from the victim and toward the strong, controlling doctor who takes over the story as a manager to lead the violated party to discovery and wholeness.[2] *Sybil* (1976) is the prototype of this small group of mass-media works. *Twin Peaks* skirts the cultural resistance mechanism in just that way—by making the story Cooper's though it does not capitulate completely to the ordinary evasions. It resolutely refuses to portray him as controlling Laura. Even the radiantly heroic Cooper must wait until he can translate *Laura's knowledge* of who killed her into terms he can express. Setting a precedent but without inviting identification with Laura, the television series retains her ownership of her own story, which no one else on the show can tell—hence the need for a prequel.

Lynch's desire, in making his own Twin Peaks film, to confront what was evaded in the series is natural, if commercially dangerous. For him, Laura as incest victim offers a superb Lynchian opportunity only glancingly exploited in the series. Characteristically, he embraces the experience of women and the feminine as his source of revelation. Here, the homecoming queen, the unequivocal social ideal of love and beauty, is revealed as the other side of the card he played in *The Elephant Man*. He uses the desirable daughter to create a narrative focus for what happens when human energy is labeled, as we saw in *Eraserhead* and *The Elephant Man* but with a difference. Spencer and Merrick are men under siege from external pressures. In this film, Lynch dares to occupy the center of the narrative with the experience of a woman who suffers from the internal wounding that is incest.

As an abusive father, Leland/BOB encapsulates the simultaneity of the dark and bright sides of cultural control. And as his violence toward his daughter conflates the surfaces and depths of culture, we see that there are no comfortable places in "normal" reality for Laura. This is because *Fire* locates itself principally at a moment in the crime that is always prior to the detectives' arrival in order to "fix" the mess—the moment of the strange and terrifying *agon* of the violated body that is beyond cure and control by social means.

Because in *Fire* we become so intimate with the problems that normality poses for the body, even physical norms become ambiguous and, at points, frightening. In *Fire* even more than in *Twin Peaks,* inside and outside are distinctions that no longer hold. In the television series, the use of wood, animal heads, and murals conflate internal and external in a darkly humorous manner that only suggested destabilization. The very walls of Laura's room in this film reiterate themselves as her experience of the interior wound when they open to admit Leland/BOB's invasive energies. The air, the purest aspect of free energy in the Lynch film—energy that is both inside and outside of us—is part of Laura's internal torment. The ceiling fan in the hall is BOB's signal that her world is imploding; the shadow side of the father's authority traps the very flow of air in a mechanism. At its extreme, the coerced air bursts into flaming holocaust. FIRE: walk with me. This is the process of which the Log Lady (Catherine Coulson) speaks when she tries to console Laura within the limits of reality as she knows it. Once again it is feminine wisdom that establishes connectedness in the Lynch narrative, for in this film only the Log Lady sees beyond surfaces. Like the FBI, she cannot keep Laura from dying, but she can offer her an empathetic awareness of her tragedy, something the FBI cannot do. The Log Lady sees the fire that is taking Laura's life, and she knows it as *this kind of fire,* not ordinary fire but the conflagration in which the energy of life turns toxic, a process in which the "wind rises" and "all goodness is in jeopardy."

Even before the Log Lady speaks to her, Laura's interior wound has led her to the conclusion that she is caught up in a flaming dance of death. She tells this to her best friend Donna Hayward (Moira Kelly) when she and Donna are casually speculating on what would happen "*if* you were falling in space" [emphasis added]. Laura, quite certain that she *is* falling, cloaks her experience in a purportedly hypothetical answer that one *would* fall faster and faster until one burst into flame forever. Her personal investment in this surmise is manifest when she wistfully adds that the angels would not come to save such a person "because they've all gone away."

However, in *Fire Walk with Me* the trajectory of the film contradicts Laura's despair and carries the spectator along with her toward a revised, affirmative understanding of survival. She is thus both right and wrong about her angel. When Laura imagines her angel as part of an idealized, impossible fantasy of "someone to watch over me," she is disappointed. When she learns a very difficult lesson about her own power to cross the boundaries of ordinary reality, she also learns through the apparition of her angel that there is a larger truth that gratifies her need for an inclusive, orderly universe. *Fire* takes us through the perilous route that she follows, one of Lynch's most traumatic evocations of the necessary encounter with base layers of the subconscious that must precede the liberating release into the higher reaches of involuntary energies.

For Lynch, as we have seen in his paintings, we are all always falling in space, but there is nothing to fear since the mysterious heart of form exists in the air, not grounded in social power as it would appear (see Chapter 1). Lynch wants to show in *Fire Walk with Me* that falling in space—what he understands as liberty—looks like death and disorientation but only from inside the flat confines of ordinary reality. In plain words, he takes a worst-case scenario and assures us that there is a way out—if we can overcome our fears of freedom.

The first thirty minutes of *Fire Walk with Me* tell us not to look to the logic of au-

Smelling the Blue Roses

thorities to deliver us. Initially the film is peopled by characters, principally FBI Special Agent Chet Desmond (Chris Isaak), who introduce us to Lynch's cosmology of multiple spaces by evoking the insufficiency—even absurdity—of ordinary negotiations in time and space by the earnest detectives. The visual evocations of the boundedness and depthlessness of their world are intensified by static editing patterns that may initially seem strangely inept but turn out to be formal echoes of the starts and stops of the sleuths' abortive efforts. Once the story moves to Laura, the editing becomes increasingly fluid, passionate, beautiful, and evocative of a momentum that will be explored below. With cinematic poetry, Lynch suggests again and anew—but with a freshness that makes it seem like the first time—not only the limits of all willful action but our freedom to get beyond it.[3]

Our first image of the brotherhood of detectives reveals Gordon Cole (David Lynch), who is about to begin the investigation into the death of Teresa Banks by summoning Special Agent Desmond. Cole stands in his office in front of a mural that recreates the surface appearance of the great outdoors. He shouts, as if across great distances, to a secretary who, when the camera pulls back, is revealed to be a few inches away from him. Cole's reality is a culturally created, flat simulacrum of time and space. The experience of depth is only betrayed by its absence and the odd excess of Cole's voice.

Cole, arguably Lynch's comedic self-portrait, is the chief officer of this network of busy investigators, working with all seriousness in the flatlands of FBI procedures and only imagining the depths of mystery beyond the reach of a reductivist logic through his designation of a Blue Rose Case. A Blue Rose Case stumps the detectives because it confounds their depthless, bounded mindset with intimations of a world with manifold layers and without neat limits; the many-layered Teresa Banks murder is a Blue Rose Case.

Parallel to the lack of spatial depth is the problem of language for the FBI. Cole's inability to hear begets his proclivity for yelling secrets and thus his need to invent a better mode of confidentiality. Therefore, he instructs Agent Desmond and his partner Sam Stanley (Kiefer Sutherland) using the body of a figure he refers to as Lil (Kimberly Ann Cole). As Cole "writes" on Lil, he transforms a human body into an animated stick figure. Lil—actually three-dimensional—has been rendered cartoonlike for his purposes. Even her gender is an enigmatic masking of what lies under her accoutrements. "Her" face is covered with theatrical white make-up; "she" wears a patently artificial red wig, black stockings and red high heels, and a loosely fitted, cartoony red dress to which is pinned an artificial blue rose (see figure 56). Lil performs a series of exaggerated theatrical gestures, which Desmond and Stanley decode as they go to work on the case. Here, language takes on the flatness of Cole's opening gesture and flattens the body itself.

Throughout their investigation, the detectives appear to be two-dimensional people trying to fathom a three-dimensional world. They stare at electric wires, and they find a two-dimensional letter "T" on a sliver of paper under Banks's fingernail. They discover that her ring—which will later play a major role in the film—is missing by looking at a photograph on her refrigerator. The photo's flat surface points to a dimensional object that baffles their flat universe. When Desmond tracks the ring to a trailer near the victim's, he disappears as he tries to pick it up, never to be seen again by the FBI, having slipped into another dimension.

56. Lil: Gordon Cole "writes" a two-dimensional body.

With the disappearance of Desmond, the seeming protagonist, we can identify with the trauma done to the circumscribed systems of the FBI detectives by the life outside them since the conventional structure of narrative has also been traumatized. This is reflected by the inability of the inconclusive fragments of information that come back to the FBI's Philadelphia offices without Desmond to take the shape of a narrative. All hope of standard coherence is lost when Philip Jeffries (David Bowie), an agent who long ago vanished mysteriously, suddenly reappears. Jeffries is a complete wild card, having nothing substantive to do with the Banks case. He disrupts the FBI and the audience, materializing and dematerializing abruptly before the eyes of Gordon Cole, Dale Cooper, and Albert Rosenfield (Miguel Ferrer), never quite explaining where he has been or even is.

Jeffries' appearance is painful for the spectator because the order of the narrative structure is destroyed as it is only beginning, rendering *Eraserhead*, in contrast, comfortable. At least *Eraserhead*'s narrative explosion comes at the end of the film. However, Jeffries' appearance does maintain a powerful kind of continuity since it is integral to the film's desire that we attend to the relationship between the detectives and larger energies. The abrupt appearance of Jeffries, stuttering incomprehensibly, presents us with a sophisticated Lynchian paradox of ordinary reality as a cultural system continually breaking down yet remaining in place.

Indeed, the entire function of the Jeffries sequence is to establish a Lynchian cosmology that prepares us for Laura's ultimate discovery of a real, if generally unseen, larger order that sustains us even when ordinary cultural systems melt down—as is the case in incest. As always, Lynch tries to free us for larger reassurances by inducing us to resist an illusory confidence in linguistic structures. Jeffries' first words to his astounded colleagues bear only the logical form of sentence syntax: "I'm not going to talk about Judy." They appear to lack any inherent connection to the characters' realities.[4] Even though later in the film the word "Judy" will be spoken again, thus redeeming language (to be discussed below), Jeffries is, at this point, an epiphany that speaks of a crisis of rational language, the foundation of detection in its limited sense.

In this scene, Jeffries doesn't know how to speak of the new spaces he has found. While he wails and stutters, "I found them!" we see on the screen the location and objects of his discoveries— the "room over the convenience store" with its aura of sensory deprivation, stained into an indeterminate beigish color, grimy, poorly furnished, and its abundance of windows covered with ripped material. Most importantly about our ability to see this room, our engagement in the processes of the film itself is supplanting our engagement in the detectives because we are empowered by the film to go beyond the kind of evidence they can find.

This "room over a convenience store," about which Jeffries tries to speak and which we see, resonates with the multiple layers of the energies beyond the borders of reason and culture. If we can allude to the conduct of our lives downstairs of our subconscious as innumerable transactions for convenience, the neglect of the room over it suggests the impoverishment of our ordinary ways of making meaning. The space immediately contiguous with expedience (convenience) gives us only the most threadbare (quasi-sinister) connections to the abundance of the subconscious (the room over it). Beyond that room is something grander and finer—the larger aspect of the subconscious, more amply present in the sumptuous Red Room.

Lynch's cosmology is there for us to see during Jeffries' disjunctive narrative. The dingy room that is an adjunct to convenience permits only a small presentiment of what lies beyond through its rag-covered windows. Here, we can once again see the importance of narrative forms to Lynch's notion of reality and its representations. The room over the convenience store contains recognizable narrative forms which differ from the "normal" narrative in that they are unbounded by detective-like reason—indeed, Jeffries is completely unhinged by it. The configuration of the energies here is marked by the asymmetrical organization of the figures, reminiscent of Lynch's representations in his paintings of reality as a flow of energy in which logical structures mysteriously retain their coherence. In this case, knowledge of his early influences directly helps in understanding his cinema.

In the space over the convenience store, order is composed of balances of slow and fast areas as Lynch learned about in the work of Francis Bacon. In the slow areas, the Little Man (Michael J. Anderson) and BOB sit near a heavy skillet of bubbling creamed corn. A little boy (Jonathan J. Leppell) and his grandmother, Mrs. Tremond (Frances Bay), sit silently. This area becomes a little faster with the movement of the characters. A woodsman (Jürgen Prochnow) moves spasmodically. The Little Man, familiar from *Twin Peaks,* rubs his fingers over a formica table. A figure in a red suit, wearing a white plaster mask with a long fingerlike nose (Carlton Russell), jumps. Sudden quick movements punctuate the scene.

In this space over the convenience store, there is what logic tells us is confusion—no discrete division between life-giving and life-destroying, fast and slow, surface and depths. But this is the scene of reality as the subconscious might represent it; in a world of flow we move easily through the spectrum of states of being. Now we are looking at still composition, now we are looking at moving images, now we are moving from surfaces into depths. An extreme close-up moves outward from an unidentified throat through its teeth and lips which produce the word "Electricity!" The little boy appears wearing a white plaster mask similar to that of the jumping figure. He lifts the mask to reveal his child's face and then lowers it. When he lifts the mask a second time, a monkey's face appears instead behind the plaster.

From this tattered and deprived space over the convenience store, BOB and the Little Man exit into the opulence of a second space, the Red Room with its brilliant coloration—a place that is mysterious, as we shall see later on, but not confused, a peaceful, joyous place in which BOB must submit to higher forces. This final transition of the images coincident with Jeffries' ravings suggests a Lynchian reality composed of spaces that interpenetrate but that are also distinct from each other—the limited space of logic and reason; the impoverished visionary space that is hidden on top of enclosures of convenience; and the vibrant beyond of the border between "convenient," ordinary life and the planes of reality in which the riches of the subconscious exist undiminished.

The FBI agents in the film cannot move easily among these spaces—later, Cooper will make a good start at doing so in the television series—but *we* can, as we are shown in this scene with Jeffries. Further, in an even more pointed way, Jeffries' visit establishes an important link between film and dreams that endures when logic cannot. As strange as this visit is, Dale Cooper expects it since he has dreamed that it will take place exactly as it transpires. Thus, at 10:10 in the morning of February 16, Cooper is alert to the event, which he believes in even though the guards never saw Jeffries enter or leave the building. Cooper's dream reality is confirmed by the videotape of a surveillance camera, a representation within the film itself of Lynch's sense that film can show the reality of dreams. The details of the tape of Jeffries' visit are as significant as the general relationship between film and the subconscious portrayed here. As the visit is about to begin, Cooper stands in front of the surveillance camera until the monitor shows his image frozen on the screen while Jeffries emerges from the elevator and rushes by the frozen image to Cole's office. Film's ability to simultaneously freeze time and record movement means it can tell us what more logical cultural channels cannot.

The stage is set for another perspective now that *Fire Walk with Me* has taken the utterly unorthodox route of evoking not one but three detectives, only to completely abandon their efforts.[5] The initial proceedings of the film sweep away rational limits to our understanding of form, not in order to do away with narrative but to permit the story to be told.

Laura opens up new possibilities and the secrets of moving among the spaces of the larger reality that are only barely imagined by the detectives. Initially, she is pessimistic about her place in what she sees as a closed and barren universe. Talking with her friend Donna, she speculates about space as a void, in which a body spins in endless random movement: "For a while you wouldn't feel anything, and then you would burst into fire forever. And the angels wouldn't help you, because they've all gone away." In this interchange, her initially flawed understanding of her situation is suggested by the contradictory visual framing of the scene. There is a tension between the serene balance of the bodies in the film frame and Laura's pessimism (see figure 57). The high-angle framing of the conversation between Laura and Donna even suggests the pres-

57. Donna and Laura: the angels have not departed.

ence of a reassuring angelic perspective from on high.[6] Through this visual perspective, Lynch embeds order and stability in the scene. This meaning, and not Laura's tragic verbal image, is the reality ultimately validated by the film. The angels are not absent in *Fire Walk with Me;* in fact, when the momentum of the film really begins in her narrative, the wave of unstable, involuntary energy in her life, moving inexorably, brings her toward her angel.

Initially, Laura's gloomy version of life seems valid. If the detectives are like paper dolls confounded by depth, Laura is a three-dimensional being living in a paper house in which BOB can violate her at every turn. He tears pages from her secret diary. He enters her body in the home of her reclusive friend Harold Smith (Lenny Von Dohlen), whose house would seem to be an inviolate shelter against the traumas of reality. However, BOB's energy invades Harold's hermitage through Laura's own pretty, blonde homecoming-queen body, erupting through her into his demonic cry of "FIRE walk with me" (see figure 58). Laura briefly attains sanctuary in Donna's arms and home, but sitting down to dinner she sees her father undergo a metamorphosis from calm, handsome, ideal daddy—"How's Donna? School? . . . Are you hungry?"—to a tyrant demented by BOB's energy, terrorizing her with a sudden diatribe about hand washing.

However, as the other spaces beyond ordinary life that we learn about in the first thirty minutes of the film become available to Laura, better possibilities emerge. Her first response toward her intuition of realms larger than the street on which she lives is fear and confusion, much as we have seen with Agent Jeffries. But for her, there is ultimately joy and celebration in her passage.

58. Laura possessed: BOB as invasive energy.

Laura is more than dubious when she receives a visitation from the space over the convenience store. Mrs. Tremond and her grandson, the little boy wearing a white plaster mask, emerge into Laura's day. The grandmother opens the way for Laura into the larger reality about which Jeffries tried to tell the FBI. She gives Laura a picture of a hallway with a door partially opening onto another, not quite visible, region and says, "I think this would look quite nice in your room." This scene between Laura, the grandmother, and the grandson is the eye-of-the-duck scene, ostensibly unrelated to the plot but which makes possible Laura's final flash of contentment at the end of the film.

Laura is drawn to her opportunity, frightened though she is by the apparitions, and hangs the picture on her wall as the old woman suggested. Later, as she sleeps, the picture becomes a passageway for her into her dreams, the darkness of the unknown, the fertile Lynchian place from which vision comes. There is no distinction made here between reality and dream; instead, dream becomes a conduit between aspects of reality, always present but only perceptible when the subconscious speaks. Through dark mazelike hallways, the dreaming Laura is guided by Mrs. Tremond toward her grandson, who snaps his fingers to produce light, an energy that conveys Laura into the Red Room.

Here, those familiar with the Twin Peaks series are ironically most at a disadvantage in viewing *Fire Walk with Me,* since it may be harder for those spectators to understand that this is not the same Red Room of the series. Lynch has directly stated that not only does everything look and sound different in the Red Room than it would in ordinary reality but also that the Red Room is a different place for everyone who enters it. It retains some resemblances with Cooper's Red Room—the one we saw in the series— and with its appearance later in the film as MIKE and BOB's Red Room. However, in Laura's dream we see *her* Red Room.[7]

Cooper's dream of the Red Room contained music and a dancing Little Man; the Little Man in Laura's Red Room doesn't dance, and the sound track contains only the sense of ambient sound in an ordinary room. Cooper's contained a classical statue of a nude female form, chairs, and the shadow of an owl; Laura's contains none of those, but instead a table with a pedestal in the form of a massive golden shell. The Red Room in the series contained a virtually silent, contemplative Dale Cooper. The Red Room here shows Cooper taking a vocally assertive role. In Cooper's dream, the interchanges occur between a sitting Little Man and Laura as he watches; in the film dream, they occur between a standing Cooper and Little Man as Laura watches. Cooper's Red Room is full of issues about phallic power relative to the image of femininity (see Chapter 3); Laura's dream of the Red Room is dominated by a feminine self-image, a large golden seashell. While Cooper's dreamtime in the Red Room takes the form of an official inquiry, Laura's dreamtime in the Red Room takes the form of a marriage proposal—the offering of a ring and the opportunity for a decision.

This "marriage proposal" is the central action of *Fire Walk with Me;* the opportunity for this marriage is an alternative for Laura to all of the self-hating sex in which she involves herself. However, although this proposal contains the prospect of freedom, happiness, and self-respect, Laura doesn't immediately recognize it as such. We too do not immediately recognize the proposal for what it is, for we, the spectators, become Laura's alter ego in decision-making as her dream sequence makes us her collaborators. In her dream, the Little Man presents the ring in a direct address to the camera—to us—as much as to the dreaming Laura. After we stare at the proffered ring with the owl hieroglyph etched into its green stone, we are directly addressed by Agent Cooper, who also stares directly into the camera (see figures 59 and 60). As he warns Laura not to take the ring, he warns us. The question is, should she/we take the ring—or the warning?

Any tendency to heed Cooper's warning in *Fire* disregards his role in this film and substitutes our memory of him from the television series. In *Twin Peaks,* the attractive detective was our guide, but this film has insistently sig-

59–60. Frame Pair: Dream marriage proposal and warning to Laura and the spectator.

naled us to shift away from identifying with him. In Laura's dream, she, not Cooper, is our point of identification. Through a multiple-perspective Laura/camera, the gaze in the dream establishes that Cooper is wrong.

The proposal is the road to choice and freedom, as compared with the suffering of Laura's life within the system. Her dream presents her with two images of herself that continue the process of recognition of this truth. In the dream there is a wounded Laura in her bed—the space of her ordinary reality that can be connected with the tormented location of the child's suffering in *The Alphabet*—and a free Laura with access to the space of the subconscious (the Red Room). The dreaming Laura who moves freely through subconscious space to the Red Room is contrasted favorably with the Laura in the bed, trapped in ordinary reality. The trapped Laura has *her* involuntary forces numbed, as represented by her deadened left arm, the side of the body traditionally identified with the heart and the intuition. (This is part of a cluster of references to numb limbs in the Twin Peaks mythology and in *Eraserhead.*) As Laura dreams, the Laura in the bed suddenly cannot move her left arm, and it is abruptly replaced by the presence of the bloodied body of a young girl lying next to her on her left—Annie Blackburn (Heather Graham)—who outwardly bears the wound that Laura's numb arm bears invisibly. Annie brings her news of the bounty of the Red Room (where the "good" Dale is). The free Laura who moves through the picture in the dream is not thus afflicted.[8]

We should realize that Cooper is not right about the ring when Laura finds it in her closed left fist. She freezes with fear, but it is also clearly a return to animation in her left hand despite her anxiety. Cooper's misplaced warning and Laura's anxiety on the basis of that warning are signs of confusion. His warning is further in doubt when, holding the ring, Laura goes to look for signs of BOB in the hallway outside her room. She is relieved to find that the ceiling fan is inert. The ring is once again connected with relief for her. Cooper warns her and us against the ring, but her dreaming reality tells us otherwise.

We can't believe a detective in this film, a rule difficult to remember despite the first thirty minutes because Cooper is already an incandescent hero in our eyes. But this is a prequel that challenges ordinary modes of intertextuality. Cooper is not yet that great detective or at least is not yet far enough along his path. In this prequel, Laura is the seeker and the secret. The choice she—not Cooper—must make invites us to see her freedom in her transfer between spaces in reality, even though from the perspective of this ordinary life that transfer has the appearance of death. This dream encourages us to arrive at a new vision in which we see her death as a death of the illusion of the literal. Laura's death is a parable confirming the reality of human freedom, of which the ring is a guarantor.

This notion of Laura's freedom in the subconscious beyond of the town of Twin Peaks is the seed that is planted in her dream and that germinates as the story progresses, culminating in the visions of the angels. At this point, Laura is confused about the message to her from her subconscious. Taking the ring seems like death. However, the promise is there. If the wounded Laura looks at her nighttime image with confusion, the dreaming Laura looks back at her with tenderness and compassion (see figures 61 and 62). Initially, Laura rejects the proposal. However, ultimately, she does take the ring and her freedom.

Laura's passage toward choice and freedom becomes visible after the dream when there is no longer a single Laura in her waking life, nor is she as disenfranchised as she was. After her dream visit to the Red Room, she increasingly acquires the hopeful power of the subconscious despite the increase in the terrors of her conscious life. The counterpoint between the two Lauras is part of the upswing of the wave of energy on which she will crest in the Red Room in the final image. Moreover, unlike in Cooper's experience in the television series, Laura's actual entrance into the Red Room is even more empowering than her dream visit. (This is probably what Lynch would have preferred for Cooper in the series.)

61–62. Frame Pair: Dream doubling of wounded and visionary Lauras.

After the dream, Laura is no less tormented in her ordinary life, but she now manifests a power of vision we have not previously seen in her. Her new powers are underscored by the editing, which evolves from the beginnings of momentum as Laura's section of the film begins and becomes beautifully fluid, most particularly in the dream itself, but also in the representation of subsequent events. The editing moves gracefully and ever more purposefully as Laura takes Donna, who is desperately curious about her best friend's nighttime prowling, into an after-hours club in Canada and we see for the first time the depths of wounded Laura's depravity and humiliation. At this club she sinks into the stereotype of the object of desire that gratuitously sexually stimulates men and women alike. However, wounded Laura abruptly becomes visionary Laura when a literal illumination (intense light) envelops her and makes her aware that across the room a drugged Donna is about to be raped by one of Laura's would-be lovers. Shocked into action, visionary Laura finds the power to protect Donna. Similarly, shortly afterward wounded Laura again transforms into visionary Laura to discover BOB's true identity when next he invades her room.

Laura's path requires that she make a painful departure from the literalness represented by Cooper's warning about the ring. To reach the freedom of her dream double, she must come to understand the ring in a more poetic sense as a unifying power. This she does as, toward the end of the film, she realizes that the ring creates a kind of continuity—she has seen it on Teresa Banks's finger and in her dream offered to her by the Little Man. She has also seen it in the strange scene in which MIKE (Al Strobel), another entity from above the convenience store, tries to warn her about her father. MIKE, as *Twin Peaks* fans know, is BOB's former partner and now seeks to impede BOB's violent career in this ordinary world. As he tries to tell Laura about Leland's multiple identity, he displays the ring.

If we are moving with the momentum of the film, we are ready to identify with Laura's revelation that the ring thus links all of its disparate but simultaneously existing spaces—the ordinary space in which Teresa lives, the Red Room of Laura's dream, and the space over the convenience store from which MIKE comes. Laura's sense of the ring as a unifying factor predicts that her taking of the ring will be a form of balance between the spaces. Cooper's reasonable warning to her is based on only fragmentary, uninformed detective knowledge. Like Laura and Cooper, we must discover in the vision of the film another less literal meaning to her death. The key to this film's rhetoric is realizing that it makes us rejoice in her rejection of Cooper's advice, as he himself, in fact, ultimately does.

Such rejoicing seems impossible when all roads lead to the boxcar in the woods where Laura winds up with high-school acquaintance Ronette Pulaski (Phoebe Augustine) after an alcohol- and drug-soaked orgy in which they are tied up for bondage sex. Bound, Laura and Ronette are easy prey for Leland/BOB, who forces the girls into the abandoned train car. In the train car, *this kind of fire* erupts—in the Log Lady's words, "not a forest fire, but a fire in the woods." But if we consider the murder scene, it becomes clear that two kinds of energy are present and that the benign form of energy is greater than BOB. Beams of light shoot up into this darkness from below—the energy of Leland/BOB—and illuminate the girls and Leland/BOB as he is driving them to the boxcar where Laura will die. However, the texture of the film is now approaching a crescendo of momentum, and beneath the despairing surface an energy is building that begins to become manifest in the appearance of beams of light from above, the presence of that stable, floating angel of which Laura has despaired. When *this kind of fire* burns there is terrible suffering but also the possibility of a sudden interface of the various spaces of reality that are usually discretely apart—the eruption from the baser levels of the subconscious into its finer realm. From a place beyond even the Red Room, the angel enters ordinary time and space. She is the revelation of an order in the universe that is always stable, regardless of what is happening in the other spaces.

The image of the larger order takes the form of an angel for Laura specifically for this narrative. Lynch is not any more committed to this as a single image of larger realities than he is to any other single image: Glinda, Merrick's mother, the womb of space in *Dune,* or Jeffrey and Sandy's robin. It is Laura's image in her story. At first, the angel is nothing but a sentimental picture in her room at home, much as John Merrick's picture of goodness was a sugary drawing of a child sleeping. Indeed, there is a clear resemblance between the sweet picture of a sleeping child in Merrick's hospital room and the etching on the wall of Laura's room of an angel presiding over a children's feast. The round-cheeked children and cherubic angel evoke a space of love and security. At the lowest ebb of her despair, the night of her death, as Laura raises her eyes to the image she sees the angel disappear. This seems to confirm her prophecy that the angels have gone away. However, the sentimentality of the image is a cue alerting us that the absence of angels is a truth that applies only to flawed social systems. The presence of the angels is a reality of the cosmos that Laura cannot see until she moves past the limits of "normal" reality.[9]

During the murder scene, Laura gets her first glimpse at an angel, her sign of the mysterious stability of falling in space. When she puts on the ring, making a leap of faith—on the strength of the apparition—her situation gets even better, albeit at the cost of unspeakable temporary affliction. At this extremity we see two visionary truths. First, in taking the ring Laura is choosing not oblivion but survival. Second, we see that this kind of death that results from the leap of faith is a peeling away of the rational illusion of boundaries. This we can see as we find ourselves occupying the perspective of a dead Laura from the camera gaze, watching Leland/BOB throw the plastic for her shroud over her—and us. There is animate intelligence beyond the ordinary space of confusion; there is abundant life in other spaces of the real.

As is typical of a Lynch film, in *Fire Walk with Me* his narration insists that we will find the larger order and move away from

After the Final No, There Comes a Yes

ordinary confusion when we open ourselves beyond the limits of language and "things like language," as Lynch has referred to logical, linear forms (see Introduction). But also characteristic is his recognition that such a letting go means the transcendence of fear. In *Fire Walk with Me,* the fear appears in its most extreme form as the fear of death. Previously, *Eraserhead* was Lynch's most daring statement of this type, a film which suggested that we will not wind up with nothingness if we lose our heads and the social construction but rather quite the reverse. With *Fire Walk with Me,* Lynch, standing on the development of this statement in his intervening films, takes a major step beyond *Eraserhead.*[10]

In *Fire,* Lynch narrates a parable in which crossing the boundaries between logic and the subconscious presents itself as a form of death. We must not take Laura's death literally because this is a movie. Simultaneously, we must not take her death literally because of the cosmology that Lynch builds into the film. In the reality of this film, our humanity is connected with a series of discrete spaces that move in and out of one another. Although there is often a "final no" in the limited space of what logic has designated as reality, there is a "yes" in other disparate, but synchronous, spaces.

When we grasp the meaning of the entire narrative, we can see that the "yes" has been there since the beginning of the film. Lynch opens with blue static, a fractal image of energy which seems boundless. The main title theme of *Fire Walk with Me* is a modal jazz composition in the style that Miles Davis pioneered in the 1960s, embodying that kind of limitless form in sound. It operates at the minimal level of musical signification: neither happy nor sad, neither major nor minor, not in any key, highly chromatic, bearing neither sharps nor flats.[11] Here is a space without defined logical shapes, but it has specific density, texture, and a form in which we can hear color and see sound. This is a representation of an important fluid space of reality.

The narrative of the bound world starts when this initial near-perfection is intersected by objects and actions circumscribed by limits. The blue static becomes available to us once it is enclosed by the parameters of a television screen on which there is no image. At the end of the main title, the television is smashed and the energy spills out of it as a feminine voice screams, "No!" (This is the initial "no" of the film; the final "no" is Leland/BOB's when he kills Laura.) The destruction of the television is the beginning of the representation in this film of the mysteries of energy and boundary that explode past the limits of the series.

The unboundedness of the music that accompanies the explosion and that dominates the first thirty minutes of the film operates in tension with the limits of the detectives at the beginning and in contrast with the appearance of melody once Laura becomes the central focus. The complexity of the oppositions between the melodic and the modal deserves a long discussion, but within the parameters of the present exposition I will just say that they exist as aural analogies to the visual evocation of levels of reality. Melody, of course, implies the bounded structuring of sound, but there is no easy dichotomy here. At the highest level of reality—the angel in the Red Room at the end of the film—there is a highly complex melodic structure that is both infinite and formal at the same time. Toward the end of the film, the seemingly irreconcilable harmonies of the melodic and the free form of the modal find an astonishing, apocalyptic moment of balance in the powerful strains of the final music.

Surprisingly, unbounded space has a form within it that is more stable than space that on the surface seems structured and neatly bounded. Within the ordinary narrative space of *Fire Walk with Me*, events come at us from all sides, motion destabilizes, and we lurch about longing to gain our balance in the confusion. This feeling of the ordinary world is crystalized by Carl Rodd (Harry Dean Stanton), the manager of the Fat Trout Trailer Camp where Banks lived. As Rodd shows the agents Banks's trailer, we cut briefly to an unidentified perspective approaching the back door of the trailer, giving us the feeling of moving through a dark maze.

It turns out to be the point of view of an even more peripheral character, a grimy, stooped old woman (Ingrid Brucato) who leaves nervously when Desmond asks her if she knew Banks. In the silence that follows this uncanny appearance, Rodd ignores the instability of ordinary life, saying, "You see, I've been places. Now I want to stay where I am." That longing for stability is at the heart of culture. Through Laura's story, we see that such a desire can only be gratified by release from rational systems. All appearances to the contrary, rational form—the mansion built by logic—is simultaneously sharply defined and unstable.

Although *Fire* is ultimately a highly optimistic picture, it derives its consolations from the hardest looks at ordinary reality. Lynch disabuses us of the conventional sense of security that we fantasize about "normal" life, which is never "as advertised" for any of the characters. Even ordinary conversations are constantly sliding into their shadow, the illogical. This happens early in the film with Sam Stanley, the literal pathologist who dithers about whether three in the morning is early or late. It happens in the scene with Jeffries. It happens aggressively during the later part of the film when Laura's life in ordinary time and space is in the final stages of meltdown.

In difficult situations ordinary language as direct assertion does not sustain us. Lynch represents this in the strange behavior of language when MIKE drives by Leland and Laura in his camper truck, striving to tell Laura about her father's alternate reality as BOB. Some of his message gets through, but the primary effect created is riot and confusion as Leland tries to drown MIKE's voice in the sound of the racing motor of his car. In the aftermath of this uproar, a shaken Laura gasps, "Who was that?" "You don't know him," Leland says assertively, followed by a quivering "Do you know him?" Later, a similar slip occurs when Laura, so high on drugs that she can hardly walk, goes with Bobby Briggs (Dana Ashbrook), her boyfriend/drug supplier, to pick up some cocaine from a drug runner. During the transaction, Bobby is forced to shoot the runner in self defense, prompting a stoned Laura to insist that Bobby has killed his friend Mike. "This isn't Mike," yells Bobby, as we might expect. However, quite unexpectedly he suddenly wonders, "Is this Mike?" although he is clearly looking at a stranger's body.

Conversely, what is ordinarily feared as instability becomes visible in *Fire* as flow, a form of order not disorientation. The rhapsodic editing and scoring of Laura's death in the boxcar is not a glorification of the nothingness and destruction of violence but rather an assertion of the structure of redemption of which this is the penultimate sign. Following BOB's atrocity is the revelation that he is unstoppable only within the confines of the rigid but penetrable realm of the social construct. In contrast, in the subconscious space of the Red Room BOB is unexpectedly docile, only a part of a larger flowing order.

The first part of the film's coda in the Red Room calls BOB to account. This Red Room is MIKE and BOB's Red Room, and it, unlike Laura's, is full of phallic mysteries because MIKE and BOB are Lynch's representations of the subconscious vision of the male enigma. Leland/BOB returns to *this* Red Room after Laura is dead. Here, he is confronted with MIKE and the Little Man, who has identified himself as "the arm," standing together as if MIKE's severed arm had been replaced. This "reunion," an inversion of castration, suggests that a redemption is already in progress.

The reckoning BOB must make calls for him to heal Leland, who is bleeding as Cooper bled in the final scene in the Red Room of the series, and to return the corn he stole. In this crucial moment of denouement, Laura, whose death at BOB's hands we have just witnessed, is not mentioned at all. Conversely, the creamed corn that is of such importance here has been only intermittently mentioned or visually represented in the film. (It too evokes a phallic mystery as semenlike seed bubbling on a stove burner in the space above the convenience store envisioned during Jeffries' sudden eruption into the FBI offices.[12]) The placement of this scene ends the film analogously to *Wild at Heart*'s conclusion with the abrupt entrance of Glinda into events, not with a rational sense of satisfaction and closure for the viewer. Yet for a spectator open to the Lynchian sensibility and vision, there is great pleasure here.

In this scene in the Red Room, MIKE and BOB perform a ritual of transubstantiation that redeems all of the chaos of the rational space of ordinary reality. The return to wholeness of the masculine creative potential occurs when BOB heals Leland's wound. This healing is represented as the return of "garmonbozia," pain and sorrow, to MIKE and the Little Man. This bodes well since feeling returns to the masculine creative potential from which it has been

disconnected in BOB's unfeeling, unrepentant acts of brutality.
Surely some parallel exists here with Laura's numb arm in her
dream and the use of Annie as a replacement for that arm.[13]

Once this healing is done, a ritual of the corn, the ingestion of
the seed, is performed—the Little Man eats the creamed corn. An
eerie texture to this act is created by the use of slow-motion reverse projection of the actor spitting the corn onto the spoon. If
we read the ingestion of the corn as an inversion of the first major
narrative image in *Eraserhead,* that of Henry Spencer expelling the
matter of potential creativity from his mouth, then we can say that
the Little Man is here preventing the social labeling of the seed. It
is another element in the film's final reassurances that energy contains its own limits, even in a reality that contains the volcanic de-
structiveness of BOB.

With this act, BOB's sowing of the seed of fear and violation is
an event that has never taken place. And abruptly we see the monkey face that had silently appeared in Jeffries' static-ridden narrative from behind a white, unarticulated plaster mask. Now there is
no mask, only a sweetly smiling monkey who murmurs, "Judy."
Jeffries lurched around the empty structure of ordinary syntax—
"I'm not going to talk about Judy. . . . We're going to keep her
out of it"—but there is absolute, poetic connection between the
word and the real in this space. The monkey's spoken "Judy" is a
representation of the simplicity and naturalness of a possible
"real word."

With the creamed corn, Lynch creates an addition to the seminal set of Lynchian images. These images—Glinda, Jeffrey and
Sandy's robin, the worms of *Dune,* the spermlike matter in *Eraserhead*—are all Lynchian nexus points for the invisible flow of energy and the limited shapes that must be part of the vocabulary of
representation. The Lynchian nexus image is always quasi-comic,
reminding us that we are dealing with human, limited form and
also reminding us of the necessary absurdity involved in the representation of the unbounded aspects of reality. The corn, like the
spermlike matter of *Eraserhead,* is a quasi-comic representation of
creative potential—specifically male—that is both reduced by labeling and larger than reason would define it.

The nexus image is an important reminder that, for Lynch, the
real is a simultaneous presence of the bound and the free, and

those images that can yield the strange truth of connection and disconnection are seminal to his mode of storytelling. This heterogeneity is the central truth of *Fire Walk with Me*. Laura comes to see this too. In the ordinary, troubled space of town life, Laura is dead. However, in the larger multi-dimensionality of the universe, *this kind of fire* cannot start let alone burn. Once Laura enters the Red Room, she can understand that she has attained fuller life.

The lyricism of the editing and music of the final tableaus marks the most intense moment of the film—a revelation of Laura's newfound balance of the open and the bound, the ultimate sign of human freedom and dignity. Rationalism might question Lynch's

63. Laura, Cooper, and the Angel: Laura redux.

final resurrection of Laura as a trivialization of the suffering of an abused child (as in the platitude, "She will meet her reward in heaven"). Alternatively, there is a logic by which Lynch could be accused of arguing for suicide. However, each of these perspectives imposes a different kind of grinding literality on the poetry of his work, the very reductive literality that he attacks. Laura's death is the center of a poetic statement that yields eternity as the refreshed present, not the hereafter. Poetically, the experience of the larger truth may seem like death when it shatters social limits, but it is actually an encounter with abundant life.

In the final tableau, we see Cooper as he was in *Twin Peaks*. He is no longer the unreliable detective who warned against the ring but an initiate into the secrets of Laura's passage. Time is quite fluid here. This is a Cooper both before and after the events of *Twin Peaks*. He glows with affection for Laura, touching her, but at arm's length, leaving her space of her own as well as affording her connectedness (see figure 63).[14] The distance, yet connection, between Laura and Cooper is a new, much more direct image of Lynch's vision of meaning than he has previously achieved. In *Fire Walk with Me,* the combination of detective and murder victim, the seeker and the secret, averts hopelessness in a single moment of resurrection. This is a Lynchian moment of resolution in which there is openness and stability in the relationship between reason (the detective) and the subconscious (the sentient center of Laura as the excluded mystery). This rapturous balance is the prelude to the white light that washes out the screen as the music soars into a sublime range, that privileged moment of multiplicity toward which Lynch and his films since *Eraserhead* continue to yearn.

However, like all of Lynch's previous closures, the burst of joy resolving into contentment suggests not the usual stasis of the Hollywood ending but the apogee of a cycle and thus the capacity for future motion. In the Lynchian reality endless energy flows through its natural cycles of turbulence and calm across the planes on which the micro- and macrorealities occur. If the wind is at its gentlest in the barely rippling draperies of Laura's angel in the final tableau of *Fire Walk with Me*, and if the simultaneity of balance occurs at its most intense, we know that this is only possible in the subconscious that momentarily escapes narrative and that almost escapes representation in the Red Room. As long as our ordinary "social realities" threaten to immure us within artificial limits, the wind will rise again and with it *this kind of fire*, particularly in the forests of the Holly-wood(s).

The Passion
of David Lynch:
The Lady or
the Highway

Through his alteration of the typical mass-media representation of the relationship between the subconscious, language, and the making of meaning in narrative film, David Lynch has changed Hollywood. He has advanced the work of Welles and Hitchcock in making the dreaming mind a force for reality rather than the distraction conventional Hollywood tells us it is. The clearest indications of a Lynchian influence—superficial imitations of the owls and idiosyncratic small towns that now abound in the media—signify little; however, there are an increasing number of more interesting, more essential signs of the crucial impact on popular culture of David Lynch's work.

For example, after *Blue Velvet*, in both good and bad commercial films, there is the explicit appearance of masculinity and femininity as roles, and an untraditional, enigmatic portrayal of the male body. By this, I do not mean the images of the feminized male body as icon of desire that have been around since Rudolph Valentino at the very least. The development to which I allude represents an increasing disturbance of the iconic "heroism" of male aggression as a "protection" from what has been portrayed as the engulfing chaos of female sexuality and energy, resistance beyond anything Hitchcock and Welles imagined, in which the spectator bears a Jeffrey-like relationship to the protagonists. Regrettably, on the debit side of the ledger is Oliver Stone's abortive attempt to achieve Lynchian freedoms of this kind in his horribly botched imitation of *Wild at Heart*, *Natural Born Killers*, which gags on its own attempts at dealing à la Lynch with the subconscious. However, on the credit side is Martin Scorsese's underappreciated *Cape Fear,* in which there is an intriguing, dangerous likeness between the upright hero and the Frank-like villain (much more dangerous than in the original version of the film) that powerfully denies the femininity of engulfing chaos.

These directors and many more suggest that the current state of mass-market filmmaking is in great part a post-*Eraserhead* phenomenon. Moreover, Lynch's influence appears to have affected more than the work of established American directors; new filmmakers, both here and abroad, seem to have taken his lead. It is as though film students learned that they could deal with the subconscious in new, more subtle and powerful ways than are available in the flashback by pushing off from Lynch's first full-length film and then taking a leap off *Blue Velvet* (and subsequent Lynch productions) into the world of the dream buried inside independent and Hollywood vehicles alike. Each new directorial sensation of the past decade has walked the path opened by Lynch. Quentin Tarantino follows in Lynch's footsteps in both *Reservoir Dogs*—with its clear homage to *Blue Velvet*—and *Pulp Fiction.* Tarantino may know little about boundary crossing, but he has gleaned much from his predecessor about representing the difference between energy and the constructed role, and about questioning the worship of controlling masculinity. Jane Campion suggests what Lynch can mean for women struggling to take their place in commercial filmmaking. She gives evidence, particularly in *The Piano,* of having learned from him how to use a female protagonist to honor the subconscious as a source of resurrection which balances the effects of the annihilating will. And because David Lynch is still in a vigorously creative period, the story of his influence remains incomplete; perhaps, like that of Hitchcock and Welles, it always will.

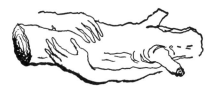

64. Log Lady logo.

In the *ideal* of completeness we find the human capacity for form, but in the *real* incompleteness of human systems, in their actual breaks and discontinuities, we find our capacity for truth.

Since this faith is so much a part of Lynch's art, there is no other statement about his work but an open-ended one and no place for him but midcareer. The reality of his struggle with the heterogeneous inconsistencies of the busy machinery of culture and the white radiance of infinity is thus represented not by the enclosed symmetry of the geometrical circle but by the inconclusive reality of the arc. This mysterious figure, the arc, contains both the sense of wholeness (the complete arc) and the implication of a larger, invisible continuum (to be discovered) of which the arc is but a fragment—Lynch's rainbow.

Nevertheless, there are usable generalizations that can be drawn from my overview of Lynch's career as a heuristic model for discussing his work. These generalizations all grow from my central thesis that a persistent thread of heterogeneity runs through Lynch's storytelling. He thrives on the tension between the two major incompatibilities in his work: nature, with its unseen balances and its mysterious, nonconscious economies; and conscious culture marked by the reductive linearities of language, with its fierce logical coherence. In the arc of work from *The Alphabet* to *Fire Walk with Me,* he embraces the profound tensions between them, tensions that remain part of the life of the work *because* they are never fully resolved. Lynch develops storytelling strategies that drift through collisions toward possible moments of equilibrium. These rare moments of balance imply the shape of the arc in their temporary interface between human determination and natural energies, but they do not abolish the perpetual vivacious tendency in life toward dissonance and apparent disorder.

Through his energetic representations of the interface between social will and nature, Lynch asserts his belief in the viability and the importance of narrative form, albeit as a form mitigated by insurgent energies. Despite all its history, especially in Hollywood movies, of enforcing will, the magic of story form emerges in Lynch's dreamlike narratives as perfectly compatible with an art that can in some ways shed the will. For this to be true, he has fastened onto everything in narrative that defeats its logic with just as much enthusiasm as he has entertained the rigid form that narrative asserts. In his hands, the collision of story with formally indigestible elements does not threaten the integrity of narrative. Like

Hitchcock and Welles, Lynch has proven that an audience's involvement with character and event can be intensified *and made more real* by giving wild, unspeakable elements their due.

Lynch's love of story, but not its tyranny, leads directly to the essential generalization that can be drawn—he has an abiding determination to revise the conventional relationship between meaning and language. His revisions of narrative form are evident in the persistence in his work of an originally conceived relationship between nature and languagelike structures as one of the major continuities in his work considered in this book. In the films I have discussed, language is the vortex of the clash between culture and the subconscious. In his narratives Lynch travels the length of this collision searching for a "real" word. At the beginning of this journey, language, in *The Alphabet,* hangs over the human condition as a seduction and a threat. The literal word is the foundation of an education that sets itself in opposition to the organic body, and in the process of division resulting from this opposition it creates a laceration of the flesh and an uproar in the dream world of the subconscious. If this is the price of meaning, then human life is essentially tragic. But Lynch does not continue in this tragic vein. Instead, he develops a larger, more comprehensive picture of language and meaning that envisions the possibility that linguistic structure can express itself both as a logical form and as a part of the powerful connected subconscious.

At the beginning of the arc of Lynch's work I have considered above, we find a short film that depicts a girl violated in her bed (*The Alphabet*); at the end of it is the portrayal of another girl, Laura Palmer, also violated in her bed (*Fire Walk with Me*). The child in *The Alphabet* bleeds helplessly under the attack of the building blocks of words; Laura is redeemed by the monkey's embodied word that balances the natural texture, body, and mood with logical construct. The voyage from the lacerating logic of language in *The Alphabet* to the redeemed word in *Fire Walk with Me* is immensely complex and involves a kaleidoscope of characters and situations. Through all of Lynch's plot actions there is an increasing richness of his depiction of the possibilities inherent in the word for some balance between culture and nature. The rumble-whoosh sound that he begins to develop in *The Grandmother* gives body and subconscious energy to the Lynchian word.

This sound is not a part of an illusionist realism in sound design, nor is it decorative or mannered. Instead, it is a part of the texture of the air in the spoken word, and it forms the heterogeneous linguistic alloy that opens language and meaning past the potential tragedy of *The Alphabet*. Music and mechanically produced light, two other prevalent alloys of air and culture in Lynch's work, also produce an augmented word. These are particularly important as modes of narrative expression in *Eraserhead, Blue Velvet,* and *Wild at Heart.* In these films, the compound of words with the body of a woman, light, and song is repeatedly used as a form of meaning that provokes liberating vision in the midst of the most constricting cultural systems.

Lynch is successful in his quest for what he envisions as a "real" word that energetically tests the potential for authenticity in popular culture. The struggle is his justification for his career in a mass media that is desperately in need of reality. But it also creates his continual risk of defining himself as irrelevant to a vocabulary heavily conditioned by an illusionist realism that takes the logic of language for the form of the actual. Narratively, this risk surfaces most drastically in the connections Lynch makes between the body of woman, the feminine glance—typically represented as the polar opposite of articulation and meaning—and authentic language. So it is not particularly surprising to find audience tolerance reaching its limit with *Fire Walk with Me,* just when Lynch finds a way to emphatically redeem the alphabet-induced damage in his first film through the name of (a) woman. When the talking monkey appears in the denouement of the film, without the plaster mask behind which it was hidden at the beginning of the narrative, and murmurs the feminine name, "Judy," it makes visible the unifying word.

As the monkey speaks, "Judy" does not take its force from a primarily linguistic, self-referential system—there is no simple grammatical referent for the name. It appears outside of the contexts of the sentence or the plot. Rather, it is part of the revelation represented by the angel, a naturally embodied Lynchian word—the dream of an organic nature fully fused with linguistic structure, falling in space, blissfully full of texture and mood, as we see it in Lynch's paintings. Perhaps it is also pertinent to mention here that this monkey has arguable roots in the paintings of Francis

Bacon. Bacon frequently painted the human face with the shadow of an animal underneath its surface, suggesting unresolvable enigmas in the fusions between humanity and nature. Lynch's image of animal nature under the mask modifies the Baconian paradigm, which is filled with a savage, utterly destabilizing energy. In speaking the feminine name, Lynch's monkey is a blissfully complete recovery of all of those feminine elements of body, subconsciousness, and plasticity, while miraculously preserving their connections with a language that in its narrowest, most mechanistic sense has seemed to exclude them.

Therefore, Lynch's achievement cannot be accurately gauged by box office numbers. The enunciation of the speaking monkey is a dazzling epiphany of hope, but the problem remains for Lynch that the coherence of his search for his real word has not achieved full integration with the popular idiom. Perhaps in *Fire Walk with Me* he has found his authentic word in his terms, but it doesn't yet translate. However, as recherché as such an image may now seem, in the long run I predict it will translate.

But the impression that Lynch has "gone too far" is built into what he is trying to do. He has already been prematurely buried for overreaching several times, notably after *Eraserhead, Dune,* and *Blue Velvet,* as well as after *Fire Walk with Me.* Nevertheless, he has returned in the past by balancing his bold leaps ahead of his time with a couple of two-steps in place. *Eraserhead* was followed by a popular success in *The Elephant Man. Dune* was followed by *Blue Velvet,* which returned his status with Academy Award nominations, although misreading of it as an incentive to perverse voyeurism too caused its own scandal. That scandal was somewhat palliated by Lynch's popular success, *Twin Peaks,* with its large audience—at least initially.

If the ambiguity of popular response to Lynch's return to the Twin Peaks mythology in *Fire Walk with Me* points toward the turmoil of the road ahead, this should be no surprise nor cause for sorrow. For there is every reason to believe in his enduring ability to create a bond of warmth between his audience and his work. The "Lynch industry" in fanzines and memorabilia has not slowed down at all. But more important than this, his post–*Fire Walk with Me* career has not slowed down. He has since developed the *Twin Peaks* episodes for syndication, each now prefaced by new pro-

logues spoken by Margaret Lanterman, the Log Lady, and has cre- Coda
ated a new film, *Lost Highway* (not yet released into general distribution at the time of writing), which is a beautiful, passionate
work full of its own kind of affirmation.

The syndication of *Twin Peaks* is more than a financially motivated re-release. Lynch's addition of the new prologues subtly alters the original episodes to reclaim what had been thought lost
when the latter part of the series veered back into conventional
heroics. Close attention to them below reveals how Lynch continues to demonstrate the resilience of his optimism. His new film,
Lost Highway, a brief examination of which follows, illuminates a
new direction for Lynch's imperative to will the loss of will within
the popular sphere—*Lost Highway* paradoxically creates hope
through identification with a protagonist who quite pointedly *cannot* find his liberation in the Lynchian manner of moving across
the borders of ordinary reality. Here, Lynch announces his faith in
the collective unconscious by permitting us to bear witness to its
abiding health regardless of the lengths to which corrupted will
may go. In expanding on these evaluations of where Lynch is to-
day, I will begin with the new prologues.

By framing Special Agent Cooper's enigmatic adventures with
Margaret's direct address to the audience, Lynch takes a new step
toward a popular way of affirming the bliss of the murmuring
monkey in *Fire Walk with Me*. This is a sign that problems with
Twin Peaks have not forced him to surrender his visionary optimism or its place in commercial entertainment. Rather, he has
moved Margaret, a beloved but somewhat peripheral—much
underused—truthteller in the Twin Peaks mythology, front and
center. As the narrator for the *Twin Peaks* episodes in re-release,
she now becomes the spectator's guide to a Lynchian relationship to the series. With this latest appearance, she becomes David
Lynch's own version of David Lynch at a feminine glance. Using
the Log Lady as a maternal lens on *Twin Peaks*, he develops his
continuing interest in the feminine sensibility as the corrective
angle of vision for an imbalanced culture. A cultural presence that
balances the tragicomic figure of the socially sacrificed Laura,
Margaret emerges from these prologues as a clear indication that
Lynch believes our relationship to reality requires that we add to
the Virgils who have guided us the feminine trail companion who

can augment the current conversation about taking charge with another conversation about letting go. Although such a sensibility is usually risky and significantly unsettling to a mass-media audience (as with Laura), Lynch and Coulson achieve a feminine guide who is a remarkably calming influence.

In her new capacity, Margaret creates a stable place inside the bounds of the normal for interfaces between the flowing energies of the real and the rigidified common idiom. The previous visionary states of Lynch's characters came and went as privileged, occasional episodes in a bound society, much as William Wordsworth evoked his visionary "spots of time" and James Joyce his "epiphanies." In contrast, Margaret Lanterman, as the maternal narrator of the syndicated series, provides an extended period for the embrace between our lives' most common elements and their most rare.

The prologues are delivered by the Log Lady in all of her mundane glory; she wears her comfy signature sweater and peers through her familiar red-rimmed glasses, sitting in her rustic cabin in front of her fireplace, a cup of tea at her side. At the same time, she holds the extraordinary log through which she conducts larger energies and visions, which are usually unheard and unspoken, into ordinary conversation. As a narrator, Margaret achieves a small perfection for Lynch in his Hollywood career.

The ordinary television narrator is a powerful illusionist device. His reality—and it is almost always a he—presents itself as more actual than the fiction it introduces, doing so by direct address to the camera and an appeal to the authority of reason not to the mythology of the story it introduces. The typical narrator adds to the typical fictional narrative even more logic than it already contains, a double dose of the dominance of rationality and social labeling. In contrast, by donning the authority of the narrator, Margaret unobtrusively turns the role inside out. As a part of the fiction herself directly addressing the spectator about the fiction, she doubles the dose of the nonrational and the subconscious.

Margaret does not offer a logical handle on *Twin Peaks* in the style of Alistair Cooke, the prototypical "host," who seeks to ground in logic the events of *Masterpiece Theatre*'s dramatization with his user-friendly plot summaries and his historical contextualizations. In contrast, Margaret never gives us a summary of events—she typically avoids any reference to the story events on the show—or any conventional historical information bearing on the story. Nor does she give us the less formal historical handle—gossip about the making of *Twin Peaks*—to satisfy the obvious hunger for such detail. Rather, she asks us to come together in a social act of letting go of labels, handles, and formal contextualizations.

Margaret, as commentator, is successful in mothering us in the most profound and fruitful Lynchian sense. Unlike the illusionist narrator, she has a very strong sense of the limits of verbal articulation in bringing us closer to the art to which she introduces us. She tells us more than once that there are many things she cannot tell us, even that she is not *permitted* to say more. Instead, she draws our attention away from words and toward our senses and our imaginations. She seeks to make us better acquainted with *Twin Peaks* by encouraging us to be detectives in the sense that Lynch originally intended Dale Cooper to be. This kind of detective yearns neither for revenge nor for final solutions. Margaret points the way for audience empathy with Cooper as the Lynchian seeker. What is creamed corn? she asks. What is a tear? "How should we interpret the happy song of the meadowlark? Or the robust flavor of a wild strawberry?" In short, we are prodded not to take charge but to let go. She reminds us that the world is a great mystery and everything we see is a clue to it, but we are likely to put the clues together incorrectly. Receptivity must balance will in interpretation. The Log Lady counsels us to seek new connections to a renewed understanding of the real.

Margaret establishes herself as a Lynchian model of a Lynchian message. She tells us that everything in the world has something to teach us, but we must become sensitive to the animate force of what we obtusely call inanimate nature; she herself exemplifies that approach. "My log hears things I cannot hear. But my log tells me about the sounds, about the new words. Even though it has stopped growing larger, my log is aware." How to take action in an animate universe is the human problem that Margaret lays out for us. The "new words" are not the syntax of language; they are the animate materials of nature that Margaret counsels us to accept as our teacher. The "new words" form a syntax of "shapes, colors, textures . . . repetitions of shapes, contrasts." She suggests that the capacity to listen to nature as we act, rather than to impose on the world as if it were not alive, is the treasure of human life, the precious something that we all seek. It is the "wrong interpretation" that makes it "so hard to find" and "so difficult to attain."

Those moments in the prologues in which Margaret comes close to directly addressing events in the series place her variously as a validation of the spirit of the early episodes and a corrective to the encroaching stereotypes that asserted themselves in the latter part of the series. In the early prologues, she has an organic connection with the events; for example, her introduction to the episode in which Laura is buried explores the uses of grieving. The grief of the characters is central to this episode, and Margaret is the voice of what is voicelessly inherent in the episode as she examines the anatomy of grieving, musing on the adaptation of the human body for tears through the tear duct as well as pondering what a tear is. She further ponders the relationship of the emotion of sadness to the physicality of the tear and ruminates on the problem of reason in grieving. Rationally, we seek to establish limits for our grief because we don't know whether it will ever end, but we don't need to. All physical processes, although beyond our will, contain a natural shape and thus a natural finitude. "Of course it will end," says the Log Lady.

By the end of the series, when derring-do heroic control has invaded *Twin Peaks,* Margaret's glance seeks to rescue us from falling into cliché along with it. For example, there is her prologue to an episode in which a death mask of Windom Earle's late wife is placed in Cooper's room as a threat. In this episode the heroic task is catching and controlling the foe, but Margaret diverts us from this illusionist plotline toward what larger engagement is still possible, such as in the physical ramifications of the death mask of Caroline left on Cooper's pillow by Earle. She points out the paradox of the death mask, which combines our desire to possess the love that has left us and the distortion of the beloved since the lack of animation in death so changes physical dimensions. Thus she asks us to forget about Earle's plans and think about his spiritual distortions, how our love of the unbound energy of life sometimes can misdirect us toward rigid form.

Her most emphatic corrective of viewer direction is in the last prologue, in which she partially rectifies the ending of the series, an ending that so profoundly disappointed Lynch. In the last episode, Cooper falls into division between an evil and a good self, a representation of multiplicity as disease that is characteristic of illusionist realism. In contrast, Margaret tells us that division is the nature of the ordinary human condition: "Where there was once one, there are now two. Or were there always two? What is a reflection? A chance to *see* two? [emphasis added] Where there are chances for reflections there will always be two or more. Only when we are everywhere will there be just one." The show demonizes Cooper's division. Margaret asks us to identify with a perspective that takes the edge off of that bipolar logic. Two does not mean logical opposition (good/bad); rather, it is one possible version of the multiplicity, that is, the heterogeneity of life. As such, it should not stimulate us to a control reflex. The answer is not control but rather more receptiveness to the energies of the Red Room.

Of course, Margaret cannot undo the imbalances of the final episodes of the series, but she is there to do what she can, much like David Lynch in Hollywood. Lynch does not control; he proposes. Here, he proposes the Log Lady as a moderator who presents an example of an ideal spectator of *Twin Peaks*—and of all of his works. By virtue of her ordinary acculturation, the Log Lady is very much of this time and place, and she knows the shapes and boundaries of ordinary life. At the same time, by virtue of her receptivity to much that is nonverbal and beyond culture, she fruitfully exceeds the limits of stereotypical priorities.

Most recently, in *Lost Highway,* Lynch has explored through a form of inversion another way of illuminating the need for receptivity. His latest is a film that never gets beyond a road of troubles and doom, as the title indicates. *Lost Highway* concerns Fred Madison (Bill Pullman), a man obsessed by a desire to possess and control his wife Renee (Patricia Arquette), a sultry redhead who reflects irreconcilable contradictions. Aloof with Fred, Renee, unaccountably, unbuttons with Andy (Michael Massee), a crude and value-free drug dealer and pimp.

Fred is doomed by his relationship to Renee not because of *her* inconsistencies but because of *his* obsessions. Through Fred's tenacity concerning Renee, instead of portraying the rewards of the will to lose one's will Lynch portrays the catastrophe of being unable to do so. Previously, the elasticity of time and space have seemed to be the way out of the maze for the hero who "lets go." However, in *Lost Highway* Lynch shows us that should time and space turn themselves inside out, so long as a person cannot be free of his own will-to-power, that person will still travel down the road to doom and destruction, the lost highway.

In brief, the story traces the life of Fred Madison, a successful jazz musician. Understated in conversation, Fred wails out his frustration at finding Renee always just beyond his grasp, when he plays his saxophone "braying like a beast," as it says in the script (p. 14). Lynch's sound design for the ringing telephone when Fred calls his wife from work complements the screaming high notes he

65. Fred obsessively craves possession of Renee.

rocks the stage with; the stylized sound of the phone ringing vainly in Fred's empty house is virtually Fred himself screaming for Renee. The self-absorbed nature of his continuous grasping for possession is particularly clear during an ignominious episode in which Renee passionlessly submits to his consummation of a sexual desire that is decidedly not mutual. In this scene, Fred's back all but eclipses Renee, as if she weren't there at all, except when we see her hand pat his shoulder with a pitying gesture that completes Fred's humiliation (see figure 65). Shortly afterward, Fred's life moves onto the lost highway when it appears that Renee has been murdered. The police certainly believe that to be the case and cart him off to jail as the prime suspect. The Lynchian enigma that suffuses this plot development is that we as the audience have no direct evidence that she is dead.

The only evidence appears to be on the last of a series of videotapes that mysteriously arrive at the Madison home in unmarked envelopes. At first, the tapes show eerie shots of the house. Why should anyone want to take these pictures? Then a new tape shows high-angle shots of Fred and Renee asleep that seem logistically impossible. Who could have raised himself to this height and taken these pictures while the Madisons slept? Renee is terrified by these tapes. Then she is no longer there, and a tape arrives for Fred alone. It shows him kneeling over Renee's dismembered corpse with a demonic expression on his face. Of importance is the difference in texture of the shots of the exterior of the house and those that represent the interior action. The exterior images are sharply defined; the interior images are so stippled by scan lines that they are no more than evocative, clear enough to startle and confused enough to be almost indecipherable—like a dream one is trying to remember.

These mysteries are left unexamined by the justice system, which sentences Fred to death, a sentence he appears to escape when he disappears from Death Row in an inexplicable way. He undergoes a painful transformation into Pete Dayton (Balthazar Getty), a young car mechanic (about eight years Fred's junior) unknown to him before his transformation, giving the astonished prison authorities no choice but to release "Pete Dayton." But Fred's escape into a time of youth and into the space of another body, free of a history that has entangled him in a fatal maze of events, nevertheless becomes another form of entrapment. After Pete's return to work, one of his regular customers, Mr. Eddy (Robert Loggia), a gravel-voiced thug who almost kills in retaliation for being tailgated, shows up with a new girlfriend, a bombshell named Alice Wakeland (also Patricia Arquette) who is a younger, blonder, and wilder version of Renee. Is she Renee? In some mysterious way, yes. A photograph in which the two appear ultimately becomes a picture in which Renee alone is present. In any case, Renee is not dead; she reappears at the end of the film. Although this doppelganger is never explained, it hovers over the film—the effect Alice has on Pete suggests Renee's continued presence in the story. Although Pete has a girlfriend named Sheila (Natasha Gregson Wagner) who loves him deeply, Fred/Pete develops the same obsession for Alice that Fred had for Renee (see figures 66 and 67). At first, there does seem to be one improvement in Fred's situation as Pete; Alice exhibits the passion for Pete that Fred craved from Renee. But eventually Alice too withholds herself, as we shall see below. Moreover, her desires, like those of Renee, translate into a dead end for Fred/Pete when she incites Pete to murder Andy, her pimp, for his money—the same Andy who was a friend of Renee's—and causes Pete to incur the wrath of Mr. Eddy. Fred subsequently defends himself by killing Mr. Eddy at the end of the film after Pete turns into Fred again. The Fred who reappears has been transformed by his metamorphosis. No longer an introvert almost constipated into agonized stasis, Fred now wears Pete's black leather jacket and emits Pete's brooding, violent energy. Now we see *Fred* kill, and again he is pursued by the police for murder. Clearly, no matter where Fred goes in the universe, one way or another his willful obsessions continue to lead to a position as one of the damned.

If *Lost Highway* were a high-concept, plot-driven film, it would take as its model the classic film noir *D.O.A.*, which depicts the world as a hell in which human beings are locked into a downward spiral of fate. An unrelieved plot of this type would seem to indicate that Lynch has capitulated to definitions of the subconscious

66–67. Frame Pair: Pete turns away from Sheila toward Alice and an old, baser desire.

that mark it as a mess of transgressive and chaotic impulses. However, the reverse is true. If *Lost Highway* is a synonym for the slippery slope down which Fred tumbles, it also testifies to his entrapment in the baser elements of his involuntary energies—his is a stunted relationship to the subconscious that has not (yet?) resulted in his emergence into the larger, more beneficent powers of the imagination. That is why he is stranded in a seemingly endless compulsive denial of human connection.

The secret of Fred's inauspicious fate is signified by the presence in the film of a vampiric-looking person known as the Mystery Man (Robert Blake), whom Fred "meets" when he attends a party at Andy's house with Renee. The Mystery Man, made up with white face and red lipstick in a manner dramatically reminiscent of Ben in *Blue Velvet,* is immediately evoked as the toxic depths of Fred's subconscious. This is made evident when the Mystery Man encourages Fred to call his home from the party, and Fred finds that the Mystery Man answers the phone call at the Madison house. When he asks how the Mystery Man got into his house, the enigmatic person responds, "You invited me. It's not my habit to go where I'm not wanted" (see figure 68). This interchange is of supreme importance in understanding where Lynch is taking us in our wild ride down *Lost Highway*. The intimation is that Fred and the Mystery Man are aspects of the same person, a new Lynchian representation of that place in the subconscious dominated by frightening elements of ourselves.

When, at the end of the film, the Mystery Man comes at Fred with a video camera grotesquely connected to him as if it were his eye, it is clear that the tapes are the productions of Fred's most toxic part of himself. Now the supposed murder of Renee leaps off the pages of the police blotter and onto the plane of imagination. Like the destruction of the baby in *Eraserhead*, the wife-murder in *Lost Highway* is a psychic drama. The tapes are exteriorizations of messages Fred's toxic will emits in Renee's direction, accounting for her terror. The tape of the murder is Fred's message to himself about how his possessive rages obliterate Renee and leave him alone with only his malignant desires, a message he takes literally, as do the police, and so does not understand. Unlike Jeffrey in *Blue Velvet*, Fred has not moved beyond the toxic, lower elements of the subconscious; indeed he has virtually become Frank. Nor has Fred chosen, as does Sailor in *Wild at Heart*, to align himself with the organic unity of life; he makes the opposite choice of annihilation.

68. Fred encounters, in a strange Mystery Man, his own toxic energies.

The audience's poetic apprehension of Fred's situation saves the moviegoer from drowning in Fred's ambiguities. Much of the film's poetry is rendered through the visual beauty of *Lost Highway*—many critics and fans will no doubt consider this Lynch's most beautiful film to date, full of the freedom of *Eraserhead*, but augmented by the richness of Lynch's experiences since then. In addition, there are also many narrative means of creating a perspective on Fred's behavior. Early in the film, we watch Fred interacting with the lower reaches of his subconscious through their externalization in the Mystery Man but refusing to recognize these forces as his own. After the humiliation of his unreturned sexual passion, we watch him perceive the Mystery Man's face where Renee's should be. Later when the Mystery Man presents himself at Andy's party, he is wearing the same shade of lipstick as Renee. The Mystery Man is similar to Ben in more than appearance; both are male projections of interior malignity onto the female (see Chapter 4). Projection is also suggested at the end of the film when Alice is conflated with the Mystery Man. After sadistically telling Pete that she will never be his possession, Alice walks naked into a nearby shack. Now that the inability to possess the woman has re-entered the story, Pete turns back into Fred, who follows Alice into the shack and finds there only the Mystery Man. Thus though it may appear on the surface to represent both Alice and Renee as the betraying femme fatale of film noir, *Lost Highway* is not misogynistic. All betrayal emanates from Fred himself, as does the violence supposedly instigated by Alice. It is the Mystery Man who hands Fred the weapons he uses, and we soon see that the Mystery Man and Fred are one and the same. Fred's craving for Renee is not love, or even lust, but rather a projection of his own inability to encounter and acknowledge in any way the baser energies of his subconscious. The film thus keeps us from identifying with Fred and invites us to identify with the freedom it gives us to see what Fred's denials have wrought.

Significantly, soon after Fred has transformed into Pete, his lust for Alice drives away the chance for connection and love that is finally offered to him in Pete's girlfriend Sheila. When Sheila walks out on Pete/Fred for betraying her with Alice once too often, the possibility for Lynch's customary heroic transcendence into the life of nature and people disappears. Furthermore, organic interconnection and the finer aspect of the subconscious represented by love are powerfully related here not only to women but to women's perception. Sheila is the only character in the film who is capable of consciously perceiving the duality of Pete's existence and who refuses to deny what she sees. (Pete's parents steadfastly turn away from *their* knowledge of his unusual situation.) Her

fleeting presence tells us how little connectedness is possible for
Fred/Pete.

Fred/Pete's rejection of Sheila for Alice/Renee (as he projects his
toxic impulses onto her) marks him as a seeker who has rejected
the feminine secret of connectedness. In so doing, he opts for the
kind of effacement of femininity that we see in Frank's penchant
for Ben in *Blue Velvet*. Natasha Gregson Wagner's resemblance to
her mother Natalie Wood, and Balthazar Getty's James Dean–like
brooding energy bring some poignant resonances to the estrangement from love in *Lost Highway*. Here, the great romance of the
1950s, *Rebel without a Cause,* is undergoing end-of-the-century
changes that suggest painful transformations of midcentury cultural fantasies about families, love, and male identity.

Fred's relationship to the Mystery Man is, of course, reminiscent of Leland's relationship to BOB in *Twin Peaks*—the demon of
the contaminated levels of the subconscious. By making the possessed character the protagonist in *Lost Highway*, Lynch gives us a
closer look at the nature of such demonic energies. We might be
traveling inside the head of—though not the story of—Walter
Neff (Fred MacMurray), Billy Wilder's obsessed insurance sales-
man in *Double Indemnity*. In inviting us into intimate contact with
such an interior landscape, Lynch links the poison of debased
imagination more clearly than ever to a denial of the importance
of feminine energy. He also clarifies his sense that in the final
analysis none of the blots upon existence represented in his films,
no matter how monstrous, indicates the kind of indelible evil that
is associated with either the religious doctrine of Original Sin or
secular pessimism about the subconscious.

The new prologues to *Twin Peaks,* Margaret's fireside chats in
front of a boarded-up fireplace that she refuses to fill with *that
kind of fire,* are advertisements for Lynch by Lynch, with the
Lynchian rumble-whoosh scoring every healing word she says.
They are Lynch's state-of-the-union addresses. Margaret is our
earthly vision indicating that everyone can be raised to the liberating paradoxes of the language of the wind. This is even true of her
opposite, the "lost" Fred/Pete who is last seen pursued by a cara-
van of police cars, inundated by the siren sound and the glamor of
the revolving police light, bellowing into the night a reverberating

"NO!" Is this Fred's negativity, his persistent denial of the higher truth, or at last a desire to put a stop to his own poisonous indulgences? Perhaps it is all three, a moment in which bloodstained past, agonized present, and possibly hopeful future are balanced. In the final frames, Fred, even though pursued by the law, is still managing to evade its clutches, thus embodying Lynch's hope and implying the possible yes after the final "NO." As Lynch phrased it for me, Fred retains eternally the possibility of reaching the humanizing level of the subconscious with its power to connect in a wholesome way. In Lynch's words, "The movie just wasn't long enough."

Fred's failures point toward the road we must not and need not take, and Lynch remains a source of faith in a terrifying world. Shall we dare to hope that—in an ever-new variety of ways—future Lynchian protagonists will continue to move us beyond the final negative into the affirmative?

Industrial Symphony
No. 1: The Dream of
the Broken Hearted

We can vividly see the connection between Lynch's conceptions of movement in painting and his development of story structure in a tape of his performance piece, *Industrial Symphony No. 1: The Dream of the Broken Hearted,* which is virtually an animated Lynch painting infused with fragments of linear narrative. *Industrial Symphony* was originally presented on stage at the Brooklyn Academy of Music in New York City on November 10, 1989, and was later recreated on videotape. The videotape was created from tapes made of four full performances from a variety of different angles. (Hard as it is to believe, we have the word of Michael Anderson, the Little Man from *Twin Peaks,* that the four performances were executed consecutively in one day.) The tape is thus not a simple recording of a staged performance but a composition for the screen. It is upon this composition, which presents ordinary life as a theatrical spectacle, that I will comment.

The piece presents a brokenhearted woman's life on the stage of her heart, on which she appears in multiple carnivalesque disguises. The piece also contains other figures that operate as doubles of her and her distressing situation—she has a double in the prologue to the performance piece and a dancing double in the piece itself, a double that is a twenty-foot-high red deer, a double that reflects her live presence in television images, and multiple doubles in the form of a platoon of Kewpie dolls that multiply her likeness in dozens of industrial parodies of her blonde, child-like appearance. Her surroundings also take on a spectacular appearance. Ordinary high-tension wires, industrial paraphernalia, and—the *sine qua non* of daily life—the car are lit and positioned to simultaneously appear as objects of use and objects to be gazed at. Construction workers and newspeople act out functional tasks that are executed in the presence of showy chorus girls and prom queens who radiate manufactured glamor. In *Industrial Symphony*, suffering is synchronously a visceral sensation and a machine-tooled cabaret act.

Taped while Lynch was working on *Wild at Heart, Industrial Symphony* narrates an alternative to the terminal moment of that film in which a woman is *almost* abandoned. Indeed, a prologue Lynch added to the taped version of *Industrial Symphony* employs the stars of *Wild at Heart* in the inversion of their film roles. In the prologue, Laura Dern is abandoned during a phone conversation with her lover, Nicolas Cage. In *Wild at Heart,* the air carries the Good Witch into a carnivalized urban setting to save the lovers; in *Industrial Symphony,* the female protagonist is abandoned to the insubstantial artifice of urban forms. The words of the phone conversation are all of her lover that is present for her, and they are inadequate. The relationship dwindles to the final click of a terminated telephone conversation. The aftermath of this click of disconnection is the main body of the video; it strips down to its essentials the mystery at the heart of this narrative—what is connection?

Lynch's answer is that connectedness does not depend on exterior social machinery. When all external show fails to sustain the protagonist, she maintains a primary (interior?) connection to the universe. To dramatize the fullness of existence, Lynch creates the visual aspects of his performance piece as compositions of levitated forms in the rippling surges of light and darkness that replicate the ground of his paintings. The pressure of the boundless on the bounded in this narrative produces the familiar Lynchian carnivalesque alterations in the appearance of the ordinary elements of cultural reality.

Industrial Symphony uses the narrative strategies of Lynch's painting to tell a dramatic story of an abandoned, brokenhearted woman. Called "a dream," the narrative creates a confluence of the fragments of rational realism with the flow of the subconscious which is typical of the dream state. In this state, the woman's wailing for her lost lover is saturated with the obvious traits of the carnivalesque: costume, disguise, and the evocation of the theatrical in the midst of ordinary life. The woman is represented as a cabaret singer, although she is not placed within the confines of a cabaret but in some boundless location that suggests an urban street. *Industrial Symphony* meditates on the road not taken in Lynch's *Wild at Heart*. Tellingly, a fundamental similarity between the two works is more important than their seemingly crucial plot differences (the loss of the beloved in the former and the reunion with the beloved in the latter); both celebrate the blessings of the real that sustain us whether a particular love relationship endures or doesn't. In *Wild at Heart,* there is a Lynchian consolation for the spectator about the blessings of the real that inform enduring love, but Lynch's sense of the blessings of the real also informs the representation of *lost* love in *Industrial Symphony.*

The main section of *Industrial Symphony* features singer Julee Cruise as the nameless, heartbroken female protagonist. She poses the question of what we are to make of the carnival of her life. With respect to conventional coding, she is a weak, ineffectual, pathetic presence. Abandoned, she does not strike out with the pluck we have been led to expect from a heroine—who might at least have the decency, if we are to take an interest in her, to be a man about her situation. Wispy and dressed in a pale, gauzy prom gown reminiscent of the styles of the 1950s, she sings about her sorrow. Suffused by pale golden misty light, she is a frail apparition in the middle of a fragmented industrial setting of wires, a tall towerlike structure of bars, an automobile body, wooden sawhorses, chemical drums, and a hospital gurney on which something lies. She doesn't *do* anything to take charge of her situation. Rather, she dreams about it, sings about it, and floats in it.

Through most of the piece, the woman sings floating high above the stage. Her theatrical levitation is part of Lynch's heterogeneous use of space and part of the carnivalesque use of the energy as well as the order of space which relates to Bakhtin's conceptualization of the carnivalesque: "*Up, down, the stairway, the threshold, the foyer, the landing* take on the meaning of a 'point' where *crisis,* radical change, an unexpected turn of fate takes place, where decisions are made, where the forbidden line is overstepped, where one is renewed or perishes" (Bakhtin p. 169). However, for Lynch, the line between the carnival and the noncarnival worlds is not a forbidden one, and the either/or of "make or break" does not apply. He uses the carnival as a lens that conveys to us the hope that remains for the hopeless.

As the woman begins to sing of her heartbreak, she sees floating, painful images of herself and her lost lover in two dancers who writhe tormented in the air, struggling with the confines of an industrial tower of bars or falling free in confusion. The pain seems to end when, later in the piece, she falls to earth and sees her situation in more grounded images—seemingly more happy—the images of popular songs from the 1950s. Situated inside a car trunk, a carnivalized reminder of the once-favored "make-out" place, the brokenhearted woman is also surrounded by the seemingly comforting images of herself transmitted to television screens by technicians with handheld cameras. Doubled by her own television image, the protagonist sings a stereotypical "remember how happy we were" song. But we soon see that when the protagonist is on the earth, instead of finding the solid place that seemed to be denied her in her floating state, we are confronted with a more insidious form of ungroundedness. Once she has landed, she is among the fragments of a faux reality evoked by bad popular songs that suggest a mindless industrial repetition of machine-made dreams.

Lynch's allusions to the fifties permit us to see that the protagonist is enthralled with clichés. Two girls dressed like prom queens sway beside the car as if they were singing backup to her performance. At the same time, a chorus line of plumed girls gyrates in the background. Reporters snap pictures, and construction workers mill about. The heroine feels happy until the performances are interrupted by toy-sized airplanes which cause a fearful dispersal of the assembled cast. As the girls, the construction workers, and the reporters run frantically seeking cover, dozens of pink plastic baby dolls descend on wires as if parachuting out of the planes.

In this transition from the clichés of bliss to the shock that evicts her from them, the protagonist is agonized by her isolation and bewildered by her lack of something to grab onto as an anchor—which had seemed to arrive in the form of popular images of love and glamor. The insubstantialness of these images suggests that they are unequal to subconscious desire; the heroine's mistaken belief that they can grant her security is the problem, not her free fall. She grasps in vain at the harmony that seems to be promised in the banal songs of young love—hair ruffled by the wind during a lakeside picnic.

But not getting what she wants leads the protagonist to something better. She finds herself with a given reality; the spinning world will contain her in a satisfactory way while she "hopes for love amid high-tension wires," as Michael Anderson felicitously phrased it for me. Our heroine receives only the fantasy of consolation from her literal interpretation of harmonious love songs that sentimentalize her situation. Acculturated to the representation of women as naturally "out of control," we may at first think that Lynch is only being stereotypical in giving us a heroine who cannot take charge of her situation. Yet, even if we are not sure exactly what the protagonist understands by the end of this dream narrative, Lynch brings important changes to the stereotype for us. It is precisely in our growing sympathy for the validity of her inability to command that we become privy to hope.

The brokenhearted woman is actually saved by what seems to imperil her. The strafing attack on her space by the toy-sized bomber planes that drop the Kewpies, seemingly innumerable machine-made replications of the protagonist, chases away the false icons of glamor and romance. Ironically, the apparent attack of the Kewpies turns into Lynch's representation of a better aspect of popular culture, the fruitful intervention of a collective unconscious chasing out mechanical repetition. The Kewpies floating in space are also cultural artifacts with an unexpectedly fresh energy that is at first misinterpreted as threatening but turns out to be toxic only to tired clichés (see figure 69). We begin to understand that the planes are a blessing in disguise, for once the delusion of coherence has passed, our heroine is free to face the real.

Now she is back in midair again, surprised by the sparkle of a shower of glitter. Less tormented, she may be opening up to a new understanding about freedom and to a receptivity to the universe unimpeded by familiar but false comforts. In this way, *Industrial Symphony* is a good example of how Lynch frequently uses a heroine, as opposed to a hero, to illuminate our grounding in the real—a mysterious floating stability in a spinning world.

The reality of being "out of control" is established at the beginning of the piece through light and sound. Through the chiaroscuro of light and dark and through music, the piece shows a universe that is primarily energy, bursting from its origins of light and sound to which narrative form is a late addition. The piece begins with piercing bursts of strobe light which cut the darkness, making visible in momentary fragments of light the objects in the *mise-en-scène*. In the initial moments of representation, light bursts are accompanied by sound vibration that is not yet music—rumble, electric static, a sound that suggests a surface is cracking. As the bursts end and we settle into a pervasive but very low-key lighting, the sound transmutes slowly into music, first as the

69. The descent of the Kewpies only seems like an attack.

twang of the bass note of a guitar, then joined by a chromatic, vibrato organ effect and an asymmetrical jazz drum interpenetrated by two levels of sirens wailing, one high-pitched and screaming, the other lower. Then, after the given energies of light and sound begin to take culturally recognizable forms, verbal articulation becomes possible.

Words do not organize this space but rather float in it, like the heroine (and like the words on Lynch's canvases). Here, words perform exactly as Julia Kristeva describes the performance of carnivalized language: "On the . . . stage of carnival, language parodies and relativizes itself, repudiating its role in representation; in so doing, it provokes laughter but remains incapable of detaching itself from representation" (p. 79). In the protagonist's opening song, "Up in Flames," the power of the lyrics to structure the situation is limited: "I fell for you, baby, like a bomb/Now my love's gone up in flames." The reference to fire in this wail about lost love is a pun on the concept of the torch song. The words considered out of context smack of parody:

My head's full of smoke, heart's full of pain
Your tender love is gone, my love remains
You shoulda shot me, baby, my life is gone
You coulda shot me, baby,
I hear those sirens scream my name
I know my love's gone up in flames.

Words ordinarily are expected to define meaning. Here they are only the best that the heroine's discourse can do under the pressure of the mysteries of overwhelming emotion. The purely chromatic music accompanying the words intensifies the impression that our heroine's "disorder" will not be brought under control.

Industrial Symphony projects onto a screen Lynch's painterlike will to lose his will, letting Hollywood's notion of reality go into free fall. It presents what we have imagined as the weak feminine position—what is as pathetic in Hollywood as an abandoned woman?—as a position of receptivity and promise. It challenges us to expand our sympathies and to let go of our daily assumptions about survival in a daring way. The piece is a marker on the boundary between what Lynch does with movie narrative in Hollywood and what he does with it when he treats film as he does his painting. It points one way toward the dynamism of his commercial movies and another toward the originality of his canvases. It is pertinent because he continues as an artist to cross and recross the border between the visual daring of his painting and photography and the conventions of Hollywood narrative. The piece is also eye-opening in its revelations about the connection between David Lynch's abiding commitment to painting and the simultaneous urgency of his drive to work in the Hollywood venue.

Notes

INTRODUCTION

1. Feminist film criticism has been largely unreceptive to Lynch's films. A typical example is Diana Hume George's "Lynching Women: A Feminist Reading of *Twin Peaks*" in Lavery's *Full of Secrets: Critical Approaches to Twin Peaks*, 109–119. On the other hand, Diane Stevenson, also in *Full of Secrets*, applauds Lynch's treatment of incest in *Twin Peaks: Fire Walk with Me* in "Family Romance, Family Violence, and the Fantastic in *Twin Peaks*," 70–81. Furthermore, Lynne Layton, in *"Blue Velvet:* A Parable of Male Development*,"* cites *Blue Velvet* as a chronicle of the problems posed by the dominant model of male maturation.

2. Readers unfamiliar with the fascinating theorization of the shot-reverse shot may wish to consult Kaja Silverman, *The Subject of Semiotics*, 201–236. Silverman gives a full account of the grammar and gender implications of this shot pattern (pp. 201, 222–236).

3. Anyone wishing to find a feminist semiotic position on the relationship between the linguistic and the real should consult Silverman's *The Subject of Semiotics*. Silverman is particularly useful for her explorations of the gendered implications of semiotics in literature and film.

1 PORTRAIT OF THE DIRECTOR

1. The struggles of Orson Welles with "the powers that were" at that time in Hollywood are painfully documented in a number of sources, noteworthy among them are: André Bazin, *Orson Welles, A Critical View*, tr. Jonathan Rosenbaum (New York: Harper and Row, 1978); Orson Welles and Peter Bogdanovitch, *This is Orson Welles*, ed. Jonathan Rosenbaum (New York: HarperCollins, 1992); and Bret Wood, "Kiss Hollywood Goodbye: Orson Welles and *The Lady From Shanghai*," *Video Watchdog* 23 (May–July 1994):

40–53. The best and most entertaining documentation of Alfred Hitchcock's creative wars is the transcription of a series of interviews with him by François Truffaut, with the collaboration of Helen G. Scott, modestly titled, *Hitchcock/Truffaut: The Definitive Study of Alfred Hitchcock by François Truffaut*, rev. ed. (New York: Simon and Schuster, 1983).

2. Other books that seek to discuss the career of David Lynch as a whole include the following: Robert Fischer, *David Lynch: Die dunkel Seite der Seele* (The Dark Side of the Soul); Michel Chion, *David Lynch*; Kenneth C. Kaleta, *David Lynch*; and John Alexander, *The Films of David Lynch*. Fischer, Kaleta, and Alexander take strictly chronological approaches to the work. Where they explore for foundations for Lynch's movies, they find them in biographical criticism, citing imagined aspects of Lynch's life as evidence, and, in the traditions of Hollywood, citing perceived influences from conventional genres. The methodologies of these critics are typical of early struggles to open up a new subject of inquiry, both in their passion to know and in the often reductive results (i.e., David Lynch must have had an unhappy childhood). Chion represents a step forward in Lynch criticism, arriving at a more complex study that is quite perceptive and helpful about the visual and aural details of Lynch's films.

Happily, there is also *Full of Secrets: Critical Approaches to Twin Peaks*, edited by David Lavery. Although a highly specialized book, dedicated only to the Lynch/Frost television series, it is, because of the heterogeneity of the critical approaches it contains, a useful introduction to all of Lynch's work. Moreover, *Full of Secrets* provides essential scholarly material in its appendices, which contain detailed cast lists and episode breakdowns for *Twin Peaks*.

3. One of the most fascinating links between Lynch's use of narrative in painting and in film is his performance piece, *Industrial Symphony No. 1*, written with Angelo Badalamenti. Interested readers may turn to the Appendix of this book for a discussion of it as a nexus point between Lynch's origins in painting and his evolution as a Hollywood director.

2 WILD AT HEART

1. Concerning the mother-daughter relationship, readers may be interested in the contrast between Lynch's film and the book of the same name by Barry Gifford on which the film was loosely based. Gifford depicts Marietta as an enervated, sexless, greying woman whose sole interest is the daughter she cannot bear to lose. Gifford's Marietta remembers a dull marriage with a man who lost his wits working with lead-based paint and finally set himself on fire. Gifford's Johnnie is the sweet, bumbling detective he is in the film, "shoe-salesman-like" as Lynch says. However, in the book his vague liaison with Marietta has all the earmarks of her previous relationship with Lula's father, one that endures through inertia. In Gifford's book, Marietta's closest rela-

tionship is with a female friend to whom she complains endlessly. Lula resembles her mother when the novel ends and Sailor leaves her in a tumbleweed landscape in which the emptiness of cultural forms makes them a cruel illusion of stability and only biologically based relationships last. Thus, Lynch's film could not be further in tone from Gifford's novel in which the absence of will means the absence of a possible future or of any connection except the regressive bond between mother and child.

2. A reading of *Wild at Heart* as a "road movie" derives from an illusionist framework that is hard pressed to deal with Lynch's portrayal of the subconscious elements in Marietta's representation and in the allusions to *The Wizard of Oz* as the spectator's (and characters') nexus with reality. In emphasizing narrative action, Kaleta fails to take into consideration Lynch's priorities and emphases. By contrast, Chion, who is quite sensitive to the central importance of Marietta and of the Oz allusions, does not make this mistake in classification: "*Sailor et Lula* [the title of the film in France] est en effet un film d'enfance, un film d'enfant voyant tout en grand et en contraste, et les références au *Magicien d'Oz* vont dans ce sens" (p. 162) [The references to *The Wizard of Oz* in *Sailor and Lula* evoke the film's central preoccupation with the innocent eye].

3. The important mother-daughter relationship in *Wild at Heart* is rare in a Hollywood film outside of the maternal melodrama. Thus readers may be interested in pondering the relationship between *Wild at Heart* and this conventional form. In the maternal melodrama, the story generally teaches us that a continuing relationship with the mother will inevitably cause damage. Thus its plot is usually a process by which the potentially disordered mother-child relationship is humbled before the restorative principle of logic represented as masculine will. *Stella Dallas* (1937) and *Mildred Pierce* (1945) are the two classic examples.

Intriguingly, the first film David Lynch ever saw, Henry King's *Wait 'Til the Sun Shines, Nellie* (1952), was a maternal melodrama, though Lynch does not remember it in detail. As both he and Peggy Reavey told me, he was not an avid movie fan as a child and did not come away from what movies he did see with scenes or performances burned into his mind. Thus, it is unlikely that there is any explicit connection between this 1950s melodrama and his movies. Nevertheless, the central project of *Wait 'Til the Sun Shines, Nellie,* a title that grows cloyingly patronizing on closer acquaintance with the film, is to carry out an exemplary patriarchal revenge on the spirited wife and mother. This particularly irritating film goes to great lengths to punish Nellie because of her yearning for horizons larger than those of a small town and to validate the dishonesty of her husband who tricks her into losing her dreams.

Interested readers may find the following selective list useful: Linda Williams, "'Something Else Besides a Mother': *Stella Dallas* and the Maternal Melodrama," *Cinema Journal* 24, no. 1 (Fall 1984): 2–27; E. Ann Kaplan, "The

Case of the Missing Mother: Maternal Issues in Vidor's *Stella Dallas*," *Heresies* 16 (1983): 81–85; Pam Cook, "Duplicity in Mildred Pierce" in *Women in Film Noir*, ed. E. Ann Kaplan (London: British Film Institute, 1978): 68–82; Linda Williams, "Feminist Film Theory: *Mildred Pierce* and the Second World War" in *Female Spectators*, ed. E. Deidre Pribram (London: Verso, 1988): 12–30; Mary Ann Doane, *The Desire to Desire: The Woman's Film of the 1940s*, (Bloomington: Indiana University Press, 1987); and Thomas Elsasser, "Tales of Sound and Fury: Observations on the Family Melodrama," *Monogram* 4 (1972): 2–15.

4. My interpretation of the purity of the sex scenes between Sailor and Lula coincides with Lynch's assessment of the scenes, as well as that of Jonathan Rosenbaum, coauthor with J. Hoberman of the first book to mention Lynch's work in detail, *Midnight Movies*. Rosenbaum does not like *Wild at Heart* but nevertheless ventured a comment about the protagonists' pristine sexuality in conversation with me. However, other critics disagree. Kathleen Murphy believes that "Like precocious preteens, their [Sailor and Lula's] climaxes come more in shared smokes and anecdotes than in their bodies' most secret places. Fucking is just the jig they do in bed . . ." (p. 62).

5. The fundamental characteristic of the eye-of-the-duck scene, according to Lynch, is its essentialness to narrative even though it is not narrative in character. As I see it, his description of this element of the film may seem whimsical, but it is *the* crucial clue to his narrative sense. Here, after all, is where the subconscious makes its deepest mark on the film and is in most tension with the plot. Significantly, even Lynch's most negative critics like this scene, though they misunderstand it as a gratuitous piece of showmanship. Murphy refers to the scene as "a sequence that is Lynch at his hallucinatory best" (p. 62). Perhaps there is a place of sensibility underneath the paroxysms of verbal abuse in which Lynch's critics really *do* understand what he is doing.

6. Given the high-voltage nature of the abortion issue, I feel that I must note here that it would be an act of resistance to the film's context to jump to the conclusion that there is any anti-abortion message in this scene. The abortion is clearly not Lula's free choice but rather a previous instance of Marietta's rage to control her daughter's life. We see Lula's pain-racked face during the abortion compressed into the outline of a medical lens. There is a similarity between this image and the image in which we see Sailor trapped within the Wicked Witch's crystal ball, both when he is in jail and when Bobby Peru is ensnaring him, suggesting that what Sailor thinks is choice is not.

7. Considering the radical responses of the preview audiences, some readers may find it as interesting as I do that criticism of *Wild at Heart* barely recognizes the presence of Farragut's death scene. For example, Kaleta doesn't mention it at all in his chapter on *Wild at Heart;* neither does Murphy, who

salivates adjectives and adverbs about everything else in her critique of the film. Alexander merely describes it in one perfunctory sentence. Chion has little more to say about the scene than that it repelled even Lynch's fans. Devin McKinney, who is more comfortable with Lynch's address to the subconscious than many critics, compares this scene with ". . . the meanest trick Buñuel ever played. . . . This is one time Lynch doesn't go as far as his predecessor" (p. 43). Indeed, we never saw how far Lynch did go. In any case, McKinney understands that the scene is not perversity on the artist's part. He likens Lynch to those artists who "took the ideals of beauty and truth, of poetry itself, crossed them with images of mutilation, deformity, and decadence, and found that beauty and truth would not only survive but thrive on them, triggering new associations and responses" (p. 42).

8. The scene of Johnnie Farragut's death is one of the few instances of structural harm done to a Lynch film by popular misconceptions of what Lynch is doing. Mary Sweeney, who worked as an associate editor on *Wild at Heart* and as the editor of several *Twin Peaks* episodes and the film *Fire Walk with Me,* told me that, as originally cut by film editor Duwayne Dunham, the dynamics of this murder were more explicit but so horrified test audiences that most of them walked out during this scene. In the original cut, after Johnnie was decapitated by a gunshot, Juana applied the bloody head directly to her body to finish off her sexual experience. The physical horror of this scene, misperceived by the test audiences as gratuitous obscenity, was in fact a searing representation of the obscenity of the controlling will that conventional Hollywood films have glamorized. Unfortunately, this excised footage no longer exists to be reintegrated into the film at some future date when audiences are better prepared to experience Lynch's artistry. However, as Johnnie's death scene exists in the final cut, it performs the same visceral function as the unexpurgated version but stops just short of the unbearable images.

9. Johnnie's death scene is of great interest within the context of Freudian glosses on scopophilia—the lust of the eyes—that have been used by feminist film critics to discuss the quasi-pornographic use of the feminine body in all Hollywood film. Because pornographic movies typically feature only the most perfunctory plot, it was customary to distinguish their gratuitous display of the erotic body from the use of the body within the parameters of a "socially redeeming" story. However, Laura Mulvey's "Visual Pleasure and Narrative Cinema," *Screen* 26, no 3 (Autumn 1975): 6–18, became a key feminist film text by asserting that all Hollywood movies use the erotic female body gratuitously. Women exist in mass-media movies, Mulvey insists, to provide male spectators a "safe" pleasure from the potentially castrating female body by constructing the female body as a glamorous spectacle at a distance from the viewer. Instead of castration anxiety, Hollywood's glamorized woman evokes voyeuristic pleasure by means of which the male spectator feels a form of

sadistic control. Farragut's death scene in *Wild at Heart* represents an interesting variation on the representation of the ideal scopophilic distance for voyeurism. Johnnie's death portrays voyeurism as captivity and simultaneously represents pornographic spectacle as precisely the road *to* castration. (The bullet to his head evokes the Freudian association between decapitation and castration.)

10. Jane Feuer's *The Hollywood Musical* provides an interesting theorization of musical movies that suggests to me the brilliance of Lynch's decision to use its conventions through allusion to the musical film *The Wizard of Oz* and to Presley's songs in *Wild at Heart*. As Feuer points out, one of the defining traits of the Hollywood movie musical is its customary reflexivity. Musicals refer to themselves as movies by being about characters who are putting on shows; they also highlight the performatory nature of character roles and even gender roles (see especially pp. 1–22 and 49–65). Finally, they are almost inevitably about the advantages of the spontaneity and direct contact with the audience in popular culture and its capacity for bonding the community, in comparison with the artifices and elitism of high culture. Indeed, Lynch reflects this understanding of popular culture's conventions when he chooses popular music and musical movies as the manifestation of the popular collective unconscious. He even follows the musical tradition of negative association with classical music by using sickeningly sweet renditions of classical pieces when the violence of Mr. Reindeer and Santos is in the air.

11. The absurdities of our conditioning to be inordinately comfortable with ruthless control in movies were brought home to me by students' reaction to *It's a Wonderful Life* in a film studies class I taught in Spring, 1994 at Mercy College in Dobbs Ferry, N. Y. In this class, every male student and an unexpected number of female students viewed this film with a sense of dissatisfaction because they missed the ordinarily obligatory scene at the end when the hero gets to wipe the floor with the villain. Resisting the patent genre conventions of this comic film, they longed for masculine control in the extreme form it takes in the gangster or adventure film—in which the protagonist, George Bailey (James Stewart), might "beat the shit out of old man Potter."

12. Readers may be interested in a sample of other critical responses to Lynch's original use of allusions to *The Wizard of Oz*. Kaleta interprets them as Sailor and Lula's misinterpretation of popular culture as a guidebook to life (p. 182). Alexander interprets them as Lynch's sellout to commercial exploitation (p. 124). Murphy, typically, is not surprised that "the patron saints of Lynch's film should be icons of arrested development" (p. 61). Chion, more in touch with what the subconscious means to Lynch, interprets the allusions as part of Lynch's creation of multiple levels of reality—his representations of the doubleness of the maternal (p. 163) and of a differently mediated vision of childhood (p. 165).

1. The Log Lady, a character that emerged for Lynch during the filming of *Eraserhead,* is an example of how his subconscious taps into basic Western traditions and transforms them. Margaret speaks in brief bursts of phrases much as Cassandra is depicted in Aeschylus's *Agamemnon* when she receives wisdom from the god Apollo. Like Cassandra, the Log Lady's powers of clairvoyance are intimately connected with a violation of her life, but she is not cursed nor is she an outcast. Cassandra, cursed with foresight because she resisted the advances of Apollo, is Aeschylus's reminder of the peril of being on the border between mundane life and something larger. The Log Lady, on the other hand, is a border marker that tells us that for every evil at the border there is also an expansion of good. Margaret has lost her husband, a logger and the great love of her life, to a fire the day after their marriage—a fire that she tells us is the devil, "hiding like a coward in the smoke." The vision—made possible by her log in the wake of the willful bursting of the air into flames that took life from across the boundaries—makes the line between energy and culture a positive if turbulent place of exchange.

2. Interviews with Lynch relative to *Dune* generally refer to his self-avowed surprise at his interest in a futuristic story. He attributes his atypical fascination with *Dune* as more a matter of the presence of unorthodox emotional substance in Frank Herbert's novels rather than their fictionalization of science. He is quoted to this effect in Paul M. Sammon's "My Year on Arrakis," *Cinefantastique* 14, no. 4 (September 1994): 31, 35. Lynch's repeated statements of this type give credibility to my surmise, parallel to that of his longtime friend and coworker Catherine Coulson, that the emotionless involutions of the UFO plot on *Twin Peaks* were much more Frost than Lynch.

3. Lynch's and Frost's versions of the character and effect of Lynch's hiatus are significantly disparate. Lynch maintains that he was deeply involved in the first seven episodes of the series and that he was forced to take time off for *Wild at Heart* because of the timing of financing. He maintains that, had he not undertaken *Wild at Heart* when he did, he would not have been able to make it at all. When I attempted to itemize with him which elements of *Twin Peaks* were contributed by which cocreator, he told me that the first seven episodes were too closely collaborative to make such an analysis, though he did take credit for the Red Room. By contrast, Frost has become increasingly bitter about Lynch. In 1991, Frost told me that, after the first seven episodes, "David left me alone." In a later interview in *Wrapped in Plastic,* a Lynch/ *Twin Peaks* fanzine, Frost is more emphatic: "When he [Lynch] got on the set, very often he threw out the script—which didn't please me all that much. But he would go off and do his own thing. He wasn't showing up all that often. He'd come in and direct an episode every once in a while. He wasn't really involved with the scripts. Then he'd go off on his own thing and leave us hanging" (no. 9, p. 2).

4. The high point of the Lynch/Frost collaboration, as I see it, occurred appropriately at the end of what I call the early episodes, when Leland dies. This episode occurs well after the truly collaborative first seven episodes, but it is still a part of the story that emerged from the original partnership. It appears just before the series collapsed into conventional heroic conflict. In the "Into the light" speech that Frost wrote for Cooper as he consoles the dying Leland Palmer, Frost finds words that quite stunningly evoke the usually unspeakable complexities of Leland/BOB: "Leland, the time has come for you to seek the path. Your soul has set you face to face with the clear light and you are now about to experience it in its reality wherein all things are like the void and cloudless sky and the naked, spotless intellect is like a transparent vacuum without circumference or center. Leland, in this moment know yourself and abide in that state. Look to the light, Leland. Find the light. . . . Into the light, Leland. Into the light." I speculate that Frost was able to articulate this Lynchian border experience clearly because Leland was dying, and thus the crossing would not violate Frost's rationalism. For Lynch, this is a state that is possible and indeed necessary for us while we live.

5. When I spoke with Frost in 1991, he told me that he and Lynch worked closely on the initial seven episodes. However, in *Wrapped in Plastic,* Frost not only takes credit for writing all the stories, but he ventures the judgment that "David's not really a writer by nature. He's a wonderful director and a great visual stylist, and he can write in collaboration with somebody. But it's good if the person he's working with has a strong sense of narrative and story, because those honestly aren't David's strengths" (no. 9, p. 3). Frost makes a credible point here, but perhaps goes a little far in underestimating Lynch's talent for working with narrative. My feeling is that Lynch's desire for heterogeneity disguises for a rationalist his legitimate and rather arresting narrative sense.

6. Of some interest regarding the value and centrality in narrative of female experience in *Twin Peaks* is the difference between the two major books published as companion volumes to the series which seem to document in print the divergences between the Lynch and the Frost visions of *Twin Peaks. The Secret Diary of Laura Palmer,* written by Lynch's daughter Jennifer, complements the initial reality of the series as an extraordinary and unusual expression from the point of view of a female subject with a distinctly feminine sense of self and eroticism. It is suffused with a sense of dreams and poetry as the source of our knowledge of reality and features the Log Lady's wisdom as one of Laura's few confirmations of her own worth.

The other important ancillary print companion to the series, *The Autobiography of F. B. I. Special Agent Dale Cooper: My Life, My Tapes,* written by Mark Frost's brother Scott Frost, is interesting in its clear distance from the beginning of the series and its resemblance in spirit to the end of the series. The book gives us a Cooper who is a rationalist fearful of losing control, whose dreams are rebuslike in character, as opposed to his dreams in the series which do not present images as a secondary form of communication to be translated into absolute significance by words. Scott Frost's book presents women as peripheral to Cooper, almost purely as the object of his controlling erotic gaze. The sole exception is Diane, Cooper's FBI associate—an *invisible, bodiless* woman—to whom he addresses his taped records of his adventures.

7. Frost has represented Lynch's revisions of scripts, particularly of the last script, as Lynch's caprice. However, my critique of the visionary necessity for Lynch's restructuring of the script notwithstanding, Catherine Coulson suggests that his changes in the final script were also a gesture of loyalty in response to the outraged feelings in the cast on the part of excluded characters. Since she was playing one of these excluded characters, she is vulnerable to the charge of self-interest here. Nevertheless, she is correct about the rituals of concluding episodes.

8. Previous books have evaluated *Twin Peaks* quite favorably but generally with little or no attention to Frost's role in the collaboration. The critics tend, therefore, to understand the show in terms of what they believe is Lynch's sensibility. However, the problem with these discussions of *Twin Peaks* as a whole solely in terms of Lynch are being remedied by new scholarly resources that will make future analysis of the collaboration among Lynch, Frost, and many other directors, actors, and writers more fruitful. Lavery's meticulous, exhaustive, and indispensable appendices in *Full of Secrets* identify *all* of the series participants and completely map all of the episodes for their many and complex incidents (pp. 196–258).

The ambitious Peaks fanzine *Wrapped in Plastic* is another invaluable source of material. Editors Craig Miller and John Thorne have published numerous revealing interviews with the *Twin Peaks* principals, including Sheryl Lee, Harley Peyton, Robert Engels, Michael J. Anderson, and Mark Frost. Even more useful for scholars are the articles comparing many of the *Twin Peaks* scripts to televised episodes, notably in nos. 16 and 21, and a discussion of Lynch's commercials in no. 19.

9. The varying claims for the origin of BOB is another indication of the cross-purposes of Lynch and Frost as collaborators. Frost is quoted in *Wrapped in Plastic* as stating that the source for BOB was in Indian stories (no. 9, p. 4). (In a telephone interview, Robert Engels told me the same thing.) However, Lynch says that BOB was created in a spontaneous moment when Frank Silva—the set dresser who ultimately was cast for the role—got caught on the set while the cameras were rolling for the pilot film and sparked Lynch's imagination. Complicating the situation is Engels's comment—also quoted in *Wrapped in Plastic*—some months after he spoke with me, referring to MIKE and BOB: " 'The origin of Mike and Bob is a planet made of corn. They fell out with each other on December 31, 1951, when Bob stole a can of corn from Mike, and the chase eventually led to Twin Peaks.' Engels

swore this is the truth, and [*sic*] he prevented this particular comment from being videotaped" (no. 10, p. 24).

10. In part, I owe my interpretation of the role of music in *Twin Peaks* to Joshua Berrett, my colleague at Mercy College.

11. Readers acquainted with my previous account of *Twin Peaks* in *Film Quarterly* (see Bibliography) will note that I have emended my transcription of MIKE's poem there, having been corrected by Lynch.

12. The speculation of Luce Irigaray, controversial French feminist, about the potential for a heterogeneous transformation of patriarchal Western culture is surprisingly congenial with Lynch's typical representation of gender in his films. As Margaret Whitford says in her Introduction to Section II in *The Irigaray Reader*, Irigaray "focuses on the double syntax, that is to say the possible articulation between conscious and unconscious, male and female" (p. 77). In "The Poverty of Psychoanalysis," also in *The Irigaray Reader*, Irigaray herself sets the structure of femininity (as she sees it)—the labial image of two lips touching—in opposition to the circle, a form that she associates with Freudian phallocentrism as expounded especially by Jacques Lacan. In the unbroken circumference of the circle, Irigaray sees patriarchal solipsism and preclusion of feminine expression. Her poetic evocation of the abundance of the feminine structure of perception, seen in the image of two lips, interfaces rather closely with Lynch's heterogeneous sense of representation: "In the two lips, the process of becoming form—and circle—is not only never complete or completable, it takes place . . . thanks to this noncompletion: the lips, the outlines of the body reflect one another, and there is born of this movement a self-perpetuating and self-developing form of desire . . . [that] never detaches itself from the matter which generates it. Form and matter—and even the distinction between the terms is blurred—beget one another endlessly . . ." (pp. 97–98). For Irigaray, unlike Lynch, the labial model of wisdom may have political consequences. Some critics believe that she is thinking in terms of lesbianism when she speaks of the benefits of a bisexual society that accepts labial as well as phallic representation. But that may, in fact, be a simplistic misunderstanding of a more abstract intent, somewhat Lynchian in attitude, about the place in the mainstream for feminine wisdom.

13. The term phallocentrism is used here as it has been used in resistant feminist readings of cultural texts that assume the organization of the human capacity for knowledge and power is dependent on either the image or the biological reality of the male member. Readers interested in further commentary on the concept of phallocentrism may be interested in the following texts: Mary Ann Doane, *Femmes Fatales;* Julia Kristeva, *Desire in Language;* Kaja Silverman, *The Acoustic Mirror;* Luce Irigaray, *Speculum of the Other Woman* and *The Irigaray Reader;* and Laura Mulvey, *Visual and Other Pleasures.*

4 *BLUE VELVET*

1. Critics have not remarked on a similar obsession with control present in both Williams and Frank. Indeed, critics are hard pressed to deal with Frank at all. Alexander accomplishes nothing in attempting to understand Frank as an Ares figure, spinning the net of Greek mythology like a cocoon around the film (p. 92). While Kaleta makes the obligatory remark about Frank's brutality, he has little else to say except in terms of story synopsis. Chion is, as always, more perceptive and less evasive and at least comments on the Oedipal resonances in the scenes involving Frank and Dorothy, though he comes to few conclusions about their function in the film (p. 112). He does, however, insightfully remark on the theatricality of Frank's behavior: "il évoque un mauvais acteur jouant un drame realiste" (p. 113) [He reminds us of a bad actor playing in a realistic drama]. Unfortunately, the most conclusive evaluation of Frank, that of Fredric Jameson, is exceptionally misdirected. Jameson sees him as a tediously repetitive character—he is referring to Frank's incessant cursing—a cliché of evil divorced from reality (historicity). Jameson is looking for some civic concern on Lynch's part, for example a representation of Frank that would arouse "the full tonal range of ethical judgments and indignations . . ." about the current drug problem (p. 536). What is to be said about such a reduced concept of ethics?

2. Lynch spends the film mapping the positions of will and subconscious energies on a continuum through the good and bad fragments of Lumberton, thus showing their commonality rather than their black and white opposition. However, there is no critical clarity about this complex Lynchian relationship between the surfaces and the depths of the town. In *Hitchcock's Films Revisited,* Robin Wood, a provocative and subtle critic, is unusually simplistic when he establishes a black and white bipolarity between innocence and evil at the center of *Blue Velvet* (pp. 44–49).

3. The insect motif in *Blue Velvet* underscores the continuity between the two fragments of the Lumberton community. The ants are hidden and marked for extermination, as are the outlaws, but ants are actually a kind of reflection from below of the surface of Lumberton, not its opposite. Ants have a highly ordered social structure that is in many ways like both sides of Lincoln in Lumberton.

4. Despite the emphatic presence of Freudian resonances, there is little reflection on Lynch's relationship to Freud in the criticism. Even Wood, who distinguishes himself by dealing with gender implications in *Blue Velvet,* does not mention Freud's name. Perhaps this critical silence reflects a widespread sense that Lynch is not a Freudian; however, it also would appear to reflect a critical confusion about what part the Oedipal allusions play in the narrative. One happy exception to this silence is Layton's Freudian analysis of the film.

5. Misunderstanding of the control issues in Lynch's films invalidates much of the criticism about his films, especially that of those critics who seek

to connect him with film noir. In "Home Fires Burning: Family *Noir* in *Blue Velvet* and *Terminator 2*," Fred Pfeil finds it only "too easy to tick off the *noir* elements" in *Blue Velvet* (p. 231). However, he could probably find those elements in James Fenimore Cooper's *Leather-Stocking Tales*, or Mark Twain's *Huckleberry Finn* for that matter—dark and light women, investigative hero, far-reaching nature of evil, homoerotic dimension, and so forth. What Pfeil misses entirely is the impossibility of categorizing Lynch as a part of the world of *noir* film as Pfeil defines it: "the hopelessly dark universe in which more consensual authorities are ineffectual, irrelevant, or corrupt" (p. 229). Authorities in *Blue Velvet* are all of the above, but Lynch sees a much larger source of hope. In linking Lynch to *noir*, then, Pfeil misses the distinction between *noir*'s anxieties about "the male protagonist's lack of control over the breakneck deviousness of its plot" (p. 228) and Lynch's assertion that lack of control is the seeker-protagonist's best hope.

6. Some representative overviews of *Blue Velvet* follow. Wood recognizes Lynch as a genius worthy of commentary but finds him flawed by homophobia. Lynch, he says, is limited by a bourgeois humanism that "enables him to identify with an abused outcast 'freak' [*The Elephant Man*] but not with any wider instance of societal oppression" (p. 46). Kaleta thinks that *Blue Velvet* is Lynch's best film, although he limits Lynch's achievement to an unprecedented honesty and boldness in discussing brutality (p. 131). He does a better service to Lynch in his extensive and highly perceptive discussion of the importance of sound in the film, which he relates to the image of the severed ear (pp. 95–97). Alexander writes that *Blue Velvet* puts us in the "realm of the senses" in which love and death are inseparable (p. 98). Chion describes the film as a vision of everyday reality (pp. 116–117).

7. Both Wood and Jameson incorrectly read the carnivalized images in *Blue Velvet* as parodic elements. Jameson refers to the film as showing "a collective unconscious in the process of trying to identify its own present at the same time that [it] illuminates the failure of this attempt, which seems to reduce itself to the recombination of various stereotypes of the past" (p. 536). Wood writes that "Lynch's fireman beaming at the audience from his itinerant firewagon is merely ridiculous, a cliché rendered laughable. . . . In *Blue Velvet*, small town values . . . are offered from the outset as patently absurd and risible, their emptiness a 'given' that precludes any need for dramatic realization" (pp. 44–45).

8. In her essay, "Word, Dialogue, and Novel," anthologized in *Desire in Language*, Kristeva uses Bakhtin's concepts about the carnivalesque to discuss novels. I have applied her discussion to narrative film.

9. In an early draft of the script, the gas Frank inhales is identified as helium, and the script calls for the actor's voice to imitate the high timbre produced by the swallowing of that gas. "The result is frightening" (p. 48). In the film, Hopper does not speak in a helium-induced voice nor is the gas

identified, producing a much more unsettling impression. The contrast between script and film sheds light on how Lynch may start with a rationalist, illusionist narrative but always moves beyond it.

10. A crucial, Lynchian difference between script and screen concerns the substitution in the film of the first dream sequence for a very talky scene. In the script, during Jeffrey's first night in Dorothy's apartment, after Frank leaves, the scene between Jeffrey and Dorothy involves a bloody unidentified object in the toilet bowl, which induces endless, ominous talk about what he knows of her situation (p. 54). All the verbiage is replaced by the crucial transition montage described above that makes sense, in visionary terms, of Jeffrey's first encounter with Dorothy.

11. Isabella Rossellini is quoted to this effect by Fischer, p. 135: "David Lynch nahm meine Schönheit und entdeckte etwas Komisches darin. . . . Das faszinierte mich . . ." [I was fascinated by the way David Lynch found something comic about my beauty].

12. The line "Now you have put your disease in me," spoken over a black screen, began in the screenplay as an interminable speech in a scene between Dorothy and Jeffrey:

> You put your disease in me . . . your semen . . . it's hot and full of disease. . . .
> Men are crazy . . . then they put their craziness into me . . . then it makes me crazy . . . then they aren't so crazy for awhile . . . then they put their craziness in me again. . . . I'm in so much darkness though with things moving . . . there is darkness sucking me. . . . It's kissing me and darkness is entering me . . . in every hole. It's opening me to a death. (p. 84)

This lurid language may always have been intended to disappear from the filmed version of *Blue Velvet*. Such bombastic dialogue is so un-Lynchian that it might have been in the script because sensationalism is useful for attracting producers, reassuring them that there will be sufficient sex in the completed film, as of course there was. In any case, this transformation of the script for the screen is another interesting insight into Lynch's art as a process, which may make the film more impressive for the reader, as it does for me.

Although Lynch has intentionally stripped the disease of a name in the film, its unnamed quality has sent some critics scurrying to put the film back under the management of linguistic order. Thus, Fischer has put forth an altogether untenable proposition, a critically irresponsible imposition on the film, that the disease is AIDS (p. 134)! (What would *that* mean for the happy ending?) Wood more understandably suggests that the word "disease" refers to sadomasochism (p. 46).

13. For those readers unfamiliar with it, the definition of fetishism will be useful in understanding castration anxiety. As Laplanche and Pontalis put it in *The Language of Psychoanalysis,* quoting in part Freud, "The two attitudes of fetishists—their *disavowal* of the perception of the woman's lack of a penis

and their *recognition* of this absence and grasp of its consequences (anxiety) 'persist side by side throughout their lives without influencing each other. Here is what may rightly be called a splitting of the ego'" (p. 119). This splitting of the ego, unnoticed by the fetishist, is an unowned masculine defense mechanism intended to simultaneously acknowledge the absence (maintain some connection with reality) and refuse to acknowledge it (assuage the male fear inspired by the female body that the penis might be removable). The fetish refers eroticism away from the actual body toward some object that can be associated with the body, like feathers or high heels—or blue velvet and a controlled gas supply. Anxiety about the possibility of castration, as Freud saw it, is related to the male child's perception of the inferior cultural status of mother within patriarchal culture. In Freudian thinking, this generates in the child's fantasy the likelihood that mother was punished by father and that too much closeness with her (identification with the feminine) might prompt the father to effect a similar castration on the son. Within the context of *Blue Velvet*, it is obvious that any images of castration relative to Jeffrey's closeness with Dorothy are only part of Frank's fantasy. The point of view in the film is that Jeffrey is more potent because of his empathy with her.

14. Lynch told me that Ben was the first character cast; before he had any other idea of what actors would be recruited, Dean Stockwell was Ben. This may surprise readers who see Ben as an intriguingly bizarre character who is, nevertheless, nothing more than a plot device for Jeffrey's discovery of Williams's partner Gordon's corruption, and a supernumerary at the location in which little Donny, Dorothy's son, is kept hostage.

Despite Lynch's strong sense about Ben, he had no deliberate plans for using him as he finally did in the film. Ben's mime of "In Dreams," the central event of the scene at his place, came about by accident; there is no song indicated for this scene in the revised third draft of the script of *Blue Velvet* (August 24, 1984). Lynch began to think about a song while he was in New York, rehearsing Kyle MacLachlan and Isabella Rossellini for the production. On a cab ride through Central Park after one of these sessions, he heard Roy Orbison's "Crying" and was attracted to it as a possible song for the scene at Ben's. However, he felt at the time that it was a little too "on the nose," too literal. Only when he purchased a Roy Orbison LP did he find "In Dreams," and immediately, as he says, "That was it." But even then, plans called for Dennis Hopper to sing the song as Frank. Hopper put off learning the song, and even though Lynch finally arranged for Stockwell, a close friend of Hopper's, to teach it to him, by shooting time Hopper still hadn't committed the song to memory. An impatient Lynch came around to see how the coaching was progressing, heard Stockwell tutorially singing the song to Hopper, and made the change on the spot.

Serendipity continues. Revised plans called for Ben to pick up a table lamp as if it were a microphone, but when the cameras were ready to roll, there was no table lamp on the set. Stockwell saw a worklight and, assuming it was there as a substitute prop, used it to Lynch's amazement and delight. To this day, Lynch has no idea who put the worklight on the set, or why it was there; nor does he care.

15. The use of light as a form of energy rather than as a moral code for "good" is tellingly illustrated in this scene. Fred Elmes, the cinematographer for *Blue Velvet,* pointed out to me that the virtual three-point lighting of this scene is distinctly unorthodox for a scene so fraught with such evil and with such "atmospheric" possibilities—i.e., "bizarre" characters. In keeping with intellectual associations between darkness and evil, the initial lighting plan called for an elaborate system of eerie shadows as the ambience for Frank, his henchmen, and Ben. The realization of the complicated initial plan was no small job since the scene was shot inside the cramped, somewhat rickety building visible in the film for the exterior shots of "This Is It!" Ordinarily, a combination of fun and spontaneous discovery is usual on a Lynch set, but the shooting of Ben's place involved major stress, and no matter how Elmes and Lynch set and reset the lights, nothing worked. When it got to be very early in the morning and tempers were frayed, in frustration because he had tried everything else, Lynch turned all the lights on. He and Elmes decided that—except for Ben's lipsync of "In Dreams"—this rather unusual solution for the lighting of a grotesque scene was exactly right. Others may be as fascinated as I am that Lynch at times begins with conventional representations and moves away only in the act of shooting a scene when his "ninety-percent solution" takes over.

16. Some readers may be interested to learn that Frank was not originally scripted to say to Jeffrey, "You're like me." Duwayne Dunham, the editor for *Blue Velvet,* told me that Frank's original line was, "You like me." The change was made during the editing process when Lynch seized on a momentary confusion about what Hopper was actually saying and realized he preferred the line that he thought he had heard the actor speak.

17. Lynch's disclaimers to the contrary, the robin was mechanical. Duwayne Dunham mentioned to me that he saw the strings controlling the "bird" in shots that were edited out of the final cut. Lynch emphatically denied that it was artificial (avoiding my eyes)—"Who started that rumor anyway?" But I'm inclined to believe that this is an instance of his fierce determination to prevent wordsmiths from reducing the mystery of his films. It is likely that he was trying to "protect" me and my readers from falling into a reductive rationalism regarding this image.

18. The tableau of the standing, mutilated, dead Gordon and the seated, mutilated, dead Don, the broken television, and the unshaded, standing electric lamp that greets Jeffrey's eyes and ours at the end of *Blue Velvet* is as reminiscent of Hitchcock as the scene at Ben's. As with the latter scene and with Hitchcock's most disturbing scenes, it is brightly lit. There is a significant

resemblance between the kind of visionary perspective we get in Dorothy's apartment at this point and the perspective that we get of Bodega Bay in *The Birds* when we see the holocaust at the gas pump suddenly from over the shoulder, as it were, of the seagulls. Over Jeffrey's shoulder, we see a visionary image of life and death in terms of electricity or energy (of which Lynch believes the world to be made) that operates independently of the life or death of bodies and machines.

5 *DUNE* AND *THE ELEPHANT MAN*

1. The book-length studies of Lynch's career are all exceedingly sympathetic in making their cases that *Dune* does not work as a film. Kaleta, for example, attributes the failure of the film to confusion engendered by the amount of expository material. He articulates the popular believe that, "The ties to the prose overburden the film with facts. The need for exposition hurts the film" (p. 85).

Lynch told me that he didn't feel the need for a cleaner, less confusing exposition of the mass of Frank Herbert's details. He expressed a different wish, that *Dune* had been more like a poem than a narrative. What he means by poetry is central to any understanding of his statement. Poetry for Lynch, as I understand him, refers to open linguistic structures—language syntax in which logical linearity is in a heterogeneous relationship with the nonrational energies of language. He also told me the film should have been more like a silent film—clearly another reference to communication less controlled by words.

Lynch also told me that he now believes that the project was not feasible, but I continue to believe that, given the freedom he needed, he could have made an interesting and effective screen version of *Dune*. He saw something that was feasible when he accepted the project, just as he saw his film version of *Wild at Heart* in a novel that only perfunctorily suggests the movie that he drew from it. There is every indication that he originally looked with as great a freedom at *Dune*.

2. The changes Lynch made in Herbert's narrative rhetoric are very suggestive. Book One of the novel is prefaced with a very pithy, forceful statement about Paul's destiny, purportedly a quotation from the *Manual of Muad'Dib* (one of Paul's holy names), written by Princess Irulan. This establishes her historical perspective on Paul's messianic destiny as the legitimate boundary of this narrative. Herbert then begins his story with the conventional immediate focus on his protagonist. The first glance we have of Paul is the scene between him and the Emperor's truthsayer as she tests him with the Box of Pain. Paul's destiny is thus rendered the reader's context and reference point in reading the novel.

Lynch's alteration of the presentation of Irulan, history, fate, and Paul changes the narrative tone. His delay in presenting Paul works to make him—

and his supposed destiny—only one element in a very complicated tapestry in which the focus is not on any one thread but rather on the overall design. Lynch's introduction to the film makes it impossible for the spectator to entertain Paul as Herbert has drawn him. It also makes it impossible for us to become engaged in the traditional heroic conquest plot which so dominates the end of the film.

3. Lynch used most of the significant female characters given to him in Herbert's book. However, the attitude toward feminine wisdom in the film differs significantly from Herbert's. In the book, this feminine power is carefully delimited by Herbert's construction of a rigidly controlled patriarchal society. The only difference between the gender structure of his fictional world and that of Margaret Atwood's feminist horror story *The Handmaid's Tale* is Herbert's approval of the arrangement that appalls Atwood. Indeed, the last sentences of the novel *Dune* find Chani, Paul's Fremen wife, being urged to accept a "Back Street" kind of life—dedicating herself to him but living on the margins of his life and letting his official wife, Princess Irulan, have him in the eyes of society. Lynch ignores Herbert's arranged marriage between Irulan and Paul as well as the rest of Herbert's gendered hierarchy.

With respect to gender in *Dune,* Alexander is very helpful. He notes the androgynous nature of the worms and the female model of wisdom in the film. Unfortunately, he immediately converts this insight into the un-Lynchian terms of domination/submission heroism: "The union of masculine and feminine energies unleashes a power *to subdue and control* [my emphasis] the monsters beneath the planet's surface (unconscious) and integrate this powerful and lethal energy into a 'conscious' force" (p. 87). His allusion to the unconscious and its connection to a combination of masculinity and femininity is helpful, unlike his suggestion that Lynch might ever represent successful human or cultural domination of that force.

4. In American popular culture, the test of a "real man," the hero, is very frequently his ability to divest himself of any identification with women. Women weaken men in action fiction. This convention is altered by the positive role of the effective vitality of Herbert's Lady Jessica and the Fremen warrior maiden Chani. But Herbert maintains a protection for men against these feminine energies, useful though they may be, through the implacable patriarchal hierarchy of Empire society, which Lynch, in contrast, weakens as a carnivalized, relative structure.

5. Chion's discussion of Lynch's poetic use of sound in *Dune* deserves attention. He is extremely helpful in defining how Lynch uses words that seem to be giving exposition for the poetic tone and texture. He comments perceptively on the sonic qualities of the exposition, which he says bombards us with words that only later take on meaning (p. 84).

6. At the end of *The Elephant Man,* Lynch adamantly disclaims any connection with Pomerance's play. A comparison between the one's film and the

other's stage play clarifies Lynch's wish to distance himself. Pomerance depicts a world incapable of love and consumed by exploitation. In his play, the answer to Treves's question of whether he is a bad man or a good man, to be discussed below, is unequivocally answered. Pomerance narrates Merrick's death as a metaphor for the repressiveness of society and the lack of human freedom.

7. At the beginning of *The Elephant Man*, Lynch claims that the papers of Sir Frederick Treves and the book about John Merrick by Ashley Montagu, *The Elephant Man: A Study in Human Dignity*, are his sources for the film. Readers curious about Lynch's use of his sources may find the following of interest. Lynch adopted Montagu's thesis about the influence of Merrick's mother and femininity on his life but generally disregarded the historical Treves's attitude toward women.

Montagu theorizes that, in order to survive the humiliation of his life as a freak and remain a loving and sensitive human being, Merrick must have been exposed to a powerful source of maternal love early in his life. According to the psychology of Montagu's assumption, maternal affection, existing beyond the conditions of mundane affairs, is the only energy capable of insulating people from society's assaults on their individuality (pp. 58–65). This thesis unquestionably has much in common with Lynch's characteristic portrayal of female wisdom and energy as part of the hero's education and support in surviving idealized social systems and their perverse shadows.

In contrast, the historical Treves is very patronizing about femininity. In his written account, he reveals a deeply Victorian view of women only as that society idealized them. He sees Merrick's relationship to his mother not as the basis of the profound strength to survive but as a frivolous fantasy about an unknown woman, the "beautiful mother" from the fairy tales and romance novels Merrick loved to read.

Similarly, Treves compares Merrick to a woman relative to the lesser character of women and to one physically beautiful attribute that Merrick had. Merrick's normal arm—coincidentally the left one, the side identified with intuition and other feminine virtues—is described by Treves in his memoirs as "a delicately shaped limb covered with fine skin and provided with a beautiful hand which any woman might have envied" (Howell and Ford p. 192). Treves depicts Merrick's love of small vanities as girlish: "Just as a small girl with a tinsel coronet and a window curtain for a train will realize the conception of a countess on her way to court, so Merrick loved to imagine himself a dandy . . ." (Howell and Ford p. 204).

Treves's patronizing attitude toward beauty and sentiment as feminine, an attitude characteristic of Victorian England, associates the marginalized Merrick with that larger population of the excluded—women. Treves's subconscious associations between women and the monstrous corroborates Linda Williams's conscious connection between them in Hollywood's monster films. Williams highlights the inadvertent revelation of Hollywood gender politics in the frequent covert identification of the creature as the alter ego of the fetishized beautiful star. Beneath *her* idealized disguise, this character too is monstrous and cannot be contained by the discourse of narrative. In contrast, while Lynch's film more openly imbues Merrick's maleness with a feminine coloration, he does it in a way that honors both Merrick and women as the saving hope of an overly reductive narrative and social discourse.

Concerning the historical "facts" of the existence of Merrick's mother, Lynch opts to take Treves's opinion that nothing can be historically verified about her or about the veracity of the story, persistently used to explain Merrick's appearance, that his mother was seriously injured by an elephant when she was carrying him. There was, however, a legend, encouraged by gossip to that effect and reported by Howell and Ford in their account of Merrick's life. They trace the actual route of a traveling circus that might have contained an elephant in its menagerie. Howell and Ford assure us that Merrick's mother might have encountered the elephant in some accidental fashion if it had escaped during one of the customary parades through town before the show and had gone on a rampage (pp. 35–42). Lynch does allude to this legend in the opening frames of the film as an imaginative history quite separate from the documented incidents in the narrative.

8. General critical response to Lynch's *The Elephant Man* is quite positive. Although Chion never satisfactorily resolves his reservations about the troubling suicide at the end of the film, he voices the majority view when he lauds Lynch for making a moving film about difference and normality that might have been quite pedestrian without his changes in the narrative from the original script (pp. 72–73). Kaleta, however, sees the film as reductive moralizing about the soul of mankind as the victim of technological progress. Unaware of Lynch's ironies, he comes away feeling that Lynch makes the good characters too saintly, the bad too beastly.

9. Bernard Pomerance seems to have missed what Lynch saw in the sources about the problems caused in *The Elephant Man* by the reductive idealization of Victorian women. In Pomerance's play, Mrs. Kendal is just another confirmation of the triviality of women in an exploitative society. During her visit to Merrick, she takes off her clothes to gratify his wish to see a naked woman, having nothing better to offer him than a chance to imitate his tormentors when she demeans herself to be stared at as he has been demeaned at the sideshow.

Worse, Pomerance disappointingly interprets Merrick's death in a way that unmistakably asserts that feminine chaos is not only a consequence of the Victorian social structure but all that we can know of the feminine. He represents Merrick's death through his own invention of Merrick's fantasy about two female freaks called the Pinheads. The Pinheads are submorons incapable of language except by rote. Their non-relationship to meaning is what defines them as Merrick's feminine alter egos. When he lies down to sleep at the end of Pomerance's play, the Pinheads appear as phantasms of his sleeping brain—the idiocy of his yearning to be normal is his internal femininity. Stretching him out into the prone sleeping position that will be death to him, they sing:

> We are the Queens of the Cosmos
> Beautiful darkness' empire
> Darkness, light's true flower
> Here is eternity's finest hour
> Sleep like other you learn to admire
> Be like your mother, be like your sire.
> (Pomerance p. 56)

All is nothingness, and nothingness is feminine.

10. During my first visit with Lynch in Los Angeles, he was generally very reserved, so I took particular note of the unpredictable moments when he would be taken by a rush of passion. One outburst that surprised me greatly occurred when we discussed Francis Bacon and narrative. Lynch suddenly retreated into himself, much in the way Henry Spencer does in *Eraserhead,* and began to *growl* about "sickeningly sweet narrative." Because of the context of our discussion, I have no doubt that he was referring to exactly the same type of narrative that we see in the pantomime at the end of *The Elephant Man,* and that he deems that kind of narrative toxic. With that in mind, I am convinced that Lynch is not including the play as the liberating collective unconscious à la Glinda in *Wild at Heart* but rather just the reverse.

6 SIX MEN GETTING SICK, ERASERHEAD, THE GRANDMOTHER, AND THE ALPHABET

1. As remembered by the closely knit group that made it, the production period of *Eraserhead* had the characteristics of a vortex—continuous motion, the impossibility of reflection, and a twenty-four-hour commitment of resources to a blind process. If there is something splendid in this overture to a number of careers in filmmaking, it ought not be too much idealized. Indeed, it appears to have taught all of Lynch's hardy band to want to make wonderful movies but within the larger sphere of the culture. The dedication of the original Lynch crew overwhelmed all aspects of their personal and creative lives. They spent their days and nights in one of the outlying buildings of the American Film Institute, leaving primarily to work at fast-food places for money to cover production costs. As remembered by Catherine Coulson, who acted as an assistant producer and also as Jack Nance's hairdresser, neither she nor Nance nor Frederick Elmes—Lynch's cinematographer for not only *Eraserhead* but also *Blue Velvet* and *Wild at Heart*—permitted their dedication to flag even though they were paying instead of being paid to make

Lynch's film. However, moved as they were by the momentum that was the *Eraserhead* process, it cannot be considered a model to be replicated.

The legend—approaching myth—of the making of *Eraserhead* veils the experience in a kind of paradisal glow, which is partly, but only partly, true. Anyone interested in Lynch and in his first film should read K. George Godwin's article, "*Eraserhead:* The Story behind the Strangest Film Ever Made, and the Cinematic Genius Who Directed It." However, Godwin's rosy-colored scenario of the experiences of those who worked with Lynch on this early masterpiece is somewhat distorted, much in the tradition of a Hollywood construct of "the happy family." In truth, the close association between Lynch, Coulson, Nance, Elmes, and a small handful of others while they shot and edited *Eraserhead* was composed of the kind of wild youthful defiance of common sense and hardships that can never come again. In Godwin's article, Coulson recounts a memory of a cozy New Year's Eve spent by her with her then-husband Jack Nance and Peggy and David Lynch (p. 72). This evening no doubt occurred, but Peggy Reavey remembers being confined to the house because there was no money for babysitters and not being able to invite guests to their home because Lynch was eternally working either on the film or for money for the film. Coulson herself told me that the years working on *Eraserhead* were extremely difficult, particularly the maintenance of the famous hairdo which caused her and Nance no end of grief. Elmes remembers, along with the challenges, a wearisome sense of endlessness about a project that could not go forward because it lived from hand to mouth economically. Moreover, none of those involved has ever been properly rewarded for all of these sacrifices.

Although *Eraserhead* continues to produce income—and Lynch voluntarily shares the income with ten of the original cast and crew—including Coulson, Nance, Elmes, and Alan Splet, who designed the sound with Lynch—the film is still shown exclusively as a midnight movie and treated as if it were a cult oddity instead of the masterpiece it is. Certainly, people in the industry have taken it seriously. In the late seventies, Stanley Kubrick told Elmes he had seen it more than 30 times, and this film impressed Mel Brooks and Stuart Corngold enough to offer Lynch the job directing *The Elephant Man.* However, its place in a general limbo continues to cause Lynch enormous pain, as was obvious while he repeated for me the well-known story of how he spent his last cent on a trip to New York so that he could audition *Eraserhead* for the Cannes Film Festival, only to have it run for a completely empty theater since the judges had already departed for France.

2. When Lynch was working on *Eraserhead,* he was constantly preoccupied with the construction and maintenance of the "baby," which was completely mechanical. According to Peggy Reavey, there is no mystery about the "baby" except the tenacity that Lynch showed in dealing with the technical challenges it posed. However, it is true, as has been reported, that the people working on

the film were sworn to secrecy. But I believe that the withholding of information does not conceal anything bizarre or strange; it is another instance, as with the robin at the end of *Blue Velvet,* of Lynch's desire to protect us from our own tendency to reduce everything to a logical explanation. Knowing that it is a mechanical device has not, however, decreased my wonder of it.

3. For readers interested in an overview of the critical reception of *Eraserhead,* I provide the following. General critical response indicates that the film is a masterpiece that changed American perceptions about the possibilities involved in filmmaking. At the same time, critics are hard pressed to say anything more concrete in articulating any specific understanding of what constitutes *Eraserhead*'s achievement. Two issues that typically emerge in extended discussion of the film tiptoe around the periphery of the film rather than engaging it. The issues pertain to the film's relationship to Lynch's life and the palpable sense of the subconscious in the film.

Lynch did marry early because of an unplanned pregnancy and the marriage did end, splintered by the strains of binding responsibility onto two young people who desired to freely explore their own possibilities. Tina Rathborne, who directed Lynch in *Zelly and Me* and also directed two episodes of *Twin Peaks,* tends to read this film as Lynch's way of dealing with some of the guilt and pain of this early experience. So does David Ansen in "The Kid from Mars," *Newsweek,* April 9, 1990. I think it is clear that Lynch used the situation of early marriage with which he was familiar, but that it is so poetically transformed that it has no resemblance to the literal events of his life.

Concerning the strong appeal to the subconscious in the film, Alexander voices the majority opinion that Lynch gives cinema new life, comparing "Henry Spencer's ordeal [with] . . . the ordeal of David Lynch 'giving birth' to his own creativity by delving into the blackness of his own psychosis" (p. 53). Kaleta's phrasing implicates the subconscious but focuses on Lynch's use of metaphor: "Like Luther's bold nailing of his philosophy on the doors of Wittenberg, Lynch has in *Eraserhead* remolded the cinematic conventions: blasting, redirecting, reforming, glorifying, and inventing. In this rough, bold film, the cinematic innovations of Lynch surface. He defines the province of contemporary film as the creation of images and metaphor" (pp. 29–39).

4. In his discussion of *Eraserhead,* Chion makes some telling remarks on the revolutionary role of sound in this film. Without referring to feminine receptivity Chion, in a parallel insight, comments on how sound creates an interior space within the externalized film narrative (pp. 54–55).

5. From my conversations with Lynch, although we did not specifically refer to chaos theory, I suspect that it would (or does) appeal greatly to him. In chaos theory, mathematics and physics are unorthodoxly joined in a discussion of the kinds of physical manifestations that do not have the regularity of shape to be accounted for by conventional physics. Chaos theory is founded on an assumption parallel with Lynch's that there are underlying forms in the

universe too complex to be charted by simple logical thinking. This resonates with what Lynch told me of his belief that mathematics might be the only way of rationally describing what the real world is like, but he doubted that we would ever be capable of developing so complex a mathematics. Here, I surmise, he is saying that mathematics is freer than language and has more poetic possibilities. Readers wishing an introduction to chaos theory might turn to *Chaos: Making a New Science* by James Gleick. But be warned—even at its most simple, chaos theory requires an understanding of advanced mathematics.

6. Lynch avows a love for factories and demonstrates his interest through the repeated appearance of machines and industrial images in his films and photographs. However, I believe he loves them in the same way that he loves the 1950s—as a mark of the finite concerning which he can posit what lies beyond. He often refers to "little factories" inside our heads that produce our own meanings. In *Eraserhead*, that production of meaning is clearly implicated in the mechanistic images that pervade the industrial city. A similar representation occurs in Lynch's most famous unproduced script, *Ronnie Rocket*. In that script, the mechanisms are depicted in the form of a transit system, and there is a relationship between electricity and the internal factory similar to the one we see in *Eraserhead*. (Electricity in *Eraserhead* is discussed at the end of my commentary on the film in the main text.)

7. According to both Reavey and Coulson, Lynch was prone to make many and constant enigmatic pronouncements about core samples in Henry's brain during the time he was making *Eraserhead*.

8. An interesting gloss on Henry's affair with his neighbor concerns Lynch's earlier plan for a film (that he never completed) under the auspices of the American Film Institute—*Gardenback*. *Gardenback* also featured a dreamlike component in a narrative of infidelity by a young newlywed man. The plot concerned a hunchback living secretly in the couple's house, which Lynch's advisers at AFI counseled him to represent as the evil that stimulated the husband to break his vows. But, as Peggy Reavey remembers it, within the context of the liberated sexual climate of the sixties, Lynch could not imagine any reality in which the hunchback or the adultery was evil. That is why he scrapped the initial project and began *Eraserhead*, in which he did not feel any unwanted pressure to apply moral judgment to Henry.

9. Godwin has suggested that there is a castration scenario in *Eraserhead*. He sees the destruction of the "baby" as a self-castration, identifying the baby as a penis, which it certainly can be said to resemble: "destroy the appetite by destroying the organ. All the poisons flood out of the dying thing and its death causes chaos. Because in destroying the penis, Henry also destroys the tool of continuity, the means by which the world (the particular inner world of the dream) is sustained. The result is death, for the nothingness of the sterile womb, Henry's Heaven, is death itself" (p. 54). Godwin's interpretation

raises many questions. If the baby is a penis, what is the sense of the representation of Mary's only relationship to it as one in which *she fills it* (with food)? Why is the streetwalker neighbor—who to all indications enjoys the male organ—disgusted by the baby? Why must Henry stifle it in order to have sex with her? Why, when the baby is destroyed, is the agony located in the planet that is associated with Henry's head? Indeed, can we really experience the cute and cuddly lady as a castrating or deathlike presence?

10. Readers interested in Irigaray's exploration of femininity and origins will find an extensive discussion of this subject in "The Blind Spot of an Old Dream of Symmetry" in *Speculum of the Other Woman.* In this essay, one of the major themes is how women in their maternal capacity are deprived of a subjectivity by being acculturated to serve as a form of origin or a conduit to it for men but not to have their own relationship to the basic matter and energy of creativity. In *Eraserhead* and *The Alphabet,* Lynch appears to suggest that female connection to origins in itself is a given. In *The Grandmother,* he seems to suggest that the attempt to reduce the maternal to nothing more than a conduit is doomed to be short-lived.

11. There is a potential biographical connection between Lynch and *The Grandmother.* He was very close to his grandmother, and the erotic elements in the short film are reflected in a poem he actually wrote to her, according to Peggy Reavey. In contrast, no one acquainted with Lynch believes that there is any biographical foundation to the abusive relationship between the protagonist of *The Grandmother* and his parents. However, both Reavey and Catherine Coulson have told me stories about Lynch's childhood that inadvertently suggest to me a different but connected relationship between the film and his life. In his childhood, order was stressed as the basis of achievement. His parents, according to report, far from treating their child violently, were calmly methodical. Whenever he wanted to do anything, his father encouraged him to first make a list of required materials. To this day, Lynch is meticulously systematic in that way. But what does a spontaneous young child feel about the constraints inherent in order itself? I surmise that the abuse Lynch envisions in *The Grandmother* is not a memory of abusive parents but of his experience of order from the perspective of the uncultivated energy fluxes of childhood.

12. *Good Times on Our Street* is the name of an elementary-school reader Lynch remembers as containing stories about Dick, Jane, and their dog Spot, mentioned by both Fischer and Chion in their biographical notes on him. Fischer quotes him as saying that these were the kind of scenes that passed for reality in both the movies and in life (pp. 14–15). Chion quotes him as saying that he was happy in the way the children in the book are when he was young (p. 16).

13. The line, "Please remember, you are dealing with a human form," is based on what Peggy Lynch actually said to David while he was positioning

her body for a shot in the film. The strange image of the face is also indebted to her. Lynch got the idea for the shot based on what she said she remembered of her father's face as he was reading her a bedtime story. Lying in her bed, looking up at the speaking face, she found the upended perspective on the features eerie.

14. In connection with Lynch's move into commercial film, readers may enjoy Chion's quotation of him on this subject: "Je ne sais pas ce qui serait arrivé si j'avais continué a faire des films comme *Eraserhead.* Je ne sais pas si j'aurais pu continuer a faire cinéma, tout simplement" (p. 63) [I don't know what would have happened if I had continued to make films like Eraserhead. I don't know if I could have continued to make any films.].

7 *FIRE WALK WITH ME*

1. My discussion of *Fire Walk with Me* assumes that the film's structure has a powerful organic integrity. This assumption intentionally disregards conjecture based on the gossip about the making of the film. It is widely known that Kyle MacLachlan restricted his participation in *Fire Walk with Me* to a fraction of what Lynch had originally intended, and so it is widely suspected that the discontinuity of the first thirty minutes was the result of half-hearted, last-minute scrambling. Even some actors assume that to be true, as I learned from Michael J. Anderson. However, Lynch is incapable of a half-hearted effort when he makes movies. Whatever might have been had MacLachlan opted for a large role, *Fire Walk with Me* is an authentic Lynchian narrative venture. The shift away from the detective's perspective, clearly mandated by the film, reveals that, working with his materials in his usual way, Lynch has made an organic film about Laura's struggle.

2. Readers may be interested to know how resistant the critics can be to recognizing that *Fire* is a film organized around the violations of incest. Happily, Diane Stevenson discusses incest at length in her article, "The Family Romance, Family Violence, and the Fantastic in *Twin Peaks*" in *Full of Secrets,* pp. 70–81, but in those full-length studies on Lynch which came out in time to consider *Fire Walk with Me,* the presence of incest in its story is barely or never recognized. In his extensive, relatively sympathetic discussion of the film, Chion mentions discontinuity in the film, his perception of a recurring image of walking, and the relationship of the film to the series, but not once does he use the word "incest" (pp. 168–185). Alexander acknowledges the incest but as an aside, as if it were just one element of the story and not its determining condition (p. 140). Furthermore, he barely recognizes that this film is about feminine perspective. The attention he pays to Laura's character analyzes her presence from the point of view of the male sensibility as if he were still talking about the series. The cultural assumption that everything coherent issues from a masculine point of view is so pervasive that critics usually are unable to make the shift in perspective even regarding those rare

249

works of popular culture that quite blatantly depart from this convention. In her book on the woman's picture of the 1940s, *The Desire to Desire*, Mary Ann Doane details how Hollywood generally helps this kind of confusion by making a norm out of male appropriation of the heroine's narrative. Chapter 2 (pp. 38–69), "Clinical Eyes: The Medical Discourse," is most pertinent to Laura's story. It very convincingly analyzes how Hollywood centralizes the role of the male doctor in controlling the stories of many women's films about sickness and women. Few notice this subordination of the heroine in her own story because it feels so right to our culture. In *Fire Walk with Me*, where Lynch energetically neutralizes this kind of male control, the opinion has been that something *doesn't* feel right.

3. There has been more freedom in Japan than in the United States or Europe to consider *Fire Walk with Me*, which had a limited run at Euro-American box offices. Chion politely details the surprisingly negative reception it drew in France, where Lynch is generally very well received. (He explains that the French critics found *Fire* to be the indulgent work of a director grown arrogant and capricious—p. 117.) In contrast, *Fire* became a raging popular success in Japan. Ron Garcia, the cinematographer of the film, has pointed out that the Japanese audience for the film is predominantly female. He surmises that the enthusiasm of the Japanese women comes from a gratification of seeing in Laura some acknowledgment of their suffering in a repressive society.

If this is the case, and it may well be, the question still remains why millions of similarly constrained women in European-based cultures were not able to find the same solace from the film. I suggest that the answer to this question lies in a structural comparison between Euro-American movies and the Japanese understanding of narrative film, which is far more inclined to the kind of heterogeneous balance to which Lynch aspires than is rationalistic Western culture. An interesting start for such a comparison might be made by consulting the poetics of Japanese film discussed in Noel Burch's *To the Distant Observer: Form and Meaning in Japanese Cinema*.

4. Lynch told me that the selection of the name Judy was random, a denial of pervasive speculation that it refers to Judy Garland and connects somehow with Lynch's love for *The Wizard of Oz*. If it does refer to Dorothy's voyage in that film—and despite Lynch's denials, it may—what seems significant is Dorothy's passage among levels of reality and its parallel in Laura's experience.

5. Some critics like to compare *Fire Walk with Me* with the ambiguous hybrid film noir/women's film classic *Laura* (1944), directed by Otto Preminger. Almost certainly, even if some of his collaborators were thinking of this film, Lynch was not when he worked on *Twin Peaks* and *Fire Walk with Me*. Or if he was, it doesn't much matter. Deliberate allusion has a minimal, playful role in his art. However, a comparison between the two films is interesting, par-

ticularly for what the critics do not say. Alexander is representative in his re-marks on the obvious similarities in the role of the female image in both films. He also notes that Jacoby is the name of the creator of Laura's portrait in Preminger's movie and the name of Laura Palmer's psychiatrist in *Twin Peaks* (p. 129). Yet he is also representative in missing the significance of the resemblances. More pertinent is that in both films the detective is incapaci-tated by the limits of the application of logic to real events. The most telling similarity between the two films is their similar evocation of the difficulty of entering into women's experience, though Lynch's is certainly the bolder and more important of the two.

6. Lynch commented on the function of the high-angle framing of the con-versation in Donna's living room to Ron Garcia, who passed Lynch's words along to me. The startling angle on the two girls was not merely an interesting image to Lynch but a way of giving us a visceral experience of the presence of the angels. I liken it to a similar shot in Hitchcock's *The Birds* that removes us, the audience, to a perspective usually beyond our limits as we see Bodega Bay from the point of view of a group of seagulls (see the discussion of *The Birds* in Chapter 1).

7. Lynch is not direct about much of what he does in his films, but he was extremely pointed about the nature of the Red Room. "It changes," he told me unequivocally, "depending on whoever walks into it." Once we get be-yond the omnipresent red drapes in every appearance of the Red Room, we can see that there are significant variations in its representation depending on who is making the visit.

8. The loss of an arm in this film, with respect to the Little Man and MIKE, functions as a castration image that associates the mutilation with too much control over women not, as in the Freudian framework, with too much inti-macy and identification with women. Clearly some sort of shift is necessary in interpreting this loss in terms of Laura. The implications of the numbed arm for her are more enigmatic than are the phallic mysteries of the Little Man, but they appear to be connected with menstrual blood through Annie's bloodied appearance in the bed, substituting for the incapacitated arm on Laura's left side just as the Little Man later completes MIKE in the Red Room. Such wounding that implicates the female genitals is ordinarily related to cas-tration anxiety for men in the influential Freudian framework of thought. However, in contrast with the Freudian framework as it has been interpreted in our culture, female blood here seems to be less a wounding than a return to vitality. In this dream, the malfunction of Laura's arm occurs immediately af-ter Cooper's rational warning about the ring and so appears to be associated with female anxiety connected with the power of rational (male?) perspec-tives in ordinary reality.

9. During my first visit with Lynch, I read to him several quotations about angels from "Sexual Difference," an essay in *The Irigaray Reader*, which had

seemed to me to interface in a fascinating way with his use of the angel images in *Fire Walk with Me*. He chose the following as the one closest to his intention: "They [angels] destroy the monstrous elements that might prohibit the possibility of a new age, and herald a new birth, a new dawn" (p. 173).

10. In Chapter 1, I compare Lynch with Orson Welles. The representation in *Fire* of a multiplicity of spaces in our reality is one specific instance of this comparison, though of course Welles is less bold in conveying these spaces. The simultaneity of the open and the closed space is quite clearly present in the final *agon* of Mike O'Hara, the protagonist of Welles's *The Lady From Shanghai*. He is tumbled about in the claustrophobic spaces of the chutes and distorting mirrors of the fun house. However, after being buffeted like a puppet cut loose from its strings—as only an element of the most limited space of reality—he leaves the enclosures of the fun house for the larger, freer (in hindsight, Lynchian) space outside. In *Fire*, Lynch challenges us much more than does Welles by asking us to understand not only the fun house of ordinary reality but also the film—and death itself—as cultural forms from which one may go on to contact with cosmic energies, like the angel.

11. My discussion of the main title music came out of a conversation with my generous colleague at Mercy College, Professor Joshua Berrett.

12. An interpretation of the creamed corn as seed and sperm was originally suggested to me by Michael Anderson.

13. Blood images that veer away from the pure biology of bleeding play a recurring role in the Lynchian vision. The chain of visionary bleeding images begins with *The Alphabet* and continues through Henry's nosebleed in *Eraserhead* when Mrs. X forces him to marry Mary, the images of the sinister Harkonnen heartplug in *Dune*, the blood from the eyes of the Bene Gesserit Sisters in the same film, Cooper's wound in the last scene in the Red Room, and Leland's wound in *Fire Walk with Me*. Since Leland/BOB is the knife-wielding aggressor in *Fire*, his wound is particularly puzzling. Some light is shed on the representation of the murderer as one who bleeds in one of the Log Lady's prologues for the rerun of *Twin Peaks* on the Bravo network:

> The heart. It is a physical organ we all know. But how much more an emotional organ. This we also know. Love like blood flows from the heart. Are blood and love related? Does a heart pump blood as it pumps love? Is love the blood of the universe?

The Log Lady's intuitive correlations suggest a Lynchian kind of nonlogic in which Leland's wound takes on a larger meaning as a stigma associated with an insult to the supply of cosmic love. Thus, the healing also assumes a resonance as part of the restoration of universal peace and love.

14. An early draft of *Fire Walk with Me*, from August 8, 1991, radically differs in crucial ways from the film as it now exists. In that draft, the script designates the ring as the mark of the victim not the visionary. In the script, our

last look at the ring is in the hospital in a scene that depicts the previously un-seen stay of Annie Blackburn in the hospital after she and Cooper leave the Red Room at the end of the series. We see an unconscious Annie with the ring on her finger. How it came to her is not explained. What we see is that it is stolen by a greedy nurse, ostensibly BOB's next victim. Annie's relationship to the ring was deleted from the final cut of the film. Similarly, although the enigmatic corn is present in the script as something BOB has stolen and must return, there is no ritual of the corn at the end. Nor does the script indicate an angel in the Red Room or anywhere else in the film.

At the end of the early script, Laura verbally tells Leland that he must kill her, and there is no penultimate scene in MIKE and BOB's Red Room. In the final image, Laura is in her Red Room sitting on Cooper's lap. Thus, in this script there is a lot less articulation of the larger cosmic framework of Laura's death and resurrection. Indeed, the script—lacking the angels, the ring as visionary power, and the corn ritual—leaves Laura not much better off than she was before. She may be in the lap of the putatively affectionate and good daddy she always wanted, but the image of affection contains the resonance of the "daddy lover" that would have defeated Lynch's peeling away of the tax-onomy of incest.

Clearly, the entrance of the angels into events galvanized the already pres-ent ring and corn, liberating the cosmology that the film now contains. The differences between script and film give us an opportunity for intuiting the narrative power that Lynch gains through his ninety-percent solution.

Bibliography

PRIMARY SOURCES

David Lynch

BOOKS

Catalogue. *David Lynch: Paintings and Drawings* at the Touko Museum of Contemporary Art (Tokyo, Japan), January 12–27, 1991.

Catalogue. *Exhibition of Photographs and Paintings* at the Sala Parpallo, Disputacion Provincial de Valencia (Spain). May–June, 1992.

Images. New York: Hyperion Press, 1994.

FILMS AND SCRIPTS

The Alphabet. Film. (Director and writer)

Blue Velvet. Film. (Director and writer)

Blue Velvet. Script. Third Draft.

Dune. Film. (Director and writer)

The Elephant Man. Film. (Director and writer)

The Grandmother. Film. (Director and writer)

Industrial Symphony No. 1: The Dream of the Broken Hearted. Videotape. (Director and writer)

Lost Highway. Film. (Director and writer) With Barry Gifford.

Lost Highway. Shooting Script. With Barry Gifford.

One Saliva Bubble. Unproduced Script. With Mark Frost.

Ronnie Rocket. Unproduced Script.

Twin Peaks. Television Serial. (Cocreator/Director/Actor) Episodes 1–29. With Mark Frost.

Twin Peaks: Fire Walk with Me. Film. (Director and writer). With Robert Engels.

Twin Peaks: Fire Walk with Me. Script. With Robert Engels.

Wild at Heart. Film. (Director and writer)

Interviews (all conducted by author)

Anderson, Michael John. Telephone interview. August 8, 1993.

Coulson, Catherine. Personal interview. March 30, 1993; Telephone interview. September 9, 1994.

Dunham, Duwayne. Personal interviews. March 30, 1993; October 9, 1994.

Elmes, Frederick. Personal interview. March 28, 1993.

Engels, Robert. Telephone interview. October 18, 1991.

Frost, Mark. Personal interview. November 22, 1991.

Garcia, Ron. Personal interview. April 1, 1993.

LaPelle, Rodger. Personal interview. August 16, 1993.

Lynch, David. Telephone interview. January 31, 1992; Personal interviews. March 29–31, 1993; April 1, 1993; January 15–18, 1996; March 13, 1996; April 12, 1996.

McGinnis, Dorothy. Telephone interview. August 16, 1993.

Nance, Jack. Personal interview. April 1, 1993.

Rathborne, Tina. Personal interview. May 19, 1993.

Reavey, Peggy. Telephone interviews. June 2, 1993; April 12, 1996.

Sweeney, Mary. Personal interview. March 29, 1993.

SECONDARY SOURCES

Ades, Dawn, and Andrew Forge. *Francis Bacon.* New York: Harry N. Abrams, 1985.

Alexander, John. *The Films of David Lynch.* London: Charles Letts, 1993.

Allen, Robert Clyde, ed. *Channels of Discourse, Reassembled.* Chapel Hill: University of North Carolina Press, 1992.

Attali, Jacques. *Noise: The Political Economy of Music.* Minneapolis: University of Minnesota Press, 1985.

Bakhtin, Mikhail. *Problems of Dostoevsky's Poetics,* edited and translated by Caryl Emerson. Minneapolis: University of Minnesota Press, 1984.

Bazin, André. *What is Cinema?* Berkeley and Los Angeles: University of California Press, 1967.

Bordwell, David. *Ozu and the Poetics of Cinema.* Princeton: Princeton University Press, 1989.

Bordwell, David, Janet Staiger, and Kristin Thompson. *The Classical Hollywood Cinema: Film Style and Mode of Production to 1960.* New York: Columbia University Press, 1985.

Bordwell, David, and Kristin Thompson. "Fundamental Aesthetics of Sound in Cinema." In *Film Sound: Theory and Practice,* edited by Elisabeth Weis and John Belton, pp. 181–200. New York: Columbia University Press, 1985.

Breskin, I. "Interview with David Lynch." *Rolling Stone,* September 6, 1990.

Bresson, Robert. "Notes on Sound." In *Film Sound: Theory and Practice,* edited by Elisabeth Weis and John Belton, p. 147. New York: Columbia University Press, 1985.

Bruce, Graham. *Bernard Herrmann: Film Music and Narrative.* Ann Arbor: UMI Research Press, 1985.

Burch, Noel. *To the Distant Observer: Form and Meaning in Japanese Cinema.* Berkeley and Los Angeles: University of California Press, 1989.

Byars, Jackie. *All That Hollywood Allows.* Chapel Hill: University of North Carolina Press, 1991.

Camper, Fred. "Sound and Silence in Narrative and Non-narrative Cinema." In *Film Sound: Theory and Practice,* edited by Elisabeth Weis and John Belton, pp. 369–382. New York: Columbia University Press, 1985.

Casebier, Allan. *Film and Phenomenology: Toward a Realist Theory of Cinematic Representation.* New York: Cambridge University Press, 1991.

Chion, Michel. *David Lynch.* Paris: Cahiers du Cinema, 1992.

de Lauretis, Teresa. *Alice Doesn't: Feminism, Semiotics, Cinema.* Bloomington: Indiana University Press, 1985.

Doane, Mary Ann. "Ideology and the Practice of Sound Editing and Mixing." In *Film Sound: Theory and Practice,* edited by Elisabeth Weis and John Belton, pp. 54–63. New York: Columbia University Press, 1985.

———. "The Voice in the Cinema: The Articulation of Body and Space." In *Film Sound: Theory and Practice,* edited by Elisabeth Weis and John Belton, pp. 162–177. New York: Columbia University Press, 1985.

———. *The Desire to Desire: The Woman's Film of the 1940s.* Bloomington: Indiana University Press, 1987.

———. *Femmes Fatales: Feminism, Film Theory, Psychoanalysis.* New York: Routledge, 1991.

Eisner, Lotte H. *The Haunted Screen,* translated by Roger Greaves. Berkeley and Los Angeles: University of California Press, 1973.

Feuer, Jane. *The Hollywood Musical.* 2d ed. Bloomington: Indiana University Press, 1993.

Fischer, Robert. *David Lynch: Die dunkel Seite der Seele.* Munich: Wilhelm Heyne Verlag, 1992.

Flinn, Caryl. *Strains of Utopia: Gender, Nostalgia, and Hollywood Film Music.* Princeton: Princeton University Press, 1992.

Frank, Elizabeth. *Pollock.* New York: Abbeville Press, 1983.

Frost, Mark. *The List of Seven.* New York: Avon Books, 1993.

———. *Twin Peaks.* Unpublished scripts for Episodes 28 and 29.

Frost, Scott. *The Autobiography of F. B. I. Special Agent Dale Cooper: My Life, My Tapes.* New York: Pocket Books, 1991.

Gifford, Barry. *Wild at Heart: The Story of Sailor and Lula.* New York: Vintage Books, 1990.

Bibliography

Gleick, James. *Chaos: Making a New Science.* New York: Viking Penguin, 1987.

Godwin, K. George. *"Eraserhead:* The Story behind the Strangest Film Ever Made, and the Cinematic Genius Who Directed It." *Cinefantastique* 14, no. 5 (September 1984): 41–72.

Henri, Robert. *The Art Spirit.* Philadelphia: J. B. Lippincott, 1923.

Herbert, Frank. *Dune.* New York: Ace Books, 1987.

Hoberman, J., and Jonathan Rosenbaum. *Midnight Movies.* New York: Harper and Row, 1988.

hooks, bell. *Yearning: Race, Gender, and Cultural Politics.* Boston: South End Press, 1990.

Hopkins, Darren. "'The Devil's In, and Can't Get Out': Re-Addressing the Work of David Lynch." Unpublished Dissertation for the Power Institute of Fine Arts, University of Sydney, Australia, 1993.

Howell, Michael, and Peter Ford. *The True History of the Elephant Man.* Middlesex, Eng.: Penguin Books, 1980.

Irigaray, Luce. *The Irigaray Reader,* edited by Margaret Whitford. London: Basil Blackwell, 1991.

————. *Speculum of the Other Woman,* translated by Gillian C. Gill. Ithaca, NY: Cornell University Press, 1992.

Jameson, Fredric. "Nostalgia for the Present." *The South Atlantic Quarterly* 88, no. 2 (Spring 1989): 517–37.

Kaleta, Kenneth C. *David Lynch.* New York: Twayne, 1993.

Kalinak, Kathryn. *Settling the Score: Music and the Hollywood Classical Film.* Madison: University of Wisconsin Press, 1992.

Kristeva, Julia. *Desire in Language: A Semiotic Approach to Literature and Art.* New York: Columbia University Press, 1980.

Lacan, Jacques. *The Four Fundamental Concepts of Psycho-Analysis.* New York: W. W. Norton, 1978.

Laplanche, J., and J. B. Pontalis. *The Language of Psychoanalysis,* translated by Donald Nicholson-Smith. New York: W. W. Norton, 1973.

Lavery, David, ed. *Full of Secrets: Critical Approaches to Twin Peaks.* Detroit: Wayne State University Press, 1994.

Layton, Lynne. "Blue Velvet: A Parable of Male Development." *Screen* 35, no. 4 (Winter, 1994): 354–372.

Levin, Gail. *Edward Hopper: The Art and the Artist.* New York: Norton, 1980.

Lynch, Jennifer. *The Secret Diary of Laura Palmer.* New York: Pocket Books, 1990.

Lyotard, Jean-François. *Discours, figure.* Paris: Klincksieck, 1971.

————. "The Dream-Work Does Not Think," translated by Mary Lydon. *Oxford Literary Review* 6, no. 1 (1983).

————. *Driftworks,* translated by R. McKeon, et al. New York: Semiotext(e), 1984.

———. "Interview with Georges van den Abbeele." *Diacritics* 14, no. 3 (Fall 1984).

———. *The Postmodern Condition,* translated by Geoff Bennington and Brian Massumi. Minneapolis: University of Minnesota Press, 1984.

———. *The Differend: Phrases in Dispute,* translated by G. van den Abbeele. Minneapolis: University of Minnesota Press, 1988.

———. *Peregrinations: Law, Form, Event.* New York: Columbia University Press, 1988.

Mancini, Marc. "The Sound Designer." In *Film Sound: Theory and Practice,* edited by Elisabeth Weis and John Belton, pp. 361–369. New York: Columbia University Press, 1985.

McClary, Susan. *Feminine Endings.* Minneapolis: University of Minnesota Press, 1991.

McKinney, Devin. "*Wild at Heart.*" *Film Quarterly* 45, no. 2 (Winter 1991–1992): 41–46.

Merleau-Ponty, Maurice. *The Primacy of Perception and Other Essays on Phenomenological Psychology, the Philosophy of Art, History, and Politics,* edited by James M. Edie. Evanston, Ill.: Northwestern University Press, 1964.

Metz, Christian. "Aural Objects." In *Film Sound: Theory and Practice,* edited by Elisabeth Weis and John Belton, pp. 154–162. New York: Columbia University Press, 1985.

Mintz, Penny. "Orson Welles' Use of Sound." In *Film Sound: Theory and Practice,* edited by Elisabeth Weis and John Belton, pp. 289–298. New York: Columbia University Press, 1985.

Modleski, Tania. *Feminism without Women: Culture and Criticism in a "Postfeminist" Age.* New York: Routledge, 1991.

Montagu, Ashley. *The Elephant Man: A Study in Human Dignity.* New York: Outerbridge and Dienstfrey, 1971.

Mulvey, Laura. *Visual and Other Pleasures.* Bloomington: Indiana University Press, 1989.

Murphy, Kathleen. "Dead Heat on a Merry-Go-Round." *Film Comment* November/December 1990, pp. 59–62.

Murray, Timothy. *Like a Film.* New York: Routledge, 1993.

Nochimson, Martha. "Desire under the Douglas Firs: Entering the Body of Reality in *Twin Peaks.*" *Film Quarterly* 46, no. 2 (Winter 1992–1993): 22–34.

———. *No End to Her: Soap Opera and the Female Subject.* Berkeley and Los Angeles: University of California Press, 1992.

Peary, Danny. "Blue Velvet." In *Cult Movies 3,* pp. 38–42. New York: Simon and Schuster, 1988.

Pfeil, Fred. "Home Fires Burning: Family *Noir* in *Blue Velvet* and *Terminator 2.*" In *Shades of Noir,* edited by Joan Copjec, pp. 227–259. London: Verso, 1993.

Pomerance, Bernard. *The Elephant Man.* New York: Samuel French, Inc., 1979.

Pond, S. "Naked Lynch." *Rolling Stone,* March 22, 1990.

Prendergast, Roy M. *Film Music.* 2d ed. New York: W. W. Norton, 1992.

Prince, Stephen. "The Discourse of Pictures: Iconicity and Film Studies." *Film Quarterly* 47, no. 1 (Fall 1993): 16–28.

Readings, Bill. *Introducing Lyotard.* New York: Routledge, 1991.

Rubin, Martin. "The Voice of Silence: Sound Style in John Stahl's 'Back Street'." In *Film Sound: Theory and Practice,* edited by Elisabeth Weis and John Belton, pp. 277–286. New York: Columbia University Press, 1985.

Schneller, Johanna. "The Secret World of Kyle MacLachlan." *GQ* 62, no. 6 (August 1992).

Silverman, Kaja. *The Subject of Semiotics.* New York: Oxford University Press, 1983.

———. *The Acoustic Mirror: The Female Voice in Psychoanalysis and Cinema.* Bloomington: Indiana University Press, 1988.

Sontag, Susan. *Against Interpretation and Other Essays.* New York: Farrar, Strauss and Giroux, 1967.

Stam, Robert, Robert Burgoyne, and Sandy Flitterman-Lewis. *New Vocabularies in Film Semiotics.* London: Routledge, 1992.

Stewart, Susan. *On Longing.* Durham, NC: Duke University Press, 1993.

Sylvester, David. *The Brutality of Fact: Interviews With Francis Bacon.* London: Thames and Hudson, 1975.

Taubin, Amy. "The Auteur as Couch Potato." *The Village Voice,* April 10, 1990.

Travers, P. "The Wizard of Odd." *Rolling Stone,* September 6, 1990.

van Alphen, Ernest. *Francis Bacon and the Loss of Self.* Cambridge: Harvard University Press, 1993.

Viano, Maurizio. *A Certain Realism: Making Use of Pasolini's Film Theory and Practice.* Berkeley and Los Angeles: University of California Press, 1993.

Weis, Elisabeth. "The Evolution of Hitchcock's Aural Style and Sound in *The Birds.*" In *Film Sound: Theory and Practice,* edited by Elisabeth Weis and John Belton, pp. 293–312. New York: Columbia University Press, 1985.

Williams, Christopher, ed. *Realism and the Cinema.* London: Routledge and Kegan Paul, 1980.

Williams, Linda. *Hard Core: Power, Pleasure, and the "Frenzy of the Visible".* Berkeley and Los Angeles: University of California Press, 1989.

Wood, Robin. *Hitchcock's Films Revisited.* New York: Columbia University Press, 1989.

Index

culinity in, 102–103, 108–110, 112–118; Frank Booth in, 28, 100–103, 107–108, 113–118, 235n.1, 236–237n.9, 239n.15; Freudian analysis of, 102–103, 235n.1, 235n.4; gender in, 37–38, 40, 102–103, 108–110, 112–118; glamor in, 111, 113, 115; impact of, on popular culture, 199–200; insect motif in, 121, 122, 235n.3; and insufficiency of language, 37–38, 109–110; involuntary bodily actions in, 38–39; Jeffrey's dreams in, 108, 116–117; Jeffrey's relationship with Sandy, 117–119; Jeffrey's report of investigation of Dorothy's house, 37–39, 109; Jeffrey's sexual relationship with Dorothy in, 40, 100, 102, 107, 108, 110–112, 119, 237n.10; Jeffrey's shooting of Frank, 118, 121; light and darkness in, 33, 99, 107, 108, 114, 121, 203, 239n.15, 239–240n.18; losing control in, 103, 106–108; Meadow Lane scene of Frank's beating of Jeffrey, 115–117, 239n.16; Mike in, 117–118; misunderstanding of, 204; music in, 105, 114, 203, 238n.14; mysteries of air in, 119–122; non-reproduction of fathering in, 108–109, 112–118; opening images of, 99, 104–106; plot summary of, 99–104; robin at end of, 119–122, 239n.17; Sandy's dream in, 109–110, 121; seeker-protagonist in, 41, 99, 101–102, 104; severed ear in, 100–104, 106, 107, 236n.6; sexuality in, 40, 102, 103, 107–108, 110–112, 116, 119, 237n.12; sound in, 105; subconscious in, 103–104, 108–110, 116–117, 237n.10; Tom Beaumont's stroke in, 105–106; will-to-control in, 107–109, 112–113, 115–116
Bodily processes. *See* Involuntary bodily processes

Brave New World (Huxley), 162
Brooks, Mel, 245n.1
Burch, Noel, 250n.3

Campion, Jane, 200
Cape Fear, 200
Carnivalesque: Bakhtin on, 29, 236n.8; in *The Birds,* 42; in *Blue Velvet,* 29, 105, 236n.7; in *Dune,* 127–129; in *The Elephant Man,* 138–44; in *Eraserhead,* 159; in Hopper's paintings, 28–29; in *Industrial Symphony No. 1,* 217–220; and language, 223; in *Twin Peaks,* 78–80, 89, 93; in *Wild at Heart,* 50, 53
Castration and castration anxiety, 132, 164, 175, 237–238n.13, 247–248n.9, 251n.8
Chaos theory, 154, 246–247n.5
Chion, Michel: on *Blue Velvet,* 235n.1, 236n.6; on *Dune,* 241n.5; on *The Elephant Man,* 243n.8; on *Eraserhead,* 246n.4; on Lynch generally, 226n.2, 248n.12, 249n.14; on *Twin Peaks: Fire Walk with Me,* 249nn.2–3; on *Wild at Heart,* 227n.2, 229n.7
Coen, Joel and Ethan, 2, 7, 9
Collective unconscious, 6, 13. *See also* Subconscious
Control. *See* Will-to-control
Cooke, Alistair, 206
Cooper, James Fenimore, 236n.5
Corngold, Stuart, 245n.1
Coulson, Catherine, 206, 231n.2, 233n.7, 244–245n.1, 247n.7
Criticism. *See* Feminist criticism; and specific films and film critics
Cronenberg, David, 2, 7, 9
Cruise, Julee, 219
Cult films, 172, 245n.1

Darkness. *See* Light and darkness
Davis, Miles, 191
Demon. *See* Possessed characters

Detectives: in *Blue Velvet,* 29, 37–39, 100, 112, 117; Cooper compared with Sherlock Holmes, 76, 77, 79, 90; in *Laura,* 251n.5; in *Twin Peaks* (TV series), 13, 39, 72–74, 76, 77, 79, 89–90, 207; in *Twin Peaks: Fire Walk with Me,* 173–174, 177–183, 186, 187, 196–197, 250–251n.5
D.O.A., 212
Doane, Mary Ann, 250n.2
Doppelganger, 96–97, 101–103, 141–142, 188–189, 208–209
Double Indemnity, 215
Doyle, Arthur Conan, 76, 79
Duck-eye scenes. *See* Eye-of-the-duck scenes
Dune: blood images in, 128, 132, 252n.13; carnivalesque in, 127–129; compared with Herbert's book, 132, 133, 136, 240–241nn.1–4; compared with other Lynch films, 126, 128, 130, 131, 137; critical responses to, 123–124, 240n.1, 241n.3, 241n.5; "director's cut" of, 124; Emperor in, 124–127; gender in, 13, 130–133, 241nn.3–4; Harkonnen in, 12, 124, 125, 128–129, 134; Irulan in, 126; Lynch's fascination with, 231n.2; maternal energy in, 130–132; Navigator in, 126–127; opening images of, 126, 137; Paul Atreides in, 13, 20, 41, 124–125, 129–134, 240–241n.2; Paul's dreams in, 130–132; plot summary of, 124–126; sound in, 133–134, 241n.5; subconscious in, 130–132; Water of Life scene in, 20, 131–132, 133; will-to-control in, 124–130; worms in, 132–133
Dunham, Duwayne, 229n.8, 239n.16, 239n.17

Ebert, Roger, 40
Electricity, 120, 161, 164, 239–240n.18

Elephant Man, The: carnivalesque in, 138–144; compared with other Lynch films, 137, 141, 143, 174–176, 190; compared with Pomerance's play, 135, 241–242n.6, 243–244n.9; critical responses to, 236n.6, 243n.8; doppelganger in, 141–142; ending of, 147; eye-of-the-duck scene in, 26, 28, 145–146; gender in, 135–136, 143–147, 242–243n.7; historical sources of, 135, 242–243n.7; involuntary bodily actions in, 39; light and darkness in, 140, 147; maternal energy in, 131, 136, 137–139, 145, 147, 242–243n.7; medicine and carnival freak show in, 138–144; Merrick and femininity in, 136, 143–145, 242–243n.7, 243–244n.9; Merrick's death in, 136–137, 145, 146–147, 243n.8, 243–244n.9; Merrick's kidnapping by night porter in, 12, 142–143; musical fantasy pantomime scene in, 26, 28, 145–146, 244n.10; opening images of birth, 137–139; plot summary of, 135–136; secret-as-protagonist and seeker-protagonist in, 41, 136; Treves's development in, 12–13, 136, 143; and Victorian attitudes, 137, 139, 143–145, 147, 242–243n.7; women's relationships with Merrick, 143–147
Elmes, Frederick, 239n.15, 244–245n.1
Energy. *See* Electricity; Wind and air images
Engels, Robert, 233–234n.9
Eraserhead: "baby" in, 151–155, 157, 158–159, 160–161, 162–164, 169, 195, 245–246n.2; "baby's" destruction in, 152, 158–159, 161, 213; blood images in, 156–157, 252n.13; carnivalesque in, 159; compared with Lynch's other films, 51, 152, 165–167, 169, 175,

251n.8; in *Six Men Getting Sick,*
171; in *Twin Peaks,* 13, 76–77,
87–92; in *Twin Peaks: Fire Walk
with Me,* 40, 174–177, 179, 249–
250n.2; vaginal images, 132–133,
163; Victorian distortions of femininity, 137, 139, 143–147, 242–
243n.7, 243–244n.9; in *Wild at
Heart,* 40, 71. *See also* Phallocentrism; Sexuality
George, Diana Hume, 225n.1
Getty, Balthazar, 215
Gifford, Barry, 226–227n.1
Glamor, 39, 48, 63, 81, 111, 113, 115,
179, 218–221. *See also* Femme
fatale
Gleick, James, 247n.5
Godwin, K. George, 245n.1, 247–
248n.9
Grandmother, The, 41, 148–149,
165–168, 172, 202–203,
248nn.10–11
Greenaway, Peter, 2, 7, 9

Henri, Robert, 7, 20, 21
Herbert, Frank, 124, 132, 136,
231n.2, 240–241nn.1–4
Heroes: conventional heroes, 11, 47–
48, 67, 70–71, 88, 93–94, 129–130,
134, 241n.4; impact of Lynch's
work on portrayal of, 199–200;
and letting go generally, 11–12, 39,
209–210; as seeker and secret generally, 40–41. *See also* Detectives;
Secret-as-protagonist; Seeker-
protagonist; and specific films
Heroines: conventional heroines, 48,
81, 92, 219, 221; in *Industrial Symphony No. 1,* 217–221; in *Twin
Peaks,* 81. *See also* Femme fatale;
and specific films
Hitchcock, Alfred, 14, 19–20, 32–34,
36–37, 41–43, 45, 61, 199, 200,
202, 239–240n.18, 251n.6
Hoberman, J., 228n.4

Hopper, Dennis, 238n.14, 239n.16
Hopper, Edward, 7, 9, 20, 21, 28–29,
126
Huxley, Aldous, 162

Incest, 167, 175–177, 183–184,
249n.2, 253n.14
Industrial images, 154–155, 159–160,
247n.6
Industrial Symphony No. 1, 41, 217–
224, 226n.3
Insect motif, 121, 122, 235n.3
Involuntary bodily processes, 38–39,
149–155, 167–168, 169–171, 186–
187
Irigaray, Luce, 165, 234n.12, 248n.10,
251–252n.9
It's a Wonderful Life, 230n.11

Jameson, Fredric, 106, 235n.1,
236n.6
Japanese film, 250n.3
Jordan, Neil, 2, 7, 9
Joyce, James, 206
Jung, Carl, 6

Kaleta, Kenneth C., 226n.2, 227n.2,
228n.7, 230n.12, 235n.1, 236n.6,
240n.1, 243n.8, 246n.3
King, Henry, 227n.3
Kristeva, Julia, 223, 236n.8
Kubrick, Stanley, 134, 245n.1

Lacan, Jacques, 8–9, 12, 15, 19,
234n.12
Ladd, Diane, 2, 62–63
Lady from Shanghai, The, 42, 252n.10
Laplanche, J., 237–238n.13
Laura, 250–251n.5
Lavery, David, 226n.2, 233n.8
Layton, Lynne, 225n.1, 235n.4
Letting go: author's process of, 1–4;
in *Blue Velvet,* 103, 106–108; and
heroes generally, 11–12, 209–210;
in *Industrial Symphony No. 1,*

Credits for Illustrations

Figure 1. Courtesy of the Australian National Gallery and Artists Rights Society.

Figures 2–4. Courtesy of Marlborough Fine Arts; and Hirshhorn Museum and Sculpture Garden, Smithsonian Institution, Gift of the Joseph H. Hirshhorn Foundation, 1972. Photographer Lee Stalsworth.

Figure 5. Courtesy of David Lynch; and the Greenville County Museum of Art, Museum Purchase: Arthur and Holly Magill Purchase Fund and a donation from Poodie, Rooty-Toot, and Bugz in memory of Jeannie Williams Styron.

Figure 6. Courtesy of David Lynch.

Figures 7–8. Courtesy of David Lynch. Photographer Catherine Coulson.

Figure 17. Courtesy of Catherine Coulson.

Figure 44. Copyright 1980 by Brooksfilm Limited.

Figure 45. Courtesy of David Lynch.

Figure 47. Courtesy of David Lynch.

Figures 49–51. Courtesy of Rodger LaPelle and Christine McGinnis, and David Lynch.

Figure 52. Courtesy of David Lynch.

Figures 53–54. Courtesy of David Lynch. Photographer Catherine Coulson.

Figure 55. Courtesy of David Lynch.

Figure 64. Courtesy of Catherine Coulson. Artist Mindy Alper.

Figure 65. Courtesy of David Lynch. Photographer Suzanne Tenner.

Figures 66–67. Courtesy of David Lynch. Photographer Suzanne Tenner.

Figure 68. Courtesy of David Lynch. Photographer Suzanne Tenner.

Figure 69. Courtesy of David Lynch.